Daylight in the Canyon
The Memoirs of Eleanor Lynde

Eleanor Lynde

Introduction by Stan Lynde

Authors Choice Press
New York Lincoln Shanghai

Daylight in the Canyon
The Memoirs of Eleanor Lynde

Copyright © 1993, 2007 by Eleanor Lynde

All rights reserved. No part of this book may be used or reproduced by any means, graphic, electronic, or mechanical, including photocopying, recording, taping or by any information storage retrieval system without the written permission of the publisher except in the case of brief quotations embodied in critical articles and reviews.

Authors Choice Press
an imprint of iUniverse, Inc.

iUniverse books may be ordered through booksellers or by contacting:

iUniverse
2021 Pine Lake Road, Suite 100
Lincoln, NE 68512
www.iuniverse.com
1-800-Authors (1-800-288-4677)

Originally published by TypeCraft

Narrative © 1993 Eleanor Lynde
Introduction © 1993 Stan Lynde

FIRST EDITION 1993

ISBN: 978-0-595-43142-7
ISBN: 0-595-43142-9

Printed in the United States of America

INTRODUCTION

Daylight in the Canyon is in every sense my mother's book, and her story. Drawn from memory, ranch records, and the pages of her diary, this book is an account of her more than fifty-year marriage to my father Myron and their more than forty years together in the sheep business.

It begins with a brief account of my father's early years, as told to and recorded by Mother, and goes on to recount her own story as she lived it, from her birth in Wisconsin to her childhood years in Hardin, Montana, to her marriage, to the birth of her children, and her often nomadic life with Dad on the vast open ranges of southern Montana.

It is a story of hope, faith, triumph, tragedy, great happiness, and at times heart-breaking sadness. It is also the story of a way of life that has passed into history now, a chronicle of lonely places and great open spaces, of mountain meadows, sage-studded prairies and badlands, and of sheep by the thousands.

The title, Daylight in the Canyon, was suggested by my sister Lorretta, who recalled my father using the phrase to wake us, his children, in the mornings of our youth. The phrase is an urge to action, to be up and doing, because when the morning light reaches the shadowed canyons day is well begun indeed for ranch people. Dad lived his life that way, and so did Mom. The legacy they left me, and my sisters Chris and Lorretta, was one of industry, character, and faith in God. We are, I believe, indebted to that legacy for who we are and what we have become.

This, then, is the story of Eleanor Lynde, my mother. I commend it to you.

Stan Lynde

ACKNOWLEDGMENTS

◆

This is a collection of my life's experiences of being a sheep rancher's wife. Each memory is so unique that many people had suggested I write them down.

Having been interested in writing since I was a child, it was natural for me to keep a diary. Then, when we retired and moved to Billings, I joined a writers' group. Professor Larry Weirather from Rocky Mountain College spoke to our group, suggesting that we write of our experiences. As he was also a neighbor, I found myself asking him for special help, which he obliged, but he soon moved to Washington.

Then I became involved in other things, but my book kept nagging me. So my friend Margaret Ping suggested I go to Professor Sue Hart from Eastern Montana College. Sue was a great help and encouraged me to continue with the manuscript.

Another person, Sherryl Hinson, spent hours typing the rough draft on her computer.

Again I came to a lagging halt, then my daughter Christine's children Shelley (Chauvin) Van and Joe Chauvin volunteered to edit and publish my story.

Along the way I was also encouraged and assisted by my children and their families (Stan and Lynda Lynde and family, Chris and Joe Chauvin, grandson Brent Chauvin, and Lorretta Lynde) and many friends.

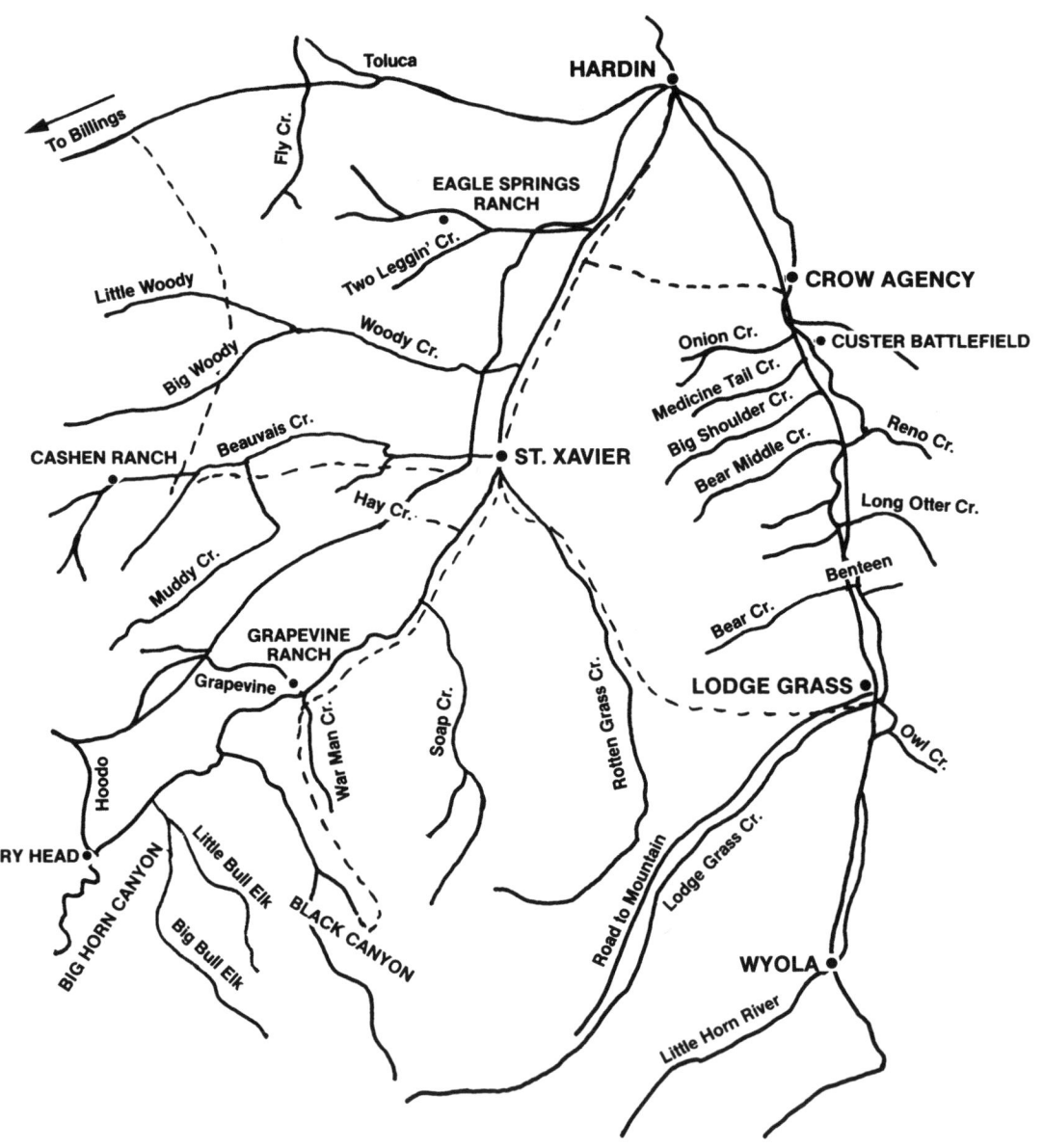

Map of areas described throughout the book where Eleanor and Myron spent their lives.

PRELUDE
By Lorretta Lynde

◆

Daylight in the Canyon is a phrase old-time cowboys used to express how late it was in the morning. Since the bottom of the canyon is the last place to get light on any given morning, this is surely the last possible time to get up and get on with the day. Myron used this phrase to wake his family and/or any hired men he had occasion to call from sleep for the start of the work day. Since Myron was an extraordinarily early riser, there were many people over the years who believed they heard this call from him while it was still the middle of the night. And indeed, it was not uncommon for him to give this call while it was still hours before official sunrise came anywhere to the land.

Eleanor Graf, age 17

EARLY LIFE OF ELEANOR LYNDE

◆

In 1916, John and Laura Staats Graf, my parents, began making plans to leave their families who owned farms near Sturgeon Bay, Wisconsin. It was a big challenge to move their six children to Birney, Montana, where they'd taken up a homestead claim. The children's ages ranged from 1 to 12 years in Spring of 1917 when the family finally boarded the train for Montana.

Problems caused them to give up the homestead and move to Sheridan, Wyoming, where John could use his trade as brick and stone mason and where the children could have good schooling. Our youngest brother was born there and was named Sheridan after the city of his birth.

However, there was little construction work, so Dad took a job in a coal mine, working until he got his finger smashed. He then got a job building a brick school in Lodge Grass, Montana. While there, he learned of brick work in the small but growing town of Hardin, which was the county seat of the newly formed Big Horn County. His first job was helping to build the new Library. Our parents liked what they learned of that growing community, so Dad built a house at the edge of town, and when school was out, moved the family there.

The seven children quickly became part of the town. They attended the Congregational Church and both the grade and high schools, taking part in sports, scouting and many of the other activities of a small town.

The large Graf yard became a popular place for all the neighbor children. They especially enjoyed the get-togethers we had in the evenings when we played strenuous games like Pump, Pump, Pull Away, Hide and Seek, Run Sheep Run and others. When it began to get dark, Dad let us have a bon fire and we'd all gather around it. There were nights when the stars seemed very close, as we tried to locate constellations.

Some nights the big kids told ghost stories, and the youngsters were almost afraid to go home and would beg for someone to walk part way with them.

Swimming in the big irrigation ditch with the neighbor kids was fun. They were Baptists, so we "baptized" each other a number of times, but I don't think that alone made us good kids. It was the community. They were all good kids, with parents who cared.

When I was ten years old, our folks bought a beautiful new Nash car, and we took a trip to Wisconsin. Much of the road was dirt, sometimes mud. When we got nearly to Minneapolis, we drove ninety nine miles on cement road. When we got back to Hardin, we really bragged about that.

Sometimes we'd take a lunch and walk down to the Big Horn River to fish. We didn't catch very many, but we had fun playing in the sand. In the winter time we'd take our sleds out, and often some farmer going to town in a big hay sled would let us hitch a ride. We all loved to skate, so we especially appreciated the town rink. I grew up with my three older sisters, so there was always someone to do things with. The two oldest sisters loved to play bridge when they had a friend come to visit, and when they needed a fourth, I was drafted.

Always I had a best friend that I shared my secrets with. I was a pretty good basketball player on the grade school team, and once I even got to travel as far as Crow Agency to play against that school. I don't remember who won, but it probably wasn't our team or I'd remember it. In high school I was a substitute, yet I was lucky enough to play quite a bit and got to go on trips to Custer and Lodge Grass.

The soda shop was a special gathering place. Each week my sisters, friends and I went to a movie. At 14, I was quite mature and began dating for movies and dances. It was a happy time when the important thing was to be invited to a party or to wonder who your date would be for Saturday night. Generally I had a boyfriend, so I didn't really fret about that. If we didn't have dates, Dad would let us sisters take the car and go wherever there was a dance. There were always enough men that we got to dance every dance. Usually one of the stags would buy our supper.

I was sixteen when I met Myron at a country school house dance. He was bringing a bunch of horses from Pryor to Lodge Grass and planned to spend the night at the Eagle Springs Ranch. When he arrived, he found the cowboys were getting ready to go to a dance at the Hart School House. He decided to go with them, but his only spare trousers were a pair of Levis.

That night I went to the dance with Tom, a young man who played in the orchestra, so that left me free to dance with whomever I wanted to. When different cowboys asked me to dance, I was pleased because they were acquaintances. But when the young man in the Levis came to ask me, I really looked him over. I didn't know him, and he was the only one there wearing Levis! I wondered why he wasn't dressed up as was the custom. He was tall and slender with dark hair and the prettiest blue eyes. He was very aware of my looking him over, and obviously felt self-conscious. But he quickly explained, "I'm from Lodge Grass and these cowboys I came with are my friends from the Eagle Springs Ranch. Their boss is Mr. Willcutt. I guess you know him and his wife and their son, Harvey. Well, they are long time friends of my parents."

The music started up. As we danced and talked, we found that we had many mutual acquaintances. He asked me for a date. That was how our romance started. Often he came to Hardin and took me to picture shows and dances. When there were dances in Lodge Grass, he'd come after me. Sometimes he'd call, asking me to come on the train and he'd meet me. He became acquainted with my family and friends. Often I was invited to his parents' ranch home, so I came to know his people and friends. His two sisters and I became good friends. Myron and I were together as often as two people living in different towns could be.

He proposed to me after a dance, but we'd never taken the time to talk about the seriousness of marriage. He'd been pressuring me, but there was a lot to think about besides just being together.

One weekend, Myron was anxious for me to come to the ranch; I thought he was probably going to press for an answer. Myron had been working as a tool dresser for the Ember Oil Drilling Co. which was drilling for oil on Lodge Grass Creek, but at this time they were shut down, so when Mr. Bill Heinrich, a rancher on Soap Creek, was ill and needed someone to lamb his sheep, Myron volunteered.

It was a beautiful spring day when Myron stopped the light wagon at the ranch house gate. I went out and climbed in to go with him up to the sheep. In the wagon, he had wood for the herder and a couple of barrels of water. On the way, we saw the many birds busy making their nests and could see the majestic mountains in the background. The whole country was becoming a beautiful spring green. Myron stopped a few minutes and went down into a coulee and came back with some pussy willows. I was thrilled. I already loved this part of the country, but now I loved it even more, especially after seeing the great array of wild flowers on the slope. But we couldn't stop to admire flowers when the herder was waiting.

When we arrived at the sheep wagon, I was introduced to the herder. He invited us in for coffee. We chatted a bit, and then the herder said, "Myron, you know that ewe with the mean looking eyes with twin lambs? Well, she's run off from them again. I need you to help me catch her, as she'll have to be hobbled until she decides to stay with them or they get frisky enough to keep up with her." Myron looked at me. "You don't mind waiting here at the wagon, do you?"

"No," I said, "You run along and do what you have to. I see dish water on the stove, so I'll do up the dishes."

After the dishes were put away, I tossed out the water and hung up the dish pan. As I stood at the door, I gazed at the beautiful panorama of Lodge Grass Creek and valley. Thoughts of what Myron would expect of a wife crowded my mind. When I said yes, I felt sure that I loved him enough. Now I questioned myself: was I really ready for marriage? I thought of my mother.

She had insisted that each of her children learn the necessary things about cooking, keeping house, gardening, canning and doing the wash. We all had to learn to milk the cow and take her to pasture and learn the necessary things about caring for chickens.

That caused me to break into a smile as I remembered that, when I was about 12 or 13 years old, Mother said, "Eleanor, it is time you learned how to prepare chicken." That was the last thing I wanted to do. None of my friends had to do it, but I went with Mother to the chicken house. After she showed me how to catch a chicken, she carried it to the chopping block and handed it to me saying, "Be sure you keep its legs together and hang onto them. Lay its head on the block, now chop its head off." Chills went up and down my spine. I didn't want to look at it—I felt like a murderer. Finally I got its head just right. But it jerked its head aside before I could come down with the ax. Now chills were really going up and down my spine, but I knew I had to stay with it. Again, I carefully laid its head on the block, just right, and it twisted. I had to do it three times before the poor chicken cooperated. Then OH! The blood!

After the headless chicken flopped around for a while, Mother came out with a bucket of scalding water and had me submerge the chicken long enough to loosen the feathers so I could pull them off. Oh, the smell! But I stayed with it. Then I had to singe the hair.

Finally I could take it to the kitchen. Mother had the cutting board ready and said, "Now take the innards out," and she showed me how to make the cut. Yuck! Another smelly job, but she stayed right with me until it was all done and the cutting board was cleaned up. Then she said, "You can go out and play now. I'll cool your chicken in cold water, and then I'll cook it, but next time you'll have to do it."

Then I thought, yes, in marriage there are a lot of those kinds of jobs and worse. I can do that, but do I want to give up the dances and the fun times? I didn't know; I simply didn't know.

Myron Lynde, age 23

EARLY LIFE OF MYRON LYNDE

◆

This is the story of my life and how I happened to become a sheep man. It seems to me life is like a card game, you are dealt a hand and you play it as best you can.

I was born to Charles Harvey Taylor and Emma Stanford Taylor in Grangeville, Idaho, on Grandfather Martin Van Buren Taylor's large ranch July 26, 1907. I was blessed with fine grandparents, uncles, aunts and a girl cousin about my age. I was the first grandson and lived on the ranch with all my family near by, so I got treated pretty special.

Shortly before I was two, my parents moved to Lewistown, Idaho. There they ran a general store. It was a small town, so I got attention from friends and customers. Here my sister Marjorie was born, but at the age of two, she died quite suddenly which was very hard on both my parents. There was much unhappiness between them, so Mother left my father and took me to Gillette, Wyoming, where we lived with her parents, Frank and Ana Stanford.

I missed my father very much, but my grandparents were good to me. My mother worked for a doctor, so I didn't see much of her because she lived at their house. My grandfather was a hostler for the railroad. Sometimes Grandpa took me to the roundhouse and let me sit in the big engine. I was sure I'd grow up to be an engineer. Granddad was also the county coroner, but that was not a job I aspired to.

Grandmother was a midwife and nurse. People in Gillette joked that they were either cared for by Ana or Frank Stanford. There was no hospital, so grandma occasionally nursed someone in her home. One time a young girl, a victim of white slavery, took poison. The doctor felt she wouldn't live, but knew that if she did, she would need a lot of good nursing, so he brought her to Grandma's house. A short time later, the girl died. I was playing on the floor near the door to her room when she raised up and fell dead. This certainly left a lasting impression; now sixty years later, it is still very clear in my mind.

That summer, Grandma decided to go to Iowa to visit family and friends and she took me along. She was always reminding me to be careful with my clothes, wanting me to be clean. Just before we arrived at the town we were to visit, she helped me into a clean white shirt, saying, "Now don't get dirty."

When the train stopped, I was standing at the steps, and the Negro porter picked me up and set me down on the platform. I carefully examined my white shirt, looked at Grandma, and said, "He didn't get me dirty." The poor woman was terribly embarrassed, as she tried to explain to the porter that it was the first time I'd seen a Negro. The porter seemed to understand and he and Grandma chuckled, but I had a feeling I'd said something wrong.

The home where we stayed had several youngsters for me to play with. One night a terrible thunder storm came up. The lightning was fierce and the loud thunder really scared everyone. Grandma gathered up the children and put us all on a feather bed. She told us not to be afraid, because when you were on a feather bed, lightning wouldn't harm you. Her story calmed all of us.

One time a group of family and friends gathered in the country for a picnic. The adults rode out in buggies, but we children were fortunate and got to ride out on a railroad hand car. This was great fun. The men looked very strong as they pumped the hand car, making it go fast, to our delight. I was sure I'd like to work as a section hand. At the picnic, we had lots of delicious food, even watermelon. But what I remembered most was "real" strawberry pop that came out of a bottle and tasted so good. The bottles were cooled in a tub with lots of ice.

In town there were nights when it was so hot no one could sleep in the house, so everyone took newspapers and spread them out on the lawn to lie on. Even then it was hard to sleep. I said, "Grandma, I'll sure be glad when we can go home." She patted me on the head and said, "Yes dear, I'll be glad when we can go home and sleep in our own beds. I'm thankful that nights in Wyoming are cool enough to sleep covered with a blanket."

One time Grandma took me to a park when we had to wait for a train. There was a slide in the park, and I was eager to try it because I'd never seen one. Down I came and lit right on my back. I cried because I was humiliated and because it hurt and had been so unexpected. Then the caretaker came and made a big show of putting more sand at the bottom of the slide so I wouldn't get hurt again. But as far as I was concerned, I'd had enough sliding for that day.

When our trip was over I was happy to get back to Gillette to our comfortable house and Granddad and he was glad to have us back too.

One vivid memory of my granddad was when he walked home with a big stock of bananas on his shoulder. At that time, fruit was shipped on the railroad in refrigerator cars, and every so many miles they would have to stop to put more ice in the cars. If any of the bananas had gotten over-ripe, they were taken out and sold. This day, Granddad bought the over-ripe bananas and took them home. Then Grandma was busy getting them around to all the neighbors. Fresh bananas were a real treat.

As the Christmas season drew near, I started looking at the catalog and decided I'd really like to have an Indian suit and a bow and arrows. In fact, it became an obsession with me. One day I saw Grandma carefully tucking a package away. I decided it must be my Indian suit, or she wouldn't have been so secretive. One day Grandma went over to Mrs. Vacey's, and I knew she'd be there quite a while, because they always had a good time visiting. I decided this would be a good time to peek in the package to see if it was really an Indian suit.

And there it was, just as pretty as it was in the catalog. I wondered if it would fit, so I tried it on. Suddenly Grandma appeared. Boy, was she mad! I received the full force of her Irish temper. I knew I'd never pull anything like that again. And then it turned out that having the suit wasn't half as much fun as wishing for it.

When Christmas came, all my naughty deeds were forgotten in the excitement of my new baby sister's arrival. Mother named her Cathryn, after my father's sister, and Mary after her sister.

When Mother was well enough, she decided to take a job in the hotel at Arvada. The wages were good and her sister Mary lived just across the street and could take care of Cathryn and me. Her son was older than me, but her daughter was just my age. It was fun having cousins to play with.

HOME IN LODGE GRASS ON THE CROW RESERVATION

In November of 1913, Mother and William Lynde were married, and we took the train to Lodge Grass. Amid the noise and steam of the engine, Bill, a tall man, carried my sister Cathryn and ushered my pretty mother as she led me, now six years old, toward the red wooden depot. At the time, Lodge Grass had no hotel, so the folks talked with the depot agent, A.G. Westwood, and he said that his family could accommodate us for a few days. Their son, Junior, and I became lifelong pals.

Dad, as I called Bill now, then contacted Mr. Perle Mapes who needed a teamster to haul ties from the Wolf Mountains to shore up tunnels in his Lodge Grass coal mine located at the edge of town (under the present School Hill).

The Mapes had built a home near the mine and were moving out of the house rented from the Indian, White Arm. He was one of the two Lodge Grass Indian Policemen. We rented the soon-to-be-vacant house and it became home. The White Arm family were good people; their daughter was about my age, and we became good friends. The Indian children went to school at the Mission near the Little Horn River, but I went to school for the White children in a small town house. I was a good student and had a real hunger for learning.

It was almost Christmas when Mother sent me to the Henman Trading Post on an errand. After Mr. Henman got the raisins Mother had ordered, he brought out a beautiful new sled which he gave to me and said it was a Christmas present. I was surprised and pleased. I thanked him and started home to show my handsome gift to Mother, disappointed because there was no snow and my new sled was hard to pull on bare ground.

I don't know when or why Dad got it in his head to make a bronco rider out of me. At age six, I certainly hadn't thought of it. But every evening, Dad would put colts in the corral for me to ride after school. I didn't like anything about it. In fact, I hated every minute of it. Other kids didn't have to ride broncs. Each evening, I dreaded the end of school, because I hated to go home, and I was actually glad if the teacher kept me after school. I vowed I'd never become a bronco rider when I grew up.

On October 16, 1914, my sister Wilma Theresa was born and soon after that, our family became acquainted with Mr. George Deputee who worked in Stevenson's store. His wife, a nice Indian lady, had died. George had a new house, and he made a deal with my folks that they could live there rent free if he could keep one room for himself. He had a Victrola and played high class music. He was well educated and had lots of books. He loved gardening and furnished us with produce and his cow furnished milk. It was a good arrangement. Mother was a fine cook and housekeeper and did lots of canning.

Our family was very hospitable, and we had a great deal of company. Mr. Deputee enjoyed all the visitors and seemed to appreciate being part of the family. He taught me many things beyond my little world. He gave me jobs, so I could make spending money, and taught me I must always pay my bills. He was a wonderful friend and influenced my life in many ways. Years later, when I was 17 and on my way home from college for vacation, and he was in the Hardin Hospital dying, I went to see him. He gave me his last precious possession, his Black Hills Gold watch with a diamond in the back. I was so touched that tears ran down my cheeks, and I wanted to cry like a baby. I vowed I'd never carry it—it was too precious—but it would forever remind me of the great man who had always had it on his person. A lump still comes to my throat when I remember the day he gave his watch to me.

Dad truly loved trading horses. Living on the Reservation was a good place to locate them, as the Indians had many horses to trade. Then Grover Swartz came to dad and told him that the government wanted to start a beef herd for the Indians. They needed to get rid of the wild horses running the range on the West side of the Big Horn River because they would need the grass for the cattle. Would Dad be interested in going in partners with him?

This was the kind of thing both men loved and they quickly gathered others to help them: Carl Cresswell, Jim Cooper, and two men who were good hands, but went by only one name. One was "Kansas" and the other was "Smokey."

Each man had to take several very dependable horses. I was only seven years old, but the men decided to take me because I was a good rider and light on a horse and could do the same work as a good man.

Rounding up horses in that big open country where there were no fences at all took a lot of strenuous riding. Several good horses were ruined because their riders expected too much from them. Finally the wild horses were gathered and delivered to the stockyard at Rowley. There they would be shipped on the railroad. As soon as they were loaded, the government paid off each of the men.

With their money, Mr. Swartz and Dad decided to build a livery barn which was badly needed for ranchers and cowboys. When the barn was completed, cowboys riding into Lodge Grass to catch a train to civilization, such as Sheridan, Wyoming, Hardin or Billings, Montana, would have a place to leave their horses until they returned. Most everyone had to make trips to Hardin, as it was the county seat for Big Horn County. The bunk room in the Livery barn was an interesting place for me because much of the time there were footloose cowboys who needed a place to stay and they'd bed down there. And there were always horses to break, so some cowboys could make a little money while they were between jobs.

It was about 1915 when a young man from Minnesota by the name of Howard Johnson arrived in Lodge Grass. He was in his late teens and hung around the barn very eager to get a job—and because he was a good worker, he was doing everything that needed doing around the barn. Everyone liked Howard. Dad brought him home to dinner and he became a part of the family. To me he became a very good friend, like a big brother, and taught me many things. He was a reliable young man and had abundant drive and energy. He'd take me with him on jobs, and he really taught me how to work. The two of us did as much work as two or three men could do. The day was never too long for us. Dad furnished the horses, and even at eight I was as good at driving a team as good as a man. The horses were too big for me to harness, but if Howard would throw the harness on them, I could handle the rest. Howard always appreciated my efforts and encouraged me to do everything I could. If I did something that Dad would be mad about, and Howard felt it couldn't be helped, he would accept the blame. He saved me from a number of whippings. No wonder I idolized him. And though he always teased me unmercifully, I really learned to take it.

In the summer of 1916, the government decided to build reservoirs so there would be plenty of water for the range cattle. Dad put in his bid and was hired. He had plenty of work horses. Howard would drive one team and I would drive another, although I was only nine years old. Then Dad hired a cowboy by the name of Jim Kincade who had decided he would rather drive a team on a dirt job than go out on a roundup.

When the Fourth of July came, everyone took time off for a big picnic at the Lynde's. Mr. Deputee always kept the yard beautiful. It was large and well shaded by the big cottonwood trees. The women brought wonderful food— even homemade ice cream.

However, I was very sick when we came in from the dirt camp, running a high fever. Then when all the people arrived, Mother made excuses for me but everyone was wondering what was causing such a high fever. For dinner they had watermelon, my favorite treat, and I was too sick to eat it.

The next day when Mother checked me, I had broken out with Small Pox, the only case of it anyone knew about. Everyone was concerned about the people who had been exposed during the picnic and wondered who would come down with it next. Jim Kincade was the only one who did, and he had been at the dirt camp, too.

Jim was still sick when it was time to put up the hay, so Howard and Dad decided to do that; they finished the reservoirs afterwards. It was a busy time and difficult to get help, so even though I was badly broken out with Small Pox, they decided to take me out to drive the stacker horse, reasoning, that I could sit in the shade most of the time.

I was sick and miserable; I had pox all over me, even on the soles of my feet, but I did my best to get comfortable as often as possible. Once I was hunkered down in the shade of the hay stack, not paying attention to much of anything. Suddenly Howard called down, "Okay, Myron, take 'er up." I jumped to my miserably sore feet, hobbled out to the horse, and started the stacker rising. Then I discovered the stacker was empty. They hadn't even gotten in with the hay. Howard began to laugh like it was the funniest thing that ever happened. I was really infuriated and yelled some very choice words at him, calling him everything that came to mind, but he thought it was so funny he slapped his leg and laughed some more. So I hollered, "Okay Howard, someday I'm going to get even with you."

Years later, Howard was riding the stacker down when something broke and Howard fell flat on the ground. He just knew I did it to get even. It took a lot of convincing and an examination of the stacker for him to believe that it truly was an accident.

As a young boy I thought it was great to hang around the livery barn because that was where the cowboys hung out. They treated me like a friend. Howard liked to box; he'd match up with someone about his size, and they'd have at it with bare knuckles. Then everyone would gather around and bet on them. I watched with mixed emotions and was happy when Howard won without getting too badly beat up. However, there were times when he would be black and blue all over, his eyes nearly swollen shut. His lips would be cut up, and his hands so badly swollen that he couldn't even tie his shoes; then I'd happily stay in the bunk room at the barn to help him any way that I could.

Dad was always buying and selling horses. Once he got a nice looking black and white pinto pony called Billy in a trade. Dad felt that I could ride him and get him gentled down so he could be sold as a kids' pony. But I was continually getting bucked off because he was so darn tricky.

One day H.W. Willcutt, foreman for the I.D. Cattle Company, came to the barn to buy horses for the cow outfit. He saw Billy and thought he was just the horse for his son Harvey. Dad told him Billy was just a little tricky. I thought, "What an understatement," but of course a horse trader's son never dared have his say, so I kept still. Mr. Willcutt was so sure Harvey could ride him that I thought, "Well, maybe he can, and if so, I'll never hear the end of it." But I liked Harvey and if he could, I'd be glad for my friend.

The next I heard of Billy, Mr. Willcutt had sold him to an out-of-state horse trader. When I saw Harvey he said that Billy was so darn tricky that he couldn't stay on him. I was glad he told me because it gave me some satisfaction. Years later, when we were both in our sixties, I was visiting with him at his ranch and he brought out a picture of a horse and asked, "Remember him?" It was Billy, and how we both laughed as the memories of all the grief that pony had caused us flooded back.

The hayloft of the barn acted as a social center. During the summer, an orchestra from Sheridan, Wyoming, was hired to play for dances held every two weeks. They would come on the evening train and play until it was daylight. About that time the morning train arrived and they could catch it back to Sheridan. It was fun for everyone, and we all looked forward to the next dance in two weeks.

Parents generally took their children to such dances. Babies were put to sleep under the benches. The other children played and imitated the adults by trying to dance. They could sleep or visit with each other, but they were not allowed to run in the dance hall. About midnight everyone paused for a supper of roast beef sandwiches, a pickle, coffee and a piece of cake, all made by women in the community.

I always worked with men, and other kids did too, like Junior Westwood. Each evening it was up to me to take the horses to the pasture which was near the Westwood Ranch, so Junior and I often got together to play and visit. His sister, Geraldine, liked to tag around after us, but we didn't appreciate it. One time we convinced Gerry that it was a lot of fun to sail on the river in a wash tub. She got in and we shoved her off. Watching her floating and bobbing down the Little Big Horn River scared us though, and we really made a mad scramble to rescue her.

When Junior and I were in our late teens, about 1925, a movie company came to Lodge Grass to make "Red Raiders." They hired the whole community as extras. The white men were hired as cavalrymen. My Dad was an officer. I was the bugler. When they took close ups of me, I was sitting on a board that moved up and down so it looked as if I was riding, and they had a fan blowing in my face. It blew my scarf and hat back like I was riding fast, and I was blowing the bugle. It did look real, but it was good that it was a silent movie, because I couldn't really blow the bugle.

Some of the movie was shot among the pine trees on the Westwood Ranch. One of the men with the company took a fancy to my white horse, and he offered me so much money for him that I couldn't refuse. I hated to give him up, but I had other horses, and I was happy when I saw him in other movies. One was a circus story. There was my horse, looking as if he was enjoying every minute of being under those bright lights in his fancy trappings.

When World War I broke out, most all of the young cowboys enlisted and they gave away much of their paraphernalia. Three of the men gave me their chaps, saddles and bridles. It was as if they wouldn't be coming back. It was a gloomy, sobering time in our small community. I felt sad as I watched these young men swing aboard the train. Worst of all was knowing my buddy Howard was leaving and it would be a long time before he came back, if he came back.

All of Lodge Grass got into the war effort. Most noticeable was the shortage of help. Young women went to ranches to help in whatever way they could. The women rolled bandages, bought War Bonds, wrote the boys' letters and did a lot of knitting for the soldiers.

At school we all did our bit, but what stands out most in my mind was the patriotism we all felt. We eagerly saluted the flag and happily said the Pledge of Allegiance every morning. We sang patriotic songs and played war games. We all learned to knit wash rags for the men. The ones I made didn't turn out very well, but I put my best effort into the project. Everyone saved tin foil and string. I don't know what it was for, but we saved it.

The cow outfits were really short of help when it was time to pull out the roundup wagons. Bill Prante, the I.D. Wagon Boss came to the livery barn to see if he could find anyone who could wrangle horses. The horse wrangler's job was to bring the horses to the rope corral in the evening so each cowboy could have a fresh mount in the morning for the long day's ride in gathering the cattle. The wrangler would watch the horses graze, but during this time it was also his job to chop wood and carry water for the cook. Sunny Jim, a handyman around Lodge Grass, said that he could chop wood and help the cook any other way, but he couldn't possibly handle the horses. I was ten years old, and I spoke up and said, "I could wrangle horses."

Prante looked at me, then looked at Dad and said, "By golly, he sure could. What do you think?" Dad kind of grinned and said, "I'll talk to his mother." I felt terribly grown up as we rode out to the roundup wagon. The work was easy for me, but lonesome. I missed my family and friends and was glad when the job was done.

Dad always had horses that needed riding, so that was part of my job. When there was a need to send a message to a distant ranch it was easy to send me. I'd get on a long-legged horse and away I would go. Often I would have to spend the night and come back the next day. It was also my job to wrangle the town milk cows. I'd take them out in the open country and turn them loose to graze. In the evening, they'd generally start back to town because that's where their calves were. I'd gather and count them, and they'd go on home. But one evening when I went after the cows, my horse bucked me off, and I was knocked unconscious way out there in the hills. The cows and my horse went into town. When it got dark everyone got concerned about me, but they didn't know where to look. Finally, at nine o'clock when the train went through Lodge Grass and blew the whistle, I came to and walked on home, afraid I'd get the devil because I was so late. I was greatly surprised because everyone was glad to see me, telling me they'd been worried and had been searching and wanting me to tell them what had happened.

I was always doing something to make spending money. When the men from the roundup wagons came into town ready for a good time, I would hurry to get my shoe shining box and shine their boots. I only charged ten cents, but they would give me a dollar and insist I keep the change. It was the same way when I was selling papers; they'd give me a big tip and then throw the papers away.

FORT KEOGH HORSES

When the war ended in 1918, Barney McLean, a young cowboy who was a friend of the family stationed at the remount station at Fort Keogh (Miles City), came back to Lodge Grass. He came to visit the folks and he told Dad, "The horses we broke there were for the French, British and U.S. Armies. Now they are to be dispersed. There's going to be a big sale and the horses will be sold to the highest bidder. They are some of the best horses you'll ever want to see; most of them are well broken. Why don't you and I go over and buy some? I'm sure you won't be disappointed. There are some that I know and will try to buy for myself. I would buy more, but I don't have much of a place to keep them, nor the money to buy more."

Dad really got enthused and he got the camp outfit ready to go. It was decided that I should go along, and the three of us could bring them back. So we piled everything we were going to need in Dad's Model T Ford and away we went to Miles City. I was very interested in seeing the Fort but more interested in seeing all those fine horses. Dad wound up buying 300 head. Every one was a good horse. Some of these horses had been artillery horses, so they were in great demand by both Indian and white farmers. The balance were Cavalry horses that would be sold to large cow outfits which always needed gentled horses.

Barney and I each saddled up a good horse; Barney took the lead and I followed in the drag. We came up Rosebud Creek following General Custer's route. Dad went ahead in the car and made camp, cooking the meals over a campfire in dutch ovens. It took us four days to get to Lodge Grass. People from all over came to look at the horses. Most who came bought and were happy to get them.

WYOMING STEERS

The spring and summer of 1919 were very dry around Arvada, Wyoming. They had no grass or water for their cattle, and even the Powder River went dry, so those ranchers had to sell their cattle. The Crow Reservation had plenty of grass, running creeks and rivers. Several ranchers in the Lodge Grass area got together and bought 1,000 head of steers, then shipped them by railroad to Parkman, Wyoming. The men drove to Parkman, ready to receive them when they arrived.

Dad sent me a telegram to bring ten head of horses and meet them there. The cattle would be taken to Pass Creek to water, and then on to Lodge Grass Basin. I was 12 years old and felt very grown up; I took my responsibility seriously. When I got the wire, I went to the pasture, gathered the horses and left early. As I rode along, I thought, "I'm glad the men have their saddles with them; I'd hate to have to saddle all these horses."

I was so eager to do this man's job that I started plenty early. I wanted to be sure to be there when they arrived, and I didn't want any of the horses to be tired when they got there. I'd ride one horse for about ten miles, then take off my saddle and put it on another and ride for another ten miles. Of course, as light weight as I was then, there was no way those grain fed horses could have grown tired.

Of course, I arrived much too early. The cattle train wasn't due until midnight. I had been told to wait at Mattie's, a cafe with a pool table. I had some money, so I ate while Mattie visited with me, showing me much kindness and respect. I felt very grown up.

By the time the cattle got into Parkman, it was dark, so the men decided to leave them in the Stockyards until daylight. The riders were tired and pitched their camp near by. In the night, the cattle could smell water. They broke out and took off towards Pass creek. The men jumped up, but no one could stop the thirsty cattle. The men found the cattle drinking the good clear mountain water which was such a treat that they drank too much. Several died and some were sick for a while.

As soon as the men got organized, they drove the cattle to the Lodge Grass Basin. There they had plenty of good grass and mountain water. Rubin Spotted Horse, a good cowboy, was hired to take care of them on the mountain for the summer, and I was to stay up there and help him. We had a cabin and Rubin did the cooking while I did chores. The steers were content in the Basin during the day, but in the evening when it was cool, they would try to come out, so we really had to watch the trails.

I found the idle time during the day very boring, so I rode around and visited ranchers and got many good meals. The ranch I enjoyed visiting the most was the Dominic Stevens Ranch. Mrs. Stevens gathered me in and treated me just like she did her own children, who were my good friends. We all went to school in Lodge Grass, and I thought Josephine Stevens was very special.

When fall came, Rubin and I were very pleased that we had every steer. For my summer's work, I received a bicycle. I proudly rode it to school, but when the fall rains and snow came, I went back to riding horses.

That winter of 1919 was the hard winter of all hard winters. The stockmen suffered terrible losses.

Snow covered the ground in October and stayed on the ground until April, and it was extremely cold. This was very unusual for the Reservation, so the stockmen had little or no hay. They had to have hay shipped from as far away as Nebraska by railroad at huge expense which bankrupted nearly every rancher. The hay was of poor quality and didn't give the livestock enough strength to pull through the winter. It was good to have Howard Johnson, my buddy, back from the Army, even though he spent all of his time hauling hay to the cattle. I went with him as often as I could, and it was awful to see the many cattle that died.

When spring came, huge trenches had to be dug to bury all the carcasses. The Indian Department cattle also died. Their losses were so great that they decided to disperse what was left of their herd.

In 1920, Mother and Dad were able to buy the old I.D. Headquarters located four miles out of town on the Lodge Grass Creek road, known as the Peanut. They changed the cabin into a barn and built a new home. They sold the Livery barn and turned to ranching but continued horse trading.

My grandparents, Frank and Ana Stanford, from Gillette, Wyoming, retired from the railroad and moved to Lodge Grass. They built a nice new house and Granddad took the job of school janitor. My two sisters stayed with them during the week and went to school. I rode back and forth on a long-legged horse after I milked the cows, but I'd get to school early enough to help Granddad with some of the janitor work. I took out the ashes, pumped the drinking water, and put it in the cooler. Granddad always kept everything sparkling clean. When school was out, I'd check with him to see what there was to do; the main thing always was to get the coal. Once that was done, I'd get on my horse and ride home in time to milk the two cows and do my chores before supper. It sure didn't take my horse long to get home, knowing good feed and his barn were waiting for him. When there were social things going on in the evening, back to town I would go.

On Fridays, my sisters would go home, so I would take the buggy. One time school let out unexpectedly on Thursday and the girls wanted to go home. I was riding Jud, a big gentle horse, so I said, "My horse is gentle; all three of us can ride him home."

I rode him right up to the back walk and Grandma came out with the girls. She helped them get up behind me. Suddenly Jud began bucking and the girls fell off. I was trying to figure why my gentle horse bucked. Then Grandma said, "I'll tell you what happened. I dumped hot ashes right where your horse was standing and forgot about it. No doubt it took a while before it got too hot."

All of us were sorry about it, but Jud was no longer standing in the ashes and seemed okay, so I said, "Well girls, get back on and we'll head for home." Theresa climbed on but Cathryn didn't. She decided she'd rather stay in town. I really couldn't blame her.

Soon my graduation day came. There were just two of us in the graduating class of 1923. Leonard Young was valedictorian and I was salutatorian and we both received scholarships from the University of Montana.

The people of Lodge Grass went all out to make our graduation special. They decorated the Little Brown Church. Our class flower was the wild Shooting Star, so the high school students went out in the hills and picked so many that the church had a lovely aroma. They also had a nice banquet for us; the whole school attended.

Whenever Leonard and I had to stand beside each other, everyone got a kick out of it. Leonard looked like the teacher and I looked like the student. He got his growth early, so he was a tall 18 year old boy and quite filled out. I was still 15 years old as my birthday wasn't until the last of July. I was younger, and I also looked like a boy. All summer I hoped I'd grow before fall, as I still had to wear knee pants; that was all there was for boys my size. When it was time for me to leave for Missoula, it was embarrassing, but I could still ride the train for half fare!

At college, Leonard and I shared a room, but we didn't see a whole lot of each other. I worked for my board by waiting tables and washing glasses. Also, whenever I had spare time, I found other jobs to earn extra money.

COYOTING

During spring break I had to leave college because the folks needed me to do the farming. Howard quit because he was going to ranch for himself. He and Hilma, a teacher, were to be married as soon as school was out.

When the spring wheat was planted, I got the haying equipment ready to start haying. If I had any spare time, there were the broncs to be broken. One time when Buck Brien and I were working with the broncs, I got a terrible kick on my shin and flew against the corral. It hurt so bad I couldn't even groan. Buck came over and looked at my sickly white face with much sympathy. "Does it hurt?" By then I had gotten my breath back and I groaned out, "Hell no, what makes you think it hurts?" Buck and I laughed over that kick the rest of our lives, at the time, it wasn't funny.

After we got our wheat cut and bound, we had to wait our turn for the threshing machine. It was a rewarding time. The neighbors all gathered to help each other, and there was always a lot of joking and camaraderie that went on—plus the wonderful food. One of our neighbors was Roy Mason. His brother Jack, who was visiting from Missouri, also came. When he was visiting with my parents, he mentioned that he planned to stay the winter if he could find a place where he could do chores for his board. This was good news to me, because I hated to be tied to the ranch just to do the chores.

It was at that time that Bobby Stovall, who was just my age, became my good friend. His family was ranching on Soap Creek. When we heard that the job of caretaker was open at the Soap Creek Oil Field, we asked for it. We got the job and we were each paid $50.00 a month. The place was quite isolated, especially in the winter, but we were happy to have a job. The cabin we lived in was just a shell and impossible to keep warm. We had no coal, so it took a lot of wood. I promised to locate and drag in the wood, chop it and carry in the water if Bobby would do the cooking. He was a good cook, so had fine meals. Our meat was venison, as there were a lot of deer around our camp. We also had a lot of trout until the creek froze over.

The coyote population had increased so much that all the ranchers were complaining about livestock losses, so a bounty had been put on them. Bobby and I had time on our hands, and we thought we could put it to good use by trapping and hunting coyotes while we were keeping a sharp eye on the oil field and its possessions.

Each morning right after breakfast, Bobby would go one way and I would go the other. We averaged ten or twelve coyotes a month. Then one morning I spotted a coyote way off. I knew I could hit him because I had a long range rifle. I got off my horse and propped my rifle so I'd be sure to hit him. Very carefully I took aim, pleased that I could get such a good shot. But something told me not to pull the trigger. I decided to sneak close. My prey stood upright—it was Bobby. He'd been on his knees skinning a coyote.

I began to shake and wasn't myself the rest of the day. In fact, it scares me yet when I think of how close I came to taking a life, and he was my best friend. There were times when I thought of telling Bobby, but I couldn't. We remained friends for a lifetime and I could never tell him how close I'd come to pulling the trigger. I still get a chill when I think of it.

We two got along very well because we'd both been raised among men (cowboys). On special occasions we'd ride into Lodge Grass, get cleaned up, get a hair cut, then take girls to a dance and spend the night at my folks. Generally we picked up a few groceries, but not many because we had to put whatever we bought in our saddle bags.

One time we decided to attend a turkey shoot. Bobby was such an excellent shot that he won four turkeys. The organizers had to bar him from further competition. But we had a good time giving the turkeys away before we hurried back to our camp on Soap Creek.

Occasionally some rider or neighbor would stop in and stay for a meal. It was pleasant to have company and hear whatever news they had. Often they brought us magazines and newspapers which were certainly appreciated. I had a great hunger for any reading material. I read and reread books. Bobby had a hobby of making things out of rawhide, such as bridles and so he didn't feel the need for reading like I did.

Our evenings were spent playing rummy. This we did with gusto, until we practically wore the spots off the cards. Being young we were happy, and each of us had a keen sense of humor, so everything was fun. Often we'd wrestle to see who would do a chore, but we were so evenly matched that it took quite a while before one of us was pinned.

Sometimes we'd ride over to Black Canyon to fish. Bill taught me how to rope a trout. The way he did it was to take some fine copper wire and fix it like a lasso; then we'd lay on the bank, and ever so carefully slip it over the trout's tail, slowly but surely keeping it moving until it reached the gills. A quick jerk, and he'd have the trout. I never could get the hang of it because I wasn't that steady. Neither did I have the patience.

When we decided that we'd made enough money, we went into Hardin and bought a new Chevrolet Roadster. It was beautiful, shiny and pretty. It had a cloth top that could be put up or down as we wished. We were thrilled with our new car and very proud that we had earned it ourselves. Of course, we wanted to show it off, so we drove it to Lodge Grass to let all of our friends and families see it. That evening, we learned of a country dance in the Wolf Mountains and decided to drive there. The mountain road had many sharp curves. We missed a bad one and wrecked our beautiful new car. We were back where we started, but thankful that neither of us had gotten hurt.

DUDE RANCHING

When spring came, Bobby and I weren't sure what we were going to do. Jack Mason was still at the ranch, so I wasn't needed to do the farming. When we stopped at Bobby's folk's ranch, his sister said that she'd hired out as a cook to the new Canyon Creek Dude Ranch on upper Lodge Grass Creek. She asked us to hire out as wranglers. This sounded good, so we hurried over there and got the job of wrangling dudes.

They put us to work right away, doing all kinds of things. We had to plant the garden and tend it, milk and take care of the two cows, etc.

The carpenter was to finish the large recreation room, so we had to haul logs. The bricklayer built a beautiful large fireplace and received a lot of praise from everyone, but it was Bobby and I who hauled the rock for it. The barn was always shiny clean and the boss got praised for it, but it was our job to clean it and keep it that way.

Another job that I seemed to fall heir to was wrangling the horses. Bobby and I were supposed to take turns going after them early in the morning before breakfast, but Bobby liked to sleep in. Not so with me. As soon as it was daylight, I was up feeling great and ready to go after the horses.

When the ranch needed ice, Bobby and I were sent to Sheridan after a truck load. When we got back, we unloaded and stacked it in the ice house, carefully covering it with sawdust to keep it as long as possible.

Finally the day came when the boss drove into the ranch with beautiful dude girls from the east, about ten or twelve of them. Bobby and I really perked up. This was why we hired out. The boss said our job was to take the girls and their chaperon on pack trips into the mountains. This was fun, even though it was hard work and a great deal of responsibility. But the girls were fun-loving as was their chaperon, so we had lots of fun.

Every so often the boss would come up to the mountains to bring us supplies and to see that everything was going as planned. Bill was the cook, but the girls willingly helped, although they didn't know much about cooking or camping. They were good sports about any hardships they had to put up with, and their chaperon also seemed to enjoy the new experiences.

I took care of the horses and helped the girls set up their range tepees each time we had to make camp. Also, I got the wood, chopped it and did the other odd jobs around camp. For instance, if we were in timber, we'd chop pine boughs for the girls' beds. They'd roll out their camp beds on them, finding the boughs a softer place to sleep than the rocky mountain ground.

Often we caught trout for the girls. They appreciated the fine job Bobby could do in frying them over the campfire in Dutch ovens, and it was a pleasant change of menu. We saw wild game such as bear, deer and elk. Of course, the girls were scared of the bears. In the evening, we'd sit around the campfire and talk, telling them exaggerated ways to save themselves if they should come upon a bear. It was all in good fun, and they seemed to enjoy the teasing.

At one camp we got on the subject of wild game, and the girls said they'd eaten both deer and elk and now they would like to eat some bear meat before they went home. We realized we'd have to get one soon because the boss wanted us back at the ranch in two days. If we didn't get there, he'd come after us, and we'd be in the dog house.

Near this camp bear were plentiful, and the girls kept after us until we decided to do it. However, we explained that meat really should be aged. But they asked, "Wouldn't it be all right if we only ate a little of it, just to say we'd tasted bear meat?"

Bobby and I talked it over. The boss had emphasized that it was our job to please the guests, so it was up to me to get the bear. I located a young one that I felt would be good meat. We skinned it and let it cool that night. The next day Bobby cut and fried some beautiful steaks and everyone eagerly ate, much more than just a taste. It wasn't long before we all had a bad case of diarrhea and everyone had to hurry off to some brush patch. After that, they lost interest in bear meat.

We'd all had a good time roaming in the mountains, but that part of their vacation was over. Now the boss would be taking them to the Indian dances, rodeos, etc., but we would have to stay at the ranch and work.

Then fall came, and it was time for the girls to leave. It was a melancholy time, like parting with good friends, but they said they would be coming back next year.

COYOTING WITH WOLFHOUNDS

Bobby and I were glad to get away from the chores of the ranch and looked forward to hunting coyotes again.

Bobby and I went back to the camp on Soap Creek, but the coyotes were all cleaned out. Then we heard that Tschirgi's sheep headquarters on Shoulder Blade Creek were having real trouble with coyotes killing their livestock and they needed a wolfer, so we rode right over to see if we could get the job.

They hired us to run their own wolfhounds. This was new and exciting. Neither of us knew anything about hunting with dogs, but the dogs knew about hunting coyotes. Soon we learned how to handle the hounds. Each dog had a personality all his own; they gave us excitement and many chuckles, and, at times, hearty laughter.

Each day we had to cook a huge pan of corn bread and cracklings to feed the dogs. However, the dogs that went with us didn't get fed until they got back to camp because they'd run better on an empty stomach. Early in the morning, before daybreak, we'd have our horses saddled, taking seven of the fourteen dogs with us. The other seven would be penned at camp to rest so they would be ready to go the next day. We caught many coyotes, so we felt we were earning our wages. We sold the hides, plus receiving the bounty placed on them. We were real pleased that we were doing so well.

At Christmas time, Bobby and I made big plans. We were to go to Lodge Grass, have dinner with my family, and take our special girls to the dance...but the cook at Shoulder Blade Camp and the five men who worked there each said they had planned to go into town. Each of them had very pressing business in Hardin, and asked if we wouldn't stay and feed the hay to the 75 head of buck sheep and the 15 head of horses, just until they could get to town, take care of their business and be right back. We said we'd like to help out, if someone could get back before Christmas as we had plans and even dates for the dance. The cook was a nice guy and he said, "Some of them will get back, and I damn sure will be back, because I only need a couple of days."

Two days went by. We weren't too surprised when no one showed, but a bit disappointed; we tried to be understanding. Anyone might have trouble and need an extra day. As each day went by, though, we became more and more disappointed. We tried to be generous. We said, "The cook is a nice guy. He wouldn't let us down. Surely he'll be here at least the day before Christmas. We can still get into Lodge Grass, get our hair cut and baths, then make it to our Christmas dinner and the dance that evening."

All Christmas Day we sat there, feeling sorry for ourselves and feeling betrayed. Finally Bobby said, "You know, in the back of that cupboard is a bottle of booze. Why don't we have a drink or two to celebrate?"

Under the circumstances, this seemed like a good idea, although neither of us had done much drinking because, being young, we had fun just being ourselves. After having one drink, we decided to have another one. As we sat there at the table talking, two of the hounds we had in the kitchen came sniffing around to see what we were up to. There was bread on the table, and we decided to put a bit of whisky on it and then give each of the dogs a taste. They howled and carried on as if they enjoyed the treat, and we had a great time laughing at their antics. Then they came back for more. After that, they staggered and really carried on. It was probably a good thing we ran out of liquor, but that was our Christmas for 1925.

When the cook got back, we accepted his apologies and the usual activities of the camp resumed. We were off to hunt more coyotes. We did very well, and the Tschirgi sheep people were pleased to be rid of the predators.

When spring came, Bobby went to his folks' ranch to help with the spring work, and I went to help my parents to get the crops in. We were really looking forward to going back to the Dude Ranch.

MORE DUDE RANCHING

It was time to get the Dude Ranch ready for guests. There were many boring things to do, but now we knew the girls and looked forward to seeing them. Some of them had corresponded with us, so we knew they were eager to get back to the ranch.

The day arrived and there was much activity at the ranch; everything was as perfect as the help could get it. The boss went to Wyola to meet the train the girls would be coming on. All the hired help were to be in the yard to greet the guests. When they climbed out of the cars, we were all happy to see each other. We all felt as if we were old friends.

The girls went to their cabins to unpack and get settled after their long train ride. But they all seemed to be looking forward to the first pack trip scheduled for the season. Of course, there were times when the boss took the dudes different places. There were trips to Sheridan, and sometimes they stayed overnight to take in something of special interest.

When they were gone, Bobby and I had some time to ourselves. We'd get on our horses and ride up in the mountains or to some place of interest to us.

One day when Bobby and I were riding up Lodge Grass Creek, we saw a young black bear, a yearling. He was going through a thick brush patch. Bobby said, "You follow him through that patch of brush. I'm going around to where he will come out and I'll rope him." I knew Bobby was a good roper, but I didn't see why he wanted to rope a bear. I couldn't question him because he was already going around the brush.

Dutifully, I followed the bear through the brush. Soon there was much snarling. Sure enough, Bobby had roped him. He'd planned to rope him around the neck, and he did, but he'd also caught his front leg. The bear was panic stricken and fighting for his life. He ran around and around Bobby's horse, causing him to become tangled in the rope. The horse was as scared as the bear was. Now Bobby was in a terrible fix and I was helpless. Neither of us carried a gun. My horse was so scared he wouldn't hold still. The bear kept slashing at Bobby. His horse was quite bloody, now. Finally, Bobby was able to get his knife out of his pocket and cut the rope in several places. As soon as the bear was loose, he ran off, taking the rope with him. We both were off our horses in a second, examining Bobby's horse. He was bleeding badly. I didn't know how bad Bobby was, but he too was bleeding. We felt it best to get back to the ranch as fast as possible. Bobby's horse was limping badly, the ranch wasn't far.

When we got there, we took the mount to the creek where he could drink, and we washed the blood off so we could get a good look at his cuts. They were bad, and we knew he wouldn't make it through the night. We felt very sad. Bobby tried to console himself. With a catch in his throat, he said, "I feel bad about losing my favorite horse, but I'm thankful he didn't belong to the boss."

Then I insisted we look at Bobby's slashes. Although they were very bloody, they weren't deep. As soon as we had them washed off, I got out the Iodine bottle and doctored him up. I bandaged his leg, which I knew would be plenty sore. I was grateful that he'd soon be okay and wouldn't have to miss any work on account of his injury. I knew I could do the work that might be difficult for him. If he had gone home, I wouldn't have wanted to stay either, because being together made everything fun.

POT OF BEANS

At the dude ranch one of our many chores was to go fishing. We went about once a week, and then the ranch cook prepared a fish fry. We liked this chore. Early nearly every morning we'd go out and catch grasshoppers. We did this while it was still cool because the 'hoppers were sluggish. We lined our bait bucket with grass so they would survive until it was time to go fishing. The dude girls would come out and help us. They thought it was great sport, and because they thought it was so much fun to run after the 'hoppers, we'd laugh with them which made it a fun chore for us.

On fishing day, Bobby and I would take our poles and mount our horses about daybreak and ride up Lodge Grass Creek. He'd take one fork of the creek and I'd take the other. One day, I chose the North Fork, leaving South Fork for Bobby. At that time, the fishing was so good we only had to fish about a mile of each canyon. By then each of us would have about 25 nice trout.

From where I was fishing, I noticed what looked like the stock of a rifle sticking out of a rock ledge, as if someone had hidden it there. I went over and pulled it out. It was rusty and must have been there a long time. I'd already gotten my quota of fish, so I tied the rifle on my saddle and went to meet Bobby.

It was about ten o'clock when we got back to the ranch. We took the fish to the cook so she could store them in the cold spring water. When we entered the kitchen, the cook had a pot of beans and ham cooking on the back of her stove. It smelled awfully good to a couple of hungry young men.

We had a cold drink and chatted briefly; then I went out and got the rusty rifle to show the boss. He was sitting at the end of the table with his glass of iced tea. I said, "Look what I found in the canyon." Everyone wondered how old it was and who could have hidden it and why they'd never come after it, etc. Suddenly there was a loud BOOM. Beans went flying everywhere. Gun smoke filled the kitchen. The cook was furious. Not only was her dinner ruined, but her favorite bean pot had a great big hole in it...and there was that terrible mess to be cleaned up.

Apologies definitely were not accepted. She didn't care if she ever saw me again. Quickly and quietly, I slipped out the door with Bill right behind me, both of us hoping she'd simmer down before dinner time. Finally, after the mess was cleaned up, everyone saw the humor in it and laughed about it.

Later that day the boss showed real interest in the old gun and I was happy to give it to him because to me it was only a reminder of the mess I'd made of the kitchen. I was always very thankful no one happened to be near the stove and the bean pot.

RE-ENACTMENT

The first three weeks of June had passed so quickly that it was nearly time for the 50 Year Custer Battle Re-enactment. Everyone was excited about it and planned to attend. Huge crowds were expected.

There was to be a carnival at Crow Agency with colorful Indians dancing. Already they had their tepees set up. The Seventh Cavalry from Texas would be there. Not only would they be putting on the re-enactment, but they would be performing drills with their horses. Bobby and I had grown up riding horses and had known just about every kind of horse, so we were really looking forward to seeing the soldiers take their horses through the drills, which would be a first for us.

In the evening there would be dancing at the Pavilion and we knew our friends would congregate there. Of course, the dude girls and all the folks from the Canyon Creek Ranch would be going.

On the morning of the 26th, everyone was excited as they prepared to leave for the re-enactment. We planned to leave as soon as they were gone. However, the boss had different ideas and he gave us orders, "I want you two to take the truck to Sheridan and get a load of ice and when you get back, I want you to hoe the garden."

Two disappointed, crestfallen young men stood there watching as the cars drove away from the ranch. Then when they were out of sight, we climbed in the truck and started for Sheridan. On the highway we met many cars loaded with people. The licenses were from all over the United States. There were banners and signs about the Battle Re-enactment. We continued on to Sheridan, feeling sorry for ourselves and very unhappy with the boss.

At Sheridan we got our load of ice, but as we drove back toward Wyola, we talked of the events at the Battlefield.

When we arrived at the Wyola railroad crossing, we noticed a freight train loading with coal and water. We decided to put the truck of ice in a well-shaded garage in town while we got on the caboose and went to Crow Agency, watched the re-enactment and saw the Cavalry put their well-trained horses through their drills. If we didn't leave the ice in Wyola, we'd never make it in time because the ranch was a 35 mile drive.

We congratulated ourselves on a brilliant idea and climbed aboard the caboose just as the train was pulling out. At Crow Agency our friends were happy to see us and we mixed in the crowd, staying as far away from the boss as possible.

Soon the re-enactment was finished and the well-trained horses did their superb drill routines. We were spellbound until it was over, but then it was time to eat a hot dog and a slice of watermelon and go over to the depot. There we discovered we'd missed the train. However, we weren't too concerned because we felt sure we could catch a ride with someone who would be going our way, so we went to look around.

Back at the carnival the rides were going, and the merry-go-round music made it all so inviting, we were glad we'd missed the train. Soon the dance band began playing at the Pavilion; we decided to dance a few dances. We were having a wonderful time. The night passed before we knew it, and still we hadn't found a ride back. It seemed that everyone was spending the night in their camps at the Crow Agency camp ground.

Early the next morning, we hurried to the depot. The first train to arrive was a freight. We counted our money and found we didn't have enough to ride the caboose. As we stood there studying the train, we noticed a hobo in an empty box car, so we climbed in with him. When we got to Wyola, we hurried to the garage where we'd left the truckload of ice. There was a big lake of water under the truck. All there was to do was get what was left out to the ranch.

When the boss got back to the ranch, he knew, but we confessed. He fired us and wrote out our checks, holding out the cost of the ice. Many of the dudes thought we should have been forgiven, but having done wrong, we expected to get fired. We got on our horses and rode to Lodge Grass. The boss had to make the long trip to Sheridan to hire two more men to take our place, and to get another load of ice.

We cashed the checks the boss gave us, but they came back marked "insufficient funds" and it was quite some time before we were able to get our money. Guess that was part of the payment for having done wrong.

SHEEP

After we got fired from the Dude Ranch, Bobby went to his parents' ranch. They were putting up hay and were short handed, so he immediately fell into a job. I went to my folks' ranch. Jack Mason was doing fine, but they could use an extra hand.

One day a big black car drove into the ranch. The two men were from Lima, in western Montana. A Mr. Price introduced himself and said, "This is Mr. Glead, my partner. We are in the sheep business. Our headquarters is in Lima, but because of drought conditions there, we've leased range from Matt Tschirgi over in the Rotten Grass country and our sheep will be shipped in on the railroad. However, as we don't know the country, we want to hire someone who does to show the camp tenders where the good water is. In fact, we could also use a good camp tender."

Of course, I asked for the job and was hired. They needed another man and I recommend my friend, Bobby Stovall, who also knew the country and was good with horses. The herders were reliable men who had been with the company for years. We got along well and I learned a lot from them.

Our headquarters was on Lodge Grass Creek and Toby Larson was herding there, lending the stability Bill and I needed. It was pleasing to work with these men. They had great respect for the company and felt sheep was the best business there was. As I worked around them, I really began liking sheep too. Lambing was a special time for me. When fall came, they shipped the sheep back to their home country, as now they had good feed on their own range.

I was working around Lodge Grass, helping at the ranch, and, of course, breaking horses. Sometimes I took odd jobs like working at the Elevator. Bobby took a job working with a man who owned race horses over in Carbon County. He really liked riding race horses. His boss had another job and couldn't take his horses on the racing circuit, but he made Bobby an offer. Bobby could use the boss's truck to haul the horses, but Bobby would have to make enough to pay the expenses. When they won big, he would have to divide with the boss.

Bobby knew the horses and was good with them, but he needed someone to go along to help handle them. Naturally, he asked me. It sounded like a good time, and Bobby was sure we could make some money.

Our first race was scheduled at the Belgrade track and we started off with high hopes. We were almost to Bozeman when we had a blowout on the truck. We got out to change the tire. The tire we took off was really worn and we were thankful we had a spare to get us into town where we could buy a tire. We looked at the spare. It sure didn't look very good, so we drove as carefully as we could. When we got to town and found out what a tire for that truck cost, we were shocked. There went most of our eating money, and we were thankful that we'd be rolling out our beds in the barn. At least we didn't have to worry about the cost of a hotel room.

Top left, Myron, age 2. Bottom left, Myron & Bobby Stoval's first car, bought with earnings from coyote hunting. Top right, Myron breaking horses at parents' ranch, age 17. Bottom right, Myron Lynde, left, and Leonard Young, right, Lodge Grass, Montana, class of 1923. Myron used to laughingly brag about being saludatorian of his class.

As the season went on, we had a little money, enough to get us on the road to small town rodeos. Some of the time we would win, but the purse would be barely enough for expenses. We had thought we'd get acquainted with some fun girls, but that wasn't working out either. Exercising and caring for four horses demanded practically all of our time.

We visited with a man from Miles City who said they had a good track and that was the place to go. He implied that we could make some money, so we headed for Miles City, as it was nearly time for their fair.

We liked the atmosphere as we exercised the horses and we had high hopes as we watched the other horses being exercised. People always chuckled when they saw one of our horses, Floppy O'Sullivan. His ears drooped and he'd lost most of the hair from his tail. He sure didn't look like much, but whenever he felt like running, he could beat most horses. At the Miles City track he seemed to have perked up. The weather was cooler, which was welcome, and we were sure our luck had changed.

Both Bobby and I were in high spirits as he and Floppy O'Sullivan trotted out to the track to line up. I felt so sure of O'Sullivan that I bet on the race. Soon they were off, and O'Sullivan was doing fine. He was running the way we knew he could run. He had the inside track and was in the lead, but Bay Beauty was coming up and was too close. Oh, Oh! O'Sullivan was pushed into the railing. Both he and Bobby were hurt. I hurried to them. O'Sullivan was skinned up, but Bobby's leg looked bad and he was taken to the hospital. I took O'Sullivan back to the stable and hurried to the hospital.

The doctor said Bobby had a bad break, and of course, was skinned up. He was put in a cast and had to stay there overnight. We were thankful that it wasn't worse, but we realized that our racing career was over with Bobby on crutches. I went back to the stables to spend the night and got everything ready to leave the first thing in the morning.

We took the horses back to their Rock Creek owner and then went on to Lodge Grass. We hadn't made the money we had hoped we would, but we'd gained some wisdom.

It was sad to part with Bobby, but he would have to stay at home until his leg was well. I worked around the ranch and took seasonal jobs around Lodge Grass. That fall there were a number of new teachers who came to town. They were all young and single, so of course town was the place I wanted to be. Naturally, all the young men looked forward to the barn dances even more.

1

ROUGH BEGINNINGS DURING THE DEPRESSION

◆

The fear was real in 1930 and '31 as the Depression worsened. Each day another company closed down because it was bankrupt. Its men, of course, were without jobs; also, they were without hope. Because they had no income, their families had to move in with relatives while the men searched for any kind of work.

We had known about these conditions but didn't realize their seriousness. Then the oil company that Myron was working for shut down operations in Lodge Grass and moved to South America. Suddenly it was our problem, and we became aware of how scarce jobs really were.

Although Myron had grown up in the Lodge Grass ranching area, he felt this kind of job was out of the question because ranchers were experiencing drought conditions and were unable to get a decent price for anything they raised. They couldn't afford to hire help so had to do all of their own work, except for exchanging help with their neighbors.

He hated to leave me in Hardin, so he convinced me it would be a good idea to elope and keep our marriage a secret until he could get a job and an apartment for us.

It did seem like the thing to do. Movie stars and a number of our acquaintances had done it. To us it was the answer, because we sure didn't want the kind of wild shivaree some of Myron's cowboy friends put on. Our trip to Roundup was short and pleasant, and we had a good time that day; but getting married in the court house by a J.P. lacked glamour. So did the two elderly witnesses, but we laughed and had a lovely dinner in the hotel dining room, which was a special treat.

A friend who lived in Billings owned a trucking firm, so Myron went to his truck depot, doing any odd chores to show the boss that he was capable of driving these big trucks. Suddenly there was a need for a driver, and Myron got the job that paid $150.00 a month—very good wages at the time. We settled into a nice little apartment on North 23rd Street that was near his work on 3rd Avenue.

Times were getting worse. Soon the trucking company was having financial problems, and the men were unable to draw complete wages. Much of the time we could afford only the barest necessities. Sometimes the landlord would have to wait for his rent, so we looked for cheaper apartments and finally found a comfortable one for $17.50 a month.

Many times the truckers and their wives would get together to share a pot of beans with a little ham and cornbread or biscuits. We managed to laugh even though we were frightened because we knew others who didn't even have a job.

Myron's job was to haul extra loads of freight, such as a minister's furniture to southwestern Wyoming or a load of tires to Butte. Most of the roads were either gravel or dirt so I was never sure when he would return. I did a lot of waiting.

One day as Myron was backing a large load of freight to the back entrance of a country store, his truck dropped into an abandoned cellar. He spent many hours trying to get out. Finally he walked to a farm to see if he could hire the farmer and his tractor to come to the store and pull him out. This caused him to be quite late with his other deliveries to by-then irate grocery men.

His other problems included muddy roads and flat tires. Waiting for trains to pass railroad crossings was the most dangerous, particularly near Laurel where the hobos had a hangout. At times they would hijack a truck that was hauling food when the truck had to stop at the crossing. This happened to a bread truck stopped at the same crossing as Myron's unmarked truck that was loaded with fruit for Yellowstone Park. He could only feel thankful that it wasn't his truck. Everyone felt deep sympathy for these hobos who turned into hijackers because they were hungry, yet we also felt compassion for the people who owned and cared for the gardens they stripped.

Pregnant with our first child, I wondered how we'd ever get a layette together, but I needn't have worried as this baby was to be the first grandchild on both sides of the family. Our greatest worry was how to save for the doctor and hospital expenses, but the boss said because Myron had plenty of back pay due him, the company would see that we had enough.

While I waited for our baby, I took long walks and exchanged visits with friends. Sometimes I went to a matinee; they were cheap and helped to pass the time. Usually in the evening I read or did hand work.

When it was time for the baby to be born, Myron became even more concerned about my being alone so he asked our friend, Helen, to stay with me. She had no children and her husband was also a trucker, so she too had been spending a great deal of time alone. She agreed to the arrangement, and we had a lot of fun as we waited.

The apartment we lived in was on the upper floor of what had been a family home. We didn't have a telephone, but the lady who lived on the first floor was kind enough to let me use her phone whenever the need arose. Apparently, Flossy was friends with everyone. There were always quite a few men around and she had many parties which often became noisy. In fact, we often found it difficult to sleep until the guests would leave in the wee hours of the morning.

It was about midnight when I woke Helen and told her it was time for me to go to the hospital. Both of us were glad that this was one of Flossy's party nights or else it might have been difficult to wake her. Helen explained that she wanted to use the phone to call a cab to take me to the hospital. As soon as she made the call Flossy became concerned, but Helen hurried back to the apartment.

When the cab honked, Helen grabbed my suitcase, and we hurried down the stairs. The driver opened the door for us, but Flossy and her friends also heard the cab and flowed out of the house. Before I could get in the cab Flossy staggered up to me. In her tipsy way, almost in tears of concern, she patted me on the shoulder, saying, "Oh! You poor dear, poor dear. You know how worried we all are about you." This was a great surprise to me because I didn't know any of the others in the group and I hardly knew her, but I said, "Well, thanks Flossy. Helen will let you know how it all goes."

Then the driver closed the door and hurried around to the driver's seat, but Flossy knocked on the window so I rolled it down. Sitting on the edge of the seat, I leaned out to hear what she had to say. She staggered closer to the cab, then kissed me, still hanging onto the cab. The nervous driver revved the motor impatiently. Again I said, "Good bye, Flossy." Tearfully, she answered in a rather quiet voice, "Good bye, Hon." Then, in a loud, commanding voice she shouted, "Hold tight, Dearie, hold tight!" and we were off. Helen and I laughed all the way to the hospital.

Our baby boy was born September 23rd at 7:00 AM. He was a very pretty baby with large blue eyes and dark hair. Several of my friends were taking nurses' training and they thought he was an exceptional child. Even the doctor remarked about how alert he was. He was a good baby and we all agreed that he was very special.

When Myron received word, he was in Wyoming. As he walked into the cafe, they called out, "Hello Dad!" By the time the boss flew down a relief driver to bring Myron back, our baby was four hours old. Our nurse friend, Verna, saw Myron go into my room so she hurried to the nursery and brought the baby to see his dad. Myron admired his son but he was so tiny; Myron seemed afraid of touching him. Just then the phone rang, so nurse Verna smiled a big smile and said, "Here Myron." He stuck out his arms and she lay his baby in them, and she was off to answer the phone. He stood there so stiff, as if the child might break and as though he just didn't know what to do about the tiny little guy in his arms.

Above, Myron and Interstate Freight Lines, Inc. truck. Right, Myron with future brother-in-law George Cooley at the Lynde ranch. Myron's location was Billings, but whenever his truck was sent through Lodge Grass, he would drive up the creek to see his parents.

Now we had to get down to the gigantic task of naming our first born son. I wanted to name him Myron Jr., but Senior said that he didn't like his name all that well. We thought of family names and finally Myron said, "I've always had such a deep feeling for my granddad Stanford. He was such a fine person and his family name will die with this generation because he was an only child. His two sons have no children so there are no male descendants to carry on the name." We named our baby Myron Stanford, to be called by his second name.

I lay in bed, happily enjoying all my beautiful flowers and lovely cards. I had a great deal of company, and my nurse friends were in my room often. I could see Twenty-Ninth Street from my window and because there were few houses on it, I could see nearly to town. I noticed about the same time every day a long line of men that reached from St. Vincent Hospital nearly to town. Curious, I asked one of the nurses and she said, "They just happen to be hungry men out of work so the hospital is furnishing them one meal a day. It is really sad. All they want is a job where they can earn their keep."

I shivered, wondering what was to become of our great nation, how the Depression would affect us, and more importantly, how would it affect the child we'd just brought into this world. But, being young, Myron and I felt that we'd make it somehow.

When Stan was six months old, the bank foreclosed on the trucking company, putting all the drivers out of work. What made it especially bad was that the men were unable to get any of the back pay that was due them, so many had to leave Billings owing apartment rent.

Myron had a good friend in Wyoming who owned a trucking firm and was willing to find a job for him; however, we decided against it because Myron had developed a kidney condition from those terribly rough roads and long working hours. The doctor said, "Stay out of those rough trucks. Life is too short, and I'm sure you can find another way to make a living."

Now the only thing left to do was to go back to Myron's parents' ranch in Lodge Grass. There he could get more rest, and the work wouldn't be quite so demanding. He could work at his own pace, and we were looking forward to the time when he could farm the small lease he'd had for years with the Indian, Otter Chief.

In about six weeks, Myron was in good health and looking forward to doing more work. He didn't know just what, but for the time being, he could farm his parents' place.

2
MY FIRST TRIP TO DRY HEAD RANCH

◆

Myron's stepfather Bill was a horse trader and was not cut out to be a farmer. The ranch wasn't producing enough to make the payments. The men staying there raised a good garden and milked a couple of cows, but they needed a boss who could go out with them to make decisions on the job. This was one of Myron's talents; he was a good organizer and a hard worker. Soon the ranch was producing enough to pay the mortgage.

Living with another family was difficult. Myron and I found that we didn't have enough privacy to talk things out, which wasn't good for our relationship; and with all of the adults around, it was impossible to discipline our child. They thought he could do no wrong. We had been working for our board, but we realized this was only temporary at best. Myron was completely well again, and he was ready to take on any kind of job that would make us a good living.

He had always been interested in sheep, and had the experience of working for two different sheep outfits for brief periods and helping with lambing for a neighbor who was ill. Sheep were down to $8.00 a head; a good deal for the buyer. Myron talked it over with his parents, explaining that they could use the equity accumulated in their ranch as security to borrow enough money to buy two bands of sheep which he would run.

They talked with their friend, H.W. Willcutt who was the foreman for the E.L. Dana Cattle Company, and he said, "I'll talk to Mr. Dana, but I feel sure that he will rent you the Dry Head Ranch and enough range to run 2,400 head of breeding ewes. But you'll have to board his cowboy who is living there, riding after his cattle."

When we received this good news, we began buying sheep. We were fortunate in finding a young man from Buffalo, Wyoming, who had inherited a sheep outfit from his father. He didn't want to be in the sheep business, so sold his sheep to Myron and his father, and they were brought to the Lodge

Grass ranch where the men lambed and sheared them. Next it was up to Myron to trail them to the Dry Head Ranch.

As we drove along on my first trip to our new place, I realized that the Dry Head Ranch was sixty-five miles from both Hardin and Billings. It was a long way over dirt roads, but if this was where the sheep would be, it would have to be my home. Anyway, it would be a new experience and if other people lived out like this, I could too. I could write letters to stay in touch. The Post Office was six miles from the ranch, and the mail came in by carrier from Kane, Wyoming, then up the canyon where there were homestead ranchers that we'd get to know.

I enjoyed the drive. Much of the country was hills and plains, but we also drove through several creeks. One small canyon had a bridge at the bottom. As we drove through, I was thoroughly enjoying the panorama of wide open country, when suddenly we drove down a small ravine right into the Dry Head Canyon. I was surprised to see a large log barn, corrals, machine shed and chicken house.

My biggest surprise, though, was the huge, three story log house. It was very picturesque with a lovely verandah and a big yard enclosed with a white picket fence. We entered the vestibule that led into the large hall, ten feet wide and forty feet long, with a five foot wide staircase leading up to the upper floors. On the right was a beautiful ballroom, twenty by forty feet, with nice shiny floors. To the left was the den with a large stone fireplace, and next to that was the dining room, both twenty by twenty. At the end of the dining room was a lovely large china cupboard. Near it was the door leading to the big kitchen and a door that led to the basement. At the back door was the wash room and the back porch. Down the back steps to the right in the apple orchard, was the old fashioned outhouse. Across the creek that meandered through the yard was a foot bridge that led to a good sized log bunkhouse.

I simply couldn't believe the size of that place. There was no house in Hardin that big; there might have been in Billings, but most rooms wouldn't be the size of those in our new house. However, I had always said that I could make my home most any place, and this was my opportunity to prove it.

Once Myron trailed the sheep to the Dry Head, we could settle down to a normal life.

Staying at the L.G. Ranch was a young man from Cleveland, Ohio, called Dude who was anxious to learn all he could about the west, and wanted the adventure of helping Myron trail the sheep to the Dry Head. Myron was well acquainted with the grazing land and stock water from Lodge Grass to the Big Horn River. He had trailed horses from Pryor to the Eagle Springs Ranch on Two Leggin Creek, but he had never trailed livestock from Grapevine Creek to the Dry Head. He said, "Dad, I know the country to Grapevine Creek so I can get that far, but from there on I'll need you, or someone, to show me where the good watering places are."

Bill answered, "I'll be there before you get to Grapevine." This satisfied

Myron, but he said, "When you come, be sure to bring us groceries because we'll be out by then. You know how hard it is to pack enough on a pack horse to last ten or twelve days."

Early the next morning, Myron and Dude saddled their horses. On their pack horse they loaded their cooking supplies, beds, range tepee and whatever else they felt they might need. When they rode out the lane, they turned and happily waved good-bye. The baby, Myron's parents and I watched until they were out of sight.

The men went through the hills until they got to the Big Horn River and then crossed the sheep over the Two Leggin Bridge where they ran right into a problem they hadn't thought about—cactus. Neither the dog nor the sheep had ever been where there was cactus, and this was a virtual cactus field. The sheep got sore footed, but they hobbled along; this was not so with the big lovable Airedale, Pete. He was eager to chase the sheep, knowing it was his job, but he had such big feet he was always getting into the cactus. He would just sit and howl until one of the men came and took out the spines. This was quite a problem until they hit upon the idea of making him moccasins by cutting small pieces of canvas out of the floor of their tepee. They'd fold the little pieces of canvas around each foot and tie them with string. At first Pete looked at his feet as if he didn't know what to think, but then he got to liking the moccasins and began jumping around like a kid with new shoes. Knowing it was his job, and with the security of the moccasins, he eagerly went to chasing sheep. But when a moccasin came off, Pete would come to a quick halt and wait until one of the men came with a spare.

When Myron and Dude reached Grapevine Creek, Bill still hadn't come as he said he would. They had already stayed in the Grapevine country longer than they felt they should. These were dry times, water and grass were scarce, and they didn't want their sheep eating up Dana's cattle range. Myron made the decision: "We've just got to move on."

Dude was the cook, and he was worried. "Well, Bill better show up soon because we're nearly out of groceries. Say, there wouldn't be any danger of him missing us if we start out?"

Myron was annoyed about the whole situation and snapped back, "He can surely follow the route the sheep have taken." So they packed up and moved on.

Soon they discovered the bad water they'd heard about. It seemed that much of the water was either alkali or gyp, and it was maddening to know that there was good water nearby, if only they could find it. They kept pushing on towards the McComas' place because Myron knew they had good water and were friends. Maybe they could even get some groceries from them. Now they had a definite goal and that cheered them somewhat.

When they got to McComas' it was very quiet; no dog barked. Myron went to the house and gave a yell, but no one answered. They looked around; there were no chickens, cows or horses. The family had moved out. They found a few edible vegetables in the garden that helped their limited diet; but most importantly, they enjoyed the good water. The sheep and horses did, too.

Now they were eating just one meal a day and pushing toward the Dry Head. Finally Dude announced, "For our noon meal today we'll be having potatoes. We've still got the old bacon rind to grease the skillet, so we'll have them fried."

The sheep were now on water and settling down to rest during the hot part of the day, so Myron said, "Okay, Dude, you can build your fire and start cooking." Neither said it, but they both knew this was the last of their food.

After they'd eaten, they felt drowsy. Knowing the sheep wouldn't travel until later in the day when it was cooler, they had a good sleep. When Myron woke up, he felt somewhat refreshed and said, "Dude, wake up; the sheep are moving out. Let's get packed up." It was then they noticed that one of the ewes had backed up to their only skillet and relieved herself. This was the last straw. Now they would just push the sheep as hard as they could until they got to the ranch.

July 4, 1933, two hungry, tired, dirty men made their entrance through the gate of the Dry Head Ranch. After a bath, shave and clean clothes, they sat down at the table to eat Mrs. Buck's good home cooked dinner and the whole world seemed much brighter. Little Stan and I were especially glad that they'd made it.

Soon the supply truck arrived loaded with groceries—and Myron's parents. They'd even brought a barber friend with them so he cut the men's hair. Things were soon back to normal.

*Ellie and Deacon at the Dryhead ranch.
Also Myron and neighbor Dave Good.*

3
LIFE AT THE DRY HEAD RANCH

◆

A friend, Roy Buck from Gillette, Wyoming, his wife Fern, and their two sons, Donald and Merlyn, were interested in moving to the Dry Head Ranch with us. Roy's concern was buying young work horses to ship to his brother in Michigan, who would then sell them to farmers for use in cultivating vineyards.

Fern was a very good cook, so she accepted the responsibility of doing the ranch cooking. The sheep company furnished all of the groceries, and I helped in whatever way I could.

The Bucks were older, and their experience and knowledge lent stability to our enterprise. We shared the huge three story log house that had been built for a dude ranch. This living arrangement worked out quite well because there was always someone at the ranch, yet neither couple had to be tied to it.

The Bucks were religious people and Roy always said grace before meals. He liked to play his guitar and Fern was fond of singing hymns. Best of all, they truly lived their religion. It was interesting to us that whenever anyone tried to take advantage of Roy in a business deal, it seemed to turn out in Roy's favor. One time when a crooked horse trader charged Roy for more horses than he received and thought he had outsmarted him, Roy was deeply hurt. But when Roy shipped the horses back east where they were in such great demand, he made a tremendous profit. After a few deals like that, all of us began to realize that we needed more of Roy's kind of religion.

When Myron got his camp set, the sheep had a herder and only needed weekly attention, so he and Roy checked the machinery that belonged to the ranch. They planned to repair it so they could start haying. Fortunately, only the mower was really broken down, and Roy, being a mechanic, soon had it ready to go. The old horse drawn rake was also usable. They got the hay cut and raked, but there was no stacker so they had to pitch it on the wagon. Then they hauled it to the barn and pitched it into the loft. It was very hard work, but the two men worked well together and finally it was finished.

July 18th was the Sheridan Rodeo, and the Buck family planned to go. They were going to meet family and many friends and also do some shopping. Since the young herder's wife was a sister to Mrs. Buck, that couple yearned to go, too. Myron volunteered, "Orville, as long as your wife wants to go so much, you can go. Ellie, Stan and I will herd. In the evening and in the morning I'll ride to the ranch and do the chores until you get back." A happy group of people hurriedly prepared for the Rodeo.

This was my first experience living out with the sheep. It was very dry and dusty, and we got awfully dirty, but I enjoyed it. Each evening we'd sit out and watch the lambs run and play. Stan would laugh and laugh as he watched them frolic about. Myron and I would be chuckling because it tickled little Stan so much.

That was a busy summer. Many acquaintances came out for a visit. Also, this was Dana's cattle range, so quite often his cowboys would stop in for a home cooked meal and generally stayed overnight. Being bachelors, they appreciated being a part of family life for a brief period.

Sometimes they'd want to hold two-year-old Stan when he didn't want to go to them. I'd tell them, "Just ignore him and pick up a magazine and look through the pages." As they held the magazine, it was natural for them to sit with their legs spread apart. Sure enough, as soon as Stan saw the magazine he'd come right over, get down and crawl between the legs so he could look at the magazine. They all remarked how unusual it was. They'd never seen a child do that, but Stan loved books at the very start of life.

The last of July, Bill Mills, one of Dana's cowboys, rode to the ranch and said, "I came over to tell you that we've got the roundup wagon out and we are rounding up the young unbroken horses. We've got them corralled now so you can come over to get the ones Roy wants."

Myron, Roy and Don, Roy's twelve year old son, saddled their horses and rode over to receive them. It was a great thrill for Don to get to eat at the roundup wagon with all the cowboys.

Roy planned to ship these horses back east in December. That meant he'd have to spend a great deal of time breaking the young horses to get them gentle and teach them to work. First he would teach them to understand the bit, and then harness them with one of our gentle team, either Jim or Nell. These two had their own ways of handling wild young horses. At first Jim would sometimes run with the young horse to work off some of the youngster's energy. Perhaps Jim could remember when he was young and the bit was first in his mouth, the harness on his back, the wagon rumbling behind him. Roy handled the reins and would sometimes pull them so the horses were very much aware of the bit. Myron sat beside Roy, ever ready to pull on the brake when the running got too rambunctious.

When a young bronco harnessed with Nell wanted to go too fast, she'd just reach over and bite him on the neck to let him know that she wasn't taking any of that nonsense. Often the men would take the horses outside the barn lot and let them go up and down the hilly terrain. Sometimes they would drive them the six miles to the Dry Head Post Office. On their return, I'd often watch them come down the canyon road at what seemed too fast a pace, but they sailed right into the barn lot and came to a halt. It never failed to remind me of the stage coach days in the movies.

When Myron had to move the sheep camps, haul wood or grain, or deliver groceries to the herder, he'd take the gentle team. But if he was just going out to the camps to see how the herders were or to find out what groceries they might need, he'd ride Flash, the saddle horse he was trying to break. That horse always kicked and tried to buck every time Myron tried to mount him, and there was one gate that he had to go through which always was a real problem.

Should the herders need only a few things, Myron would ride his lovable, faithful saddle horse given to him by his good friend, Frank Greenough, who had named him Deacon—a very appropriate name. If a herder happened to need some wood, Myron would tie his rope around some branches and drag them into camp. Nothing upset Deacon. When horse and rider had to swim the river, Deacon would swim high so Myron didn't get wet.

One time when Myron was tending camps with Deacon, evening came on too fast, and Myron was caught in the pitch blackness of a cold night. Suddenly he realized that he didn't know where he was. He was completely lost and hadn't the slightest idea of how to get home. Though horses have a homing instinct, Myron wondered if Deacon had been at the Dry Head long enough to know how to get back to the ranch buildings. Greatly concerned, Myron patted him on the neck and said, "Deacon old boy, I sure don't know where we are or how to find our way home, so I am going to turn you loose and hope that you know." The horse took off, traveling through a canyon and several coulees. When Deacon stopped, he was at the ranch gate. Myron was surprised they'd gotten home so quickly. The dear old fellow got special attention and an extra ration of oats that night.

In the early fall, the Dana Cattle Company suggested that Myron and Roy go up in the mountains and cut timber for corral poles needed at the Grapevine Ranch, as part of their lease payment on the Dry Head Ranch. It was a grueling job because the mountain trails were so steep and treacherous. They took a camp outfit up there and did their own cooking as they cut the poles and snaked them down the mountain. This took them eight days. Then the Dana men came and loaded the logs on trucks and hauled them off—a mighty welcome sight to Myron and Roy, as they were behind with their own work.

Now it was the last part of September and time to trail the lambs to Tschirgi's camp on Shoulder Blade, near Garryowen. The same lamb buyer was buying all the lambs and wanted to ship them from Tschirgi's, so Myron and the herder, Ed, started out. Instead of a pack horse, Myron decided to take the team and a two wheeled cart in order to haul groceries and a barrel for good water. Also, the cart would go through the coulees without any problems.

When the men were ready to leave, we realized we had only one loaf of bread for them. Quickly Fern stirred up a big batch of bread because Roy said that he'd drive us out to see how they were doing and take the freshly baked bread.

The lambs had been traveling fine, but when we got to where Myron planned to camp, there was no camp. We saw the two-wheeled cart, but no team or Myron. And we couldn't see Ed and the sheep. Soon we saw Nell, one of the team, staked nearby. Then way up on a high hill we saw Myron riding Jim toward us. We still couldn't see the sheep or Ed and the saddle horse, Deacon.

Myron said, "I've lost Ed and the sheep. When we started out this morning, I pointed out this high hill and told Ed this is where we would camp. Then I went the longer way with the cart. When I got here, I couldn't see him or the sheep. I've been hunting for them ever since."

Roy stood there scanning the country. "I've noticed that at times Ed gets confused as to directions. When he's herding, it hasn't made any difference, but with trailing, I can see where it really does."

Myron was greatly concerned that something might have happened to Ed, like a fall or a heart attack; and he knew that the only food he had was his lunch at noon, so he said, "Roy, how about driving us on top of that high hill. From there we will be able to see a lot of country." Hobbling Jim, Myron got in the car.

We could see a lot of country, but not Ed or the sheep. Now it was getting dark and all of us were even more worried. Finally the men decided that if Ed was cold, he would surely build a fire and we'd be able to see it. We kept driving around the hills, hoping to see a fire. Finally, we went over to the McComas' place where we could get out of the car, go inside their cabin, have a fire, and be out of the chilly night air. Every so often the men would think of some place they hadn't looked, and off they would go. Surely if Ed saw car lights, he would come toward them.

It was a very long night and each of us kept silently praying for Ed. Finally, at daybreak, the men could see him and the sheep a long way off, not at all where they should have been. They came back to the McComas' cabin and Fern, the children, and I got in the car, and we all drove to where Ed and the sheep were. The first thing Myron said was, "Ed, what in the world happened? Why are you way over here when we were to camp over there just below that high hill?"

Ed took off his hat and scratched his head, "Well, I just got lost and when I realized it I decided to let the sheep bed down here. I unsaddled my horse, put his hobbles on him and me and my dog just snuggled together and covered up with the saddle blanket, using the saddle for a pillow. I had a good night's sleep."

We all sighed and shook our heads. The poor old man had used good judgment, but he had no idea how much trouble he'd caused or what a terrible night we'd all been through, especially Myron. But all he said to Ed was, "You stay here with the sheep and I'll go and get our camp outfit and cook you some breakfast."

Roy drove back to the cart and dropped Myron off, and the rest of us went back to the ranch because there were plenty of chores to be done, and all of us were mighty hungry. We knew that we didn't have to worry about Ed because Myron probably wouldn't let him out of sight.

When it was nearly time for the sheep to arrive at the Two Leggin Bridge, Myron's father and mother came after Stan and me at the Dry Head. After we'd herded the lambs across the bridge, they took Stan and me into Hardin. There we visited with family until Myron and Ed trailed the lambs to Shoulder Blade where the buyer was to receive them. There they found that, because it was such a dry year, Tschirgis were going to keep their lambs on the mountain another month hoping for fall rains. That meant we would have to wait too. Ed had plans to go back east, so Myron would be herding.

I decided that if Myron would be herding and sleeping in the range tepee, then I'd take two-year-old Stan out there and stay with him. When I saw how dusty and dirty it was and listened to the ever blowing wind, I wondered if I'd made the right decision, but I knew I had when I thought how much worse it would have been for Myron if we hadn't been with him. I set about making our camp as comfortable as possible and tried desperately to keep the dirt out of the food as I cooked over the campfire. I tried to wash Stan's clothes, especially the diapers, but found it impossible to keep soot off of them as I had to use the big dutch oven for washing. Then, because I had no clothesline or pins, I spread them on sagebrush to dry. The dust was bad, and I had to watch like a hawk as the eternal wind would catch them and blow them out of the country. I spent a lot of time that fall chasing my laundry.

That wind was mighty cold much of the time, so often Stan and I would have to stay in the tepee snuggled down under the covers. He disliked the quiet, so I'd read to him out of magazines. I guess he just liked to hear my voice. I had brought tablet paper, a coloring book, pencil and crayolas so he could scribble and draw. And he had a few little cars and toys to keep him entertained. When it was warm enough, we went for walks—anything to pass the time.

After a week of dust and dirt, we were able to borrow a sheep wagon from Tschirgis. That was heavenly. No more did I have trouble keeping dirt out of the food or have to cook over a campfire with all the smoke, soot and ashes. Now I had a real stove with an oven to cook on. We had a comfortable table where we could eat like a family, and the nice bed was great. I had a real washtub, so we could take baths and wash clothes and be as clean as we wanted to be. I even appreciated having a linoleum floor to scrub. Our little family had a real home.

During the time we lived there, we had a trapper friend from Crow Agency who would stop in for a visit and coffee. Mr. Christianson, who was riding after his cattle, often stopped for a chat, too. Myron's parents came out and brought groceries, so we didn't feel isolated, even though we didn't have any near neighbors.

After about three weeks, the Tschirgi herders started coming in. They were glad to be down off the mountain into bright sunshine again; they'd gotten very tired of all the fog up there.

The lamb buyer came to receive the lambs, and back to the Dry Head we went because a lot of work was waiting. It was now November, and Myron had to get the winter feed hauled before bad weather really set in.

It was December before Myron and Roy were able to haul a huge pile of logs in; the furnace used to heat two floors of this large house was wood burning. Myron and I decided that when the Bucks left for Michigan, we'd move our bedroom into the den. That way we'd only have to keep three rooms warm.

Myron, Stan and herder Truman.

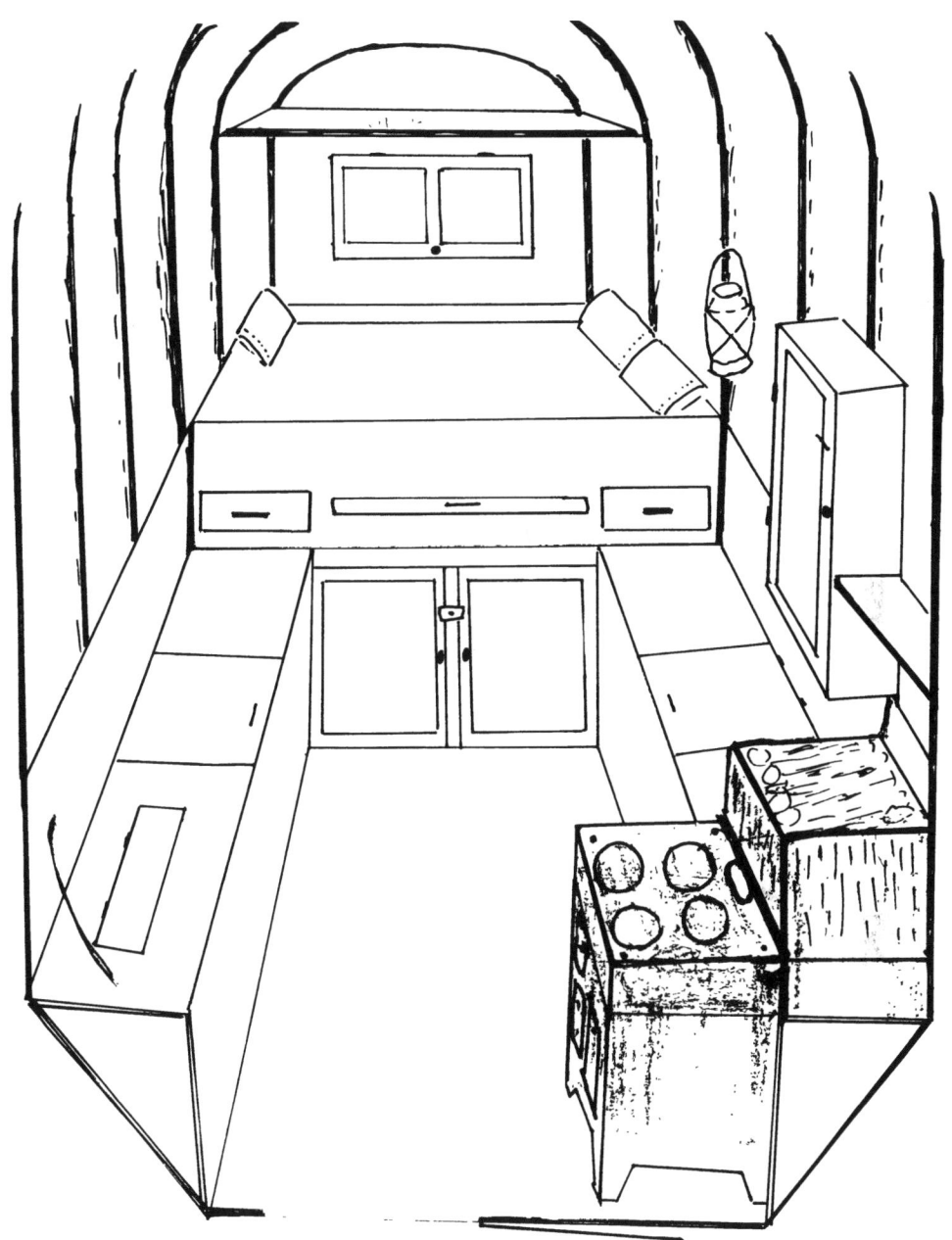

View of inside of sheep wagon as drawn by Eleanor Lynde.

Dryhead Ranch house.

4
BUCKS GO TO MICHIGAN

◆

When school was out for Christmas vacation, the Bucks planned to leave for Michigan in their car. The horses would be shipped on the railroad, and Roy had other horses he'd purchased in Lodge Grass. Because we were going there for Christmas, and because Myron knew how to go across country to the Spotted Rabbit Crossing where the horses could swim the Big Horn River, Myron told Roy he'd take the horses to Lodge Grass and help him ship them.

Stan and I rode over with the family in the car; however, I was quite concerned about Myron swimming the Big Horn River when there were chunks of ice floating in it. He tried to convince me that he'd be all right because Deacon was a good swimmer and swam high out of the water. I wasn't completely convinced but consoled myself that Toots Brown's camp was near the crossing. Other than that, I'd pray that the Lord would take care of him.

It took Myron two long days to reach Lodge Grass. After spending the first night at Toots Brown's camp where he and his horses had a good rest, he made it to the Lodge Grass Ranch just before dark. He was terribly chilled, but after eating his supper he felt refreshed.

He looked at me and said, "Well, I guess if we are going to the dance as planned, I'd better get my oxfords out of the saddle bags."

He put on his hat, overshoes, and coat, and went down to the barn. He picked up his saddle bags and found that, as they had gotten wet when he crossed the river, they were frozen quite solid. He brought them to the house and we starting thawing out the shoes. We weren't able to dry them in time for the start of the dance, and Myron was so drowsy that we gave up on the whole idea of going.

After a nice Christmas, we went back to the Dry Head Ranch. We did appreciate Charlie, the Dana cowboy, staying there looking after things while we were gone, and we were pleased to look after his things so he could leave.

It was good to get back, but now I had full responsibility for all the cooking, and I soon learned about cooking for unexpected guests. The ranch was on the main road, and everyone had to drive through the barn lot right by the house. Knowing they were welcome, they stopped to tell us what news they had and find out what was new with us. Of course when anyone came it was ranch etiquette to always ask them to come in and share our meal, or if it was evening, to spend the night. Whenever I cooked a meal, I never knew if we'd be alone, with our hired man and cowboy Charlie, or if there would be others.

Before, Mrs. Buck had accepted the responsibility. Now that I had to be hostess, cook and dishwasher, it was quite a different matter—but it was good for me.

STRANGE GUEST

It was the last part of January, cold, with some snow on the ground. The wind was blowing—a normal condition in our part of the country. I had grown used to it, except when it blew violently and the big log house swayed and pebbles blew off the rim rock onto the tin roof. It bothered me some in the day, but more so at night. This night it seemed worse than ever as I tossed restlessly in bed and wished I could sleep as peacefully as Myron and Stan did. I heard the wash tub as it swung back and forth where it hung against the wall on the back porch and wondered if I should get up and bring it in the house. But I thought of all the reasons why I shouldn't. Realizing how cold it was outside, I snuggled down and covered up my head, hoping that would help me go to sleep.

Suddenly I heard the dog bark viciously, as though a stranger was out there. I strained my ears to hear. I thought someone knocked, but all I could really hear was the big old cottonwood tree branches scratching against the house and the other usual noises. I looked at the clock; it was midnight. I decided I must be wrong. No one would come at that time of night, so it must be a deer or some kind of wildlife.

I heard it again, only it was more distinct this time, so I reached over and shook Myron awake. "Wake up. Someone is knocking at the back door."

He listened. "I don't hear anything. It must have been the wind."

"It was more than the wind. The dog barked so savagely; then there was a distinct knock."

Wearily he said, "Oh Ellie, go to sleep. It could only have been one of the cowboys. He probably went to the bunkhouse and will tell Charlie his problem. If it was a neighbor and they were in need, they'd have continued to knock or they would have opened the door and given a yell or call until we answered."

Knowing he was right, I convinced myself it was my imagination, so I dropped off to sleep.

When morning came, Myron went out to the bunkhouse to see if we had anyone extra for breakfast, but the men hadn't heard anything unusual. Dismissing all of the night's adventures from my mind, I went about preparing breakfast. After the men had their second and third cups of coffee, it was light enough for them to start their day. Myron grabbed the milk bucket and started to the barn. The wind was blowing, swirling snow about him. It was still quite dark in the large barn, and he wished that he had taken the lantern.

Myron had to walk past several empty horse stalls before he got to where the cow was stabled. As he walked past the first two stalls, an eerie feeling came over him. Quickly he turned to look back in the direction he'd come. There, between him and the door—his only avenue of escape—stood a man with a rifle pointed right at him. He was unknown to Myron and looked strangely out of place because he was dressed in a straw hat and a yellow slicker. In December, local men wore felt hats or scotch caps pulled over their ears and warm sheepskin coats.

Quickly Myron said, "Hello there. I didn't see you as I came by the door." He hoped his friendly greeting would encourage the man to put his gun down.

No answer. He just stood there holding his gun. Many things flashed through Myron's mind. Should he throw his empty milk bucket at him? But instead he asked, "Where did you come from?" Still no answer. Then Myron noticed that there wasn't an extra horse in the barn. He said, "Where's your horse?"

Now the man lowered his gun so it was pointed toward the floor. He looked out the door as he answered. "He's out there in that open machine shed." Myron was surprised. Definitely this fellow was no cowboy because cowboys always unsaddled their horse and saw that it was watered and fed before they did anything else.

"Why didn't you put him in the barn and feed him?"

"I was afraid you wouldn't like it," the stranger answered.

Now Myron was convinced that he didn't belong in this country or he would have known of ranch people's hospitality.

Myron continued, "Why don't you go and get your horse, put him in a stall, and we'll feed him some hay and oats. Then you and I will go in the house, and my wife will cook you some breakfast."

When he brought the stranger to the house, Myron called, "Ellie, here's a man who needs some breakfast." I went to the door to see who it was, and Myron said, "This is my wife. What's your name?"

The man said, "My name's Bronco Bill." I could see that Myron was surprised, but he didn't say anything.

Soon I was ready to serve the man a breakfast. He was ravenous. We were sure he hadn't eaten for quite some time. I thought that when he got through eating, he'd either go out to the bunkhouse or be on his way. When he was finished, he didn't thank me as everyone else did.

Myron got up when the stranger did. "Bronco Bill's horse has some bad saddle sores, so we are going out to doctor him."

I knew things weren't just right, but I went about my work knowing I'd find out in due time. Then I noticed that Charlie was walking out to the barn with them. Then Leo joined them.

It wasn't long before Myron came in with the bucket of milk and said, "There is something awfully fishy about this guy. I guess you noticed his clothes. Well, his horse is a beautiful thoroughbred mare, his saddle and bridle are a good outfit, but he's been riding that horse without a blanket, and man, oh man, that mare's got bad saddle sores. She really shouldn't be ridden for quite some time, at least until she's healed, but he says he must be riding on."

"I asked him, 'What about those sores on your horse?' and he said, 'She's made it this far, by damn; she'll make it okay the rest of the way.' Then when he became aware that Charlie was a real cowboy, he began talking of all the broncs he'd ridden, saying, 'They don't call me Bronco Bill for nothing,' but all of his conversation didn't make much sense."

When Myron went back out to the wood pile where the men were, he could see that Charlie was very tired of the wild tales Bronco was telling. He suggested, "Myron, now that you have this great bronc rider, I think he ought to pay for his breakfast by riding that bronc you got tied in the barn. He needs a good workout and you have other things to do."

Bronco started towards the barn, and the other men went with him. Myron became concerned because he was afraid the situation was getting out of hand. This man definitely was not a bronc rider and Charlie knew it and was just trying to get Bronco Bill to quit bragging about the wild broncs he'd been riding.

When they got to the barn, Bronco stepped inside his horse's stall, picked up his saddle and threw it on, cinched it, put the bit in his horse's mouth and climbed on with his gun across his lap saying, "I best be getting along."

Myron was terribly concerned about the horse and said, "I'd like to see you stick around a while to get those sores healed on your horse."

"Nope, I got to go."

Charlie realized what they'd done and looked at Myron, wishing he would do something, but all Myron could think of was the terrible sores on that poor horse so he said, "Just a minute Bronco and I'll give you a saddle blanket so your horse's back won't get any worse." But Bronco just rode off, as if he hadn't said anything. Helpless, they stood there watching him ride over the hill.

Finally Charlie blurted out, "My God, my God! In all of my life I've never seen saddle sores like that horse has. What kind of a human would do that to an animal?"

Myron agreed. "He just isn't normal. I'm sure that he stole that beautiful mare."

A couple of days later, when Myron and the men were out in the corral repairing a broken post, two strange riders rode up to them. They got down off their horses and introduced themselves. One was a sheriff from Wyoming and the other was an attendant at the hospital for the insane. The Sheriff said, "We are trailing a man who has escaped from the institution. He is dangerous and has killed two men. He has stolen a thoroughbred mare from a rancher who wasn't home, as he had driven into town after supplies. His hired hand was out riding, and the escapee went into the bunkhouse and stole some old clothes and a rifle. The only other thing that these people missed was an old yellow slicker and a straw hat."

Later we heard that Bronco had ridden over to our neighbor's place, and when Jim saw that mare, he made a deal with Bronco by trading him an old but good horse with a saddle blanket and a little money to boot for the thoroughbred.

Late the next day, three men rode by the corral. The sheriff and attendant didn't stop, just waved, but they had their man and we were very relieved, especially when we thought of what could have happened.

A NEIGHBOR'S VISIT

I was glad that Monday was a beautiful February day because I needed to wash clothes. The gasoline-powered washing machine sat outside on the porch because of the exhaust and noise. Myron and the hired man were about a mile from the ranch, cutting logs to build a sheep shed. Stan was playing with his little cars alongside of the porch.

Everything was going along quite well. I was pleased because I was anxious to finish to have time to prepare a good dinner for the hungry men. Suddenly I heard our dog bark. I looked up and saw a neighbor, Hank Lane. He was a bachelor who was almost a hermit and stayed mostly to himself. I suppose part of the reason was that he'd immigrated from France and spoke very broken English. He'd married, but she'd only lived with him long enough to get his money. There were reports of his being mean to his animals, and he was very difficult for his neighbors to get along with, being so unpredictable.

He seldom stopped at ranches to share a meal. Since the primitive dirt road leaving the canyon led through our barn lot, I felt sure he was just passing through.

I was busy threading the clothes through the ringer when I heard someone call, "Mrs. Lynde." Surprised, I jumped. I'd forgotten about Hank until he'd gotten right to the porch.

At first I tried to chat with him and let my noisy machine continue, but this didn't work at all because he talked such broken English that I had to listen carefully. So I shut off the washing machine motor. When he didn't leave, I wearily sat down on the steps in the pleasant sunshine. He sat down beside me.

I knew that Hank was a bachelor, so I tried to make allowances for his being so dirty. Not only were his clothes dirty, but they were also greasy. He chewed tobacco which caused his big bushy mustache to become quite stained. He had repaired his cowboy boots, but even that he did in a slipshod way. He'd used a strip of harness leather, cutting off chunks and tacking them on the heels of his boots in squares, never bothering to really trim them to the shape of the heels. Naturally, dirt and manure was caught there. His old leather vest was spotted with grease that had been accumulating for years and his shabby old felt western hat matched.

His ever-ready pistol was strapped to his waist and his cutting bullwhip lay coiled at the foot of the steps with his faithful dog lying there watching it. He sat on the steps with me and we visited. Even though I couldn't understand everything he said, I could tell that he liked me and seemed to appreciate the fact that I took time to visit with him. While I was anxious for him to leave, I liked myself for having made his life a little less lonely for that brief period.

My morning had really slipped away, but I hadn't realized just how much until the men suddenly arrived for dinner. Myron graciously asked Hank to stay for dinner, but he said, "I didn't know it was so late. I have to be getting on." In the end, Myron persuaded him to stay.

While the men visited and washed up, I dashed into the house, poked some kindling into the old cook stove, made some coffee and warmed up the leftovers. By the time the men came into the dining room, I had the table set. Then we all sat down to dinner with our very special guest.

For a long time afterwards the men had a great time teasing me. They accused me of having such a good time entertaining my new gentleman friend that I'd completely forgotten to cook dinner for them. It became quite a joke with us, especially if dinner was a bit late.

Hank also made moonshine during prohibition. Many old timers thought whisky was a cure-all for everything, so when Myron developed a toothache, he rode over to Hank's place for "medicine." When Myron came back, he was so happy and carefree he didn't care if he had a toothache. But when the painkiller wore off, he was in real misery and had to make his way to the dentist.

TRAPPER BEN

We were having a good deal of trouble with coyotes and bobcats killing the young lambs. When Trapper Ben heard about it, he wanted to come out and trap, so Myron said that we would board him and he could keep all of the animal hides he took. He had very good results, so he stayed out for about two months or so. Finally he decided that he'd take his hides and go into town, sell them and visit family.

He got himself all cleaned up, but decided that his hair was much too long and it made him look shabby. He asked Myron to cut his hair.

Myron just laughed and said, "Ben, you've got to be kidding. You know better than to ask ME to cut hair. I don't know how. I've never cut any in my life."

Ben simply wasn't taking no for an answer. "Oh! Sure you can. Anyone can cut hair. I don't want to go home looking like a tramp. I want to look nice for my best girl."

Again Myron tried to convince him, "Really, I've never cut anyone's hair."

Ben went into the kitchen, found a dish towel and put it around his neck, came back to the dining room, put his clippers and scissors on the table, straddled a chair backwards and said, "There's nothing to it. Now just take a little off all the way around. Go ahead."

Myron stood there and stared at Ben's scissors and clippers. Finally he felt that he ought to give it a try, so he began taking off a little hair all the way around. Soon he noticed it wasn't even and tried to even it up. Ben sat there content and happy. Every now and then he'd sing a little ditty, "Hello, Ma, hello Pa." Then he'd chatter about how good it was to be going home.

Myron continued to labor away. After a great deal of effort he laid the clippers down and signed, "Well, Ben. I guess I'm through."

Ben jumped up and went to look in the mirror. He came stomping back, fuming. "The only reason you're through is that you've run out of hair! That is the damnedest haircut I've ever saw! My God! I'm ashamed to go home and have Mama see me looking like this!"

Myron tried to apologize, but Ben wouldn't listen. He was too deeply hurt. He had wanted to look special for his best girl and now he looked his worst with no way to remedy it until his hair grew a little.

He clamped on his hat and walked out the door. Poor Ben had to learn the hard way that everyone couldn't cut hair, especially Myron.

Ben was gone about two weeks, and when he came back he said that he'd had a barber work on his hair so he looked real good. He'd had a nice vacation and was glad to be back.

HENRY MILLER

Henry was a rather dignified and charming bachelor. He was probably thirty five years old. His speech suggested he was from the South, but he never talked about himself. This tall slender man had the kind of manners that gave us the feeling his upbringing was better than average. Everyone liked him. He, too, was a homesteader and was never too busy to help out a neighbor, so during lambing when it was necessary for us to hire extra help, it was natural that we hire him. Myron appreciated his dependability and his sense of humor. Henry was someone you could have fun with.

One evening, the men had just sat down to supper when a car drove in. It was two lawmen. Myron went out to greet the guests and asked them to come in and eat. Most of our men were finished with their meal and carried their plates to the kitchen. Henry and a couple of the other men were still at the table. I quickly set clean plates for our guests and carried in the food just as Myron and his guests seated themselves. Myron introduced the men and they began their meal.

These lawmen were from Hardin and we'd known them for years so they felt free to talk with us. John asked, "Did you know that Bud and I have been appointed Federal Officers? We'd like to stay all night, if you can put us up."

Myron looked at John and said, "Sure, fellows; we can put you up and want to help you any way we can."

John smiled and said, "That leads up to the next thing. Could we borrow a couple of horses? We've gotten a report that there is a whisky still up there in the Gill Creek country, so we've got to check it out."

Bud sighed, "I sure hope that we get evidence this time because that country is so hard to get into. It's nearly impossible by car."

Henry finished his supper, then took his plate to the kitchen and left. Charlie and Jim finished and went to the bunkhouse.

Early the next morning, the law officers ate a quick breakfast and were on their way just as it was getting daylight. The crew came in right at six o'clock for their breakfast. Henry was a little late, so the other men finished and went out to their work. Myron went with them, giving them instructions so they could start their day.

I poured Henry a second cup of coffee. He seemed tired and wasn't in any hurry to go to work. Noticing his red eyes I said, "Looks as if you lost some sleep."

He leaned back in his chair, "Yes, I sure did. I had some moving to do, and I did some other things too." He didn't look right at me as he usually did but looked down and kind of grinned, so that was the end of our conversation. He took his plate to the kitchen and went out the door.

Late that afternoon, the two federal men came riding back to the ranch. I began preparing them something to eat and the men were washing up when Myron came in and asked, "Did you fellows have any luck?"

John sighed. "No, someone must have gotten word to the moonshiner because his still and everything is gone except a ton of sugar."

The federal men hurried through their early supper. They were tired, so they piled into their car and started their long drive back to Hardin.

It was just after that when Henry came to the house and asked me, "Could I get some matches? I seem to be out."

I got the box of matches. As Myron came in the door he said, "It's a damn shame those federal men came all the way out here, spent the day looking for evidence and someone had already tipped the bootlegger off."

All Henry said was, "Wow! That was close." Then he and Myron walked out the door, back to the sheep.

I stood there a moment as it dawned on me. I wouldn't have thought that Henry was a bootlegger!

Myron at the Dryhead ranch.

5
HERDING FOR TSCHIRGI

◆

When Roy Buck and his wife first agreed to come to the Dry Head Ranch, Bill, Myron's stepfather, had painted a rosy picture for Roy. He promised he could keep his horses there and he could have a share of the sheep profits.

That fall when Roy went over to Lodge Grass to settle, up he came back disappointed, telling us that he decided to move his family to Billings where he could use his carpenter skills and have shorter hours. The boys could have better schools and all of them could enjoy church life again.

Then Bill came to the ranch and announced that he had sold the sheep and bought cattle. Myron and I were shocked because we had not been consulted. Myron said that he wasn't interested in cattle so he wanted out—and wanted his share of the money the partnership had made. He knew that the sheep had made a good profit and felt that our share would give us enough to live on until we could decide what we wanted to do.

But Bill said, "There isn't anything left. There was the down payment on the cows and I needed a new car. Then there were the payments on the machinery I bought for the Lodge Grass Ranch."

Myron and I were deeply hurt because we'd put in long hours, and the only wages we'd drawn were just enough to get by on. Now Bill had sold the sheep without consulting us, and we were fully aware that there had been no written agreement. We had been too trusting and had nothing in our name.

The situation was understandably tense. Myron said, "Well, I can see where that leaves us, so long as we don't want anything to do with the cows. At least I think that we are entitled to sheep herder wages and that old Model A Ford."

When the Bucks moved out, we packed our few belongings and helped Bill, the hired man, and the herder trail the sheep to the Two Leggin Bridge where the buyer was to receive them. Myron drove the truck, pulling first one wagon to where we'd camp at night and then going back to pick up the other wagon and take it to where that band would spend the night. Stan and I rode with Myron in the truck. Of course, I did the cooking for the men.

When finally we reached the Two Leggin Bridge, there was a brief wait so we went on to Hardin to my parents' home.

Jobs were still plenty scarce, but Myron went up town to see if he could find anyone who needed a hired hand. There he ran into Bill Prante, an old friend who was the sheep foreman for the Tschirgi Ranch.

As they were visiting, Prante mentioned that he'd come to town to hire a herder. Myron asked for the job and Prante said, "Gosh! We are only paying the single herders twenty dollars a month and board. But I guess we could pay a married herder thirty dollars a month if they bought their own groceries."

This was good news to us. Now we'd have a place to live where we could be a family, and we could save our precious cash until spring when we planned to start raising wheat and hay on the Indian lease we had with Chester Otter Chief on Lodge Grass Creek. I was really looking forward to moving to the Indian lease because it had a nice little new house which would be a real home to us.

But for now we had a herding job and were very thankful. However, the job was far from being easy. The grass was short those dry years and the sheep had to keep traveling to get enough to satisfy their hunger. Myron had to stay right with the sheep or they'd trespass on a neighbor's range.

Our home was a sheep wagon which was comfortable for one man but a bit crowded for the three of us. Stan, now three years old, would have liked to have been more active. When he tired of his toys and books, I encouraged him to draw or color with his crayolas. He found this was a good way to pass the time.

Since Stan grew awfully tired of being cooped up, he spent as much time out of doors as was reasonable; but that too was lonely, for he liked to be with people. To entertain him, we played a game of drawing. One of us would draw the head of a man and the other one would draw the body. We'd keep that up until we couldn't think of any more details or tired of the game. Often Stan would draw on his own to help pass the time. Of all of Stan's toys, I think he loved best his little rubber characters like Mickey and Minnie Mouse, Pop-Eye, Wimpy and Olive Oyl, and also the Big Bad Wolf. They were the nearest things he had for playmates. He was a happy child, but he was most happy when his Dad and the dog Benny came home.

I was always looking for hand work and quickly ran out of anything I brought with me. Soon I discovered the sacks that the sheep salt came in were of a strong coarse material, a little like linen, so I used them to make dresser scarves and pillow cases. They were very pretty when embroidered with colorful thread and trimmed with a crochet edge.

Bill and Hazel Prante were very good to us. Now and then, they'd drop in to visit and sometimes stayed to eat. If the weather was cold, Myron and Bill would stretch out on the bed and Stan would climb up there with them while

Hazel and I fixed supper. Although it was crowded, we laughed and joked and had a good time.

We saw very few people. Occasionally the trapper or a cowboy looking for a stray horse or cows would drop in and have coffee or a meal. Then we'd have a good visit. Each scrap of news was very welcome because we had no radio and always seemed to be out of fresh reading material. We never missed a chance to trade reading material with other herders; it didn't matter what it was, detective magazines or whatever. Even the girlie magazines were read. Actually, I learned more from them than I really wanted to know.

At night we went to bed early. Stan liked the foot of the bed because there he could have his toys to sleep with. When it was very cold, he'd sleep in the middle. Myron slept on the outside of the bed so he could get up quickly if the sheep should move off the bed ground. That meant he slept closest to the lantern, which also meant that, for our evening entertainment, it was Myron who read out loud to Stan and me.

On cold nights, Myron would bank the fire with coal about nine o'clock and then get up at midnight and bank it again. Then we'd get up about five to cook breakfast so it would be over with when the sheep started moving off the bed ground.

One day Hazel Prante found it necessary to make a trip to Billings. She felt that she didn't drive well enough to go to the city alone, so she asked me to go along. Very early the next morning, we dressed in our town outfits. We wore hats and gloves. I even wore high heels; I really felt dressed up. I decided to have Stan wear his navy suit with a white shirt and a blue tie. The outfit was especially becoming because it brought out the blue in his eyes.

Fortunately, we had no trouble on the long, dusty road. Since we were able to finish our errands before noon, Hazel decided that we should have the special treat of eating in one of the best dining rooms in town. We chose the Grand Hotel. We laughed because we'd been in the hills so long that we felt very "countrified." Having joked about it, we decided that if we put on our best manners no one would know that we were fresh out of the hills.

It was thrilling to walk into the beautiful dining room. The host greeted us warmly and showed us to a very nice table, all set with beautiful white linen table cloth and napkins. The pretty china and silver sparkled.

The waitress was a sweet girl, eager to please. She brought Stan a high chair and gave him special attention. They seemed to take a genuine liking for each other. Hazel had already decided that we should order their best dinner. I ordered chicken and dumplings, because lacking refrigeration, we hadn't been able to have chicken at camp.

I remarked, "It's interesting that being in a lovely restaurant like this and being treated like we are somebody makes me feel quite elegant."

Hazel chuckled and said, "After all, we don't look like sheep herders, so I'm sure no one will know our secret." We just sat there smiling.

All of us enjoyed our lovely dinner and it was almost time to start our 125 mile trip back because we did want to get out to camp before dark.

As we rose from the table, our little waitress was right there to help Stan down. She said, "You know, I think you are a very nice little boy. Where do you live?"

Quickly, I answered for him, saying, "Wyola."

However, Stan felt that he had been asked so he should answer. In a rather loud voice, he proudly said, "We live in a sheep wagon. My daddy is a sheep herder."

Both Hazel and I saw the humor in it and we didn't dare look at each other until we got out of the restaurant. We laughed all the way home—about how it served us right for trying to put on airs.

One snowy day, Stan and I took a walk in the hills. When we got back, we decided that the snow was just right to make a snowman so we rolled two huge snow balls for the body and another for his head. When we had them put together, we found some rocks and sticks to make his eyes, nose and mouth. We had lots of fun, but we'd gotten awfully wet. I started to look at my watch to see if it was time to go in and discovered that my watch was gone. It had been a gift and much more expensive than I could afford, so I was frantic to find it.

I thought of the long walk and of all the area we'd covered that afternoon. Thinking of the tiny watch, I sighed. It would be very difficult to find.

Too soon it was dusk. The sheep, Myron, and the dog Benny arrived. I had no idea where I'd lost my watch, but if it was near the wagon the sheep would surely trample it in the snow. In the morning Myron would feed the sheep their cotton seed pellets and there would be more milling around, so I might as well forget it. But I couldn't. Then I remembered the woman in the Bible who had lost a coin, and how she had hunted for it until she found it. I decided that was exactly what I would do. Even if the sheep had trampled it down, I'd look until I found it or what was left of it.

Morning dawned, a beautiful day, and as soon as Stan was ready to play, I took him outside. While he was running and playing, I walked around part way up a small hill and looked back toward the wagon. Half way between the snowman and the wagon was a good sized patch of sage brush. Something sparkled. I rushed over—and sure enough it was my watch. I was a very happy young lady and wished I had someone to rejoice with me, but I was so happy praising the Lord and so thankful for my good fortune that I really didn't need any help!

One day Hazel came with Bill for a brief visit and brought me a pattern for a hook rug. I appreciated her visit and her thoughtfulness in bringing me the gift. I happened to have my rug hook with me, but I didn't have any yarn. However I read in one of the farm magazines that rags cut on the bias could be used in place of yarn. With this in mind I gathered up the few rags that I had and started on the rug, but they were such little pieces that they kept me constantly threading the needle. Luckily, on our weekly trip to Lodge Grass,

I mentioned my problem to a friend and she gave me a whole dress cut on the bias.

I was thrilled as I carefully cut away, making long strips and then carefully winding them up in a ball. That afternoon Myron happened to be herding near the wagon and he watched me tediously cut away on my strips.

Finally he said, "I can show you a way to fold that material so you won't have to do much cutting." I couldn't see how he could make my job easier, but I gave him the dress. He folded the material and I handed him the shears. He snipped a few times, and my eyes opened wide with horror. He had ruined my beautiful piece of cloth! I had only tiny little strips. Myron saw my anger and he didn't even stop to apologize but hurried out to his sheep. I had all I could do to keep my tears from spilling over. Little things came to mean so much to me when we lived in such isolation.

While we were herding, our little old Model A Ford really began to give us trouble. We decided to use some of our precious savings to trade it off on a very nice used Chevrolet. The former owner had given it such good care that the paint was just as shiny as it was when it was new. We proudly drove it back to camp. Bill Prante happened to drop by the next day, and we proudly showed it to him. He said he thought we got a darn good buy on such a nice car.

Soon he starting laughing and laughing. We stood there and stared at him. Finally he explained. "You people take the cake. You are the only couple that I know with a job where they are earning thirty dollars a month and board themselves—and you still have enough to buy a new car!" Then he laughed again.

Most of the time we left our car at the Tschirgi Ranch where it could be kept out of the weather. Our friend John worked there. He had a lady friend he liked to visit about once a week, but he didn't have transportation, so Myron made a deal with him. John could use our car to visit his special lady every week—if he would bring our car out to camp once a week and stay with the sheep while we hurried into Lodge Grass to get our mail. This worked well for all of us. John only went as far as Wyola, but he always kept our car shined up and full of gas. Having him care for the sheep even for such a short time meant a lot to us, and we always came back to camp rejuvenated.

We subscribed to *Colliers Magazine* which was running a continued story by Earnest Haycox. We were so anxious to see what happened next that I'd read it out loud on our way back to camp. Reading while we bounced over those very rough roads didn't do much for sentence rhythm, but it was fun and made the trip go faster.

The first part of February the ranch decided that it was getting close enough to lambing that they would move the sheep into the ranch where they could feed them beet pulp that had been trucked in from the sugar beet factory. This was good feed for ewes that were about to lamb, although that wasn't expected until April.

It was an extremely cold day when John, the camp tender, showed up. Myron told him that some of the ewes would be lambing soon.

John looked surprised. "Impossible. This bunch of sheep aren't bred to lamb until May." Myron insisted, "I want you to go and tell the boss. If they are born out here in this cold without shelter, they won't survive."

The next day, Bill Prante came to our camp and was very surprised to find that several lambs had been born during the night. Myron reported, "All of the lambs are doing okay except one, and it got separated from its mother." So Myron, young Stan, and Bill walked through the sheep searching for it.

Of course they were concerned for the lamb, because he needed the nourishment from his mother's milk in order to survive, and Stan sensed the concern. Putting himself in the lamb's place, he looked up at the men with what seemed to him a brilliant thought and said, "Well, if you can't find the lamb's mother, maybe you could find his daddy."

Often Myron would let Stan hold the reins as if he were driving the big gentle Percheron team that was pulling the empty sleigh back to the camp, and he felt very grown up. He'd scold that big team in his baby voice and away they would go back to the barn. Myron would take them to water, unharness them and pour out their oats while Stan watched as if he wanted to be sure he remembered everything he saw.

As the days lengthened, one could see different signs of spring. This made us more and more anxious to move to our leased place on Lodge Grass Creek where we could have a real home, and Myron was mighty anxious to get started farming on his own.

Myron, Ellie and Stan, age 4.

6
FARMING ON LODGE GRASS CREEK

◆

    Finally the long awaited April arrived. We packed our few things, thoroughly cleaned the sheep wagon, climbed into our car and left the Tschirgi Ranch.

    It was a thrilling day when we moved into the little white house leased from the Crow Indian, Chester Otter Chief. It was a cute little house. Its two porches and four small rooms reminded me of a child's play house, but seemed spacious after the sheep wagon. It was wonderful to have neighbors close enough that we could walk to their houses to visit. Also, now that we were only three miles from town we could pick up our mail every day.

    We bought secondhand furniture and happily accepted any that others wanted to give away. Myron even bought me a used pedal sewing machine which had been a dream of mine. He also build a cumbersome cupboard. He was ashamed of it, but I loved its roominess. I painted it and all of the other furniture apple green which gave a matched look and I sewed matching curtains for the cupboard and windows. Once our shiny new linoleum was in place, we felt our home very attractive.

    Stan missed having a dog for a playmate, so Myron located a black shepherd pup that Stan promptly named Oscar. Both of us were surprised at the choice of names because he hadn't known anyone who had that name. We never knew just where Stan got his ideas. Oscar was so strong that, at times, Stan had trouble playing with him. That pup wanted love and attention so much that when our four year old tried to pet him, he'd jump up on Stan and knock him down. Then there would be a lot of hollering until one of us got to the scene of the scuffle and scolded the dog. Soon Oscar learned not to be quite so aggressive and became part of our family.

    Each time we went to town we saw many Indians Myron knew. He could understand much of their language and could talk sign language with them.

But when Myron was farming he was away from home so much I was a bit concerned that one of our Indian neighbors or one of his friends would come to our house and try to talk to me. Of course I had never learned their language, and many of the old time Indians had never learned to speak English.

One day an elderly Indian rode his black and white pinto horse to our house. He rode with the air of one who had spent a lifetime riding bareback. Bird Far Away was a tall, well built man who carried himself very straight. His braids had been thick, long and black, but now were streaked with gray and had thinned considerably. He wore a black, tall, cone shaped hat, known as a Reservation hat, along with his Levis and moccasins. His shirt was light in color and he had a kerchief tied about his neck and wore a dark vest.

Fascinated, I watched the pinto splash through the mud, water and patches of melting snow as he came nearer to the house. Bird Far Away's faithful horse was thin, for he had not had oats all winter. I was drawn to this proud man who had seen much trouble.

"A-ho," came the guttural call from the gate. I knew that I had to go out to see what he wanted and was hoping that he'd become my friend, but Myron told me that he didn't speak English. Just how could I make a friend if I couldn't talk to him?

When I walked the brief distance to the gate, I greeted him, "Hello."

He sat on his horse looking me over for what seemed a long time, then nodded as if he approved, saying, "Where's My Boy?"

Knowing he wanted Myron, who had been his friend since he was a child, I pointed in the direction he had gone and said, "Fix fence." Satisfied, he rode off. I was pleased because I felt that I'd made a friend.

What Bird Far Away wanted was for Myron to lease his place. As I came to know him and his wife, Whoop That Sings, I found the language barrier was not as difficult as I had thought.

One day the men had just finished the noon meal and were leaving to go out to the hay field. I was picking up the dishes when I heard an Indian lady's voice and glanced out the window just as Myron came to the door.

He said, "Ellie, here is Bird Far Away's wife, Whoop That Sings, and her five year old granddaughter. They've walked all the way out from town. They haven't had anything to eat or drink." Then he hurried out to his waiting men, and they went off to the hay field.

Knowing the three mile walk could be very tiring and dusty, even for a young person, I quickly got each of them a glass of water to drink and offered to let them wash up, but Whoop That Sings waved her hand to show me that she felt washing was quite unimportant at a time like this. Wearily she sat down at the table as I hurried to get dishes and hot food for them. She signed, "My tired, my tired."

Hungrily they began eating. From the size of the dinner the child consumed I wondered when they'd last eaten. The grandmother and child chatted in their language as they ate. From their expressions I knew they had enjoyed the food.

Getting up from the table, the child said something to the grandmother and went out to play with Stan under the big box elder tree. Whoop That Sings got up from the table, stretched and patted her stomach. Then without a word she walked into the living room, took off her soiled blanket, stretched out on the couch, covered herself with her blanket and dropped off to sleep.

When I looked in on her I had to smile. Even though we couldn't understand each other's language, I had been a good hostess. Then I broke into a big grin as I thought of my fastidious aunt from the east who was scared of Indians and wondered what she would say or do if she should walk into my living room and see Whoop That Sings stretched out, taking her nap on my couch.

As the time neared to plant our wheat crop I became concerned as to how Myron would get the job done. We had no machinery. When I asked, he replied, "Well, I've made a deal with Jay Sharp, the fellow who owns the grocery store and also owns a farm several miles up Lodge Grass Creek. Up until now he's had to hire a man to put in his crops with his own machinery, but when I talked to him I suggested a deal where I would put in his crop and then he'll let me use his machinery to put in my crop at night and on Sunday. That way, we'll each get our crops in about the same time."

The wheat was beautiful. As we watched it grow, we had many plans for the money it would bring in. Then one day, as Myron drove up the road, he was shocked to see our beautiful green field turned black. He could hardly get there fast enough to investigate, and when he was on the scene, he was horrified to see that the shoots were covered with Mormon crickets. The field was completely destroyed, and along with it, our dreams and even our garden.

We were crushed because we'd spent our money putting in our crop. Now what were we going to do? We did feel fortunate that we had a good hay crop stacked before the crickets came, but because of hard times, others couldn't afford to buy it. Besides, there was plenty of hay in the country.

One day a neighbor had to make a trip to Billings and asked Myron to ride along. There Myron found he had time on his hands. With finances constantly on his mind, he decided to talk with a banker about buying some cows for his fall pasture since we had plenty of hay to winter them. He was uneasy about talking to a banker when all he really had was an idea, but reasoned that the banker could only say no. Besides, nothing ventured, nothing gained.

When the banker said, "Yes," Myron could hardly believe his good fortune. He was even more surprised when the banker added, "I'll loan you enough to buy fifty head of cattle as soon as you send your three references."

Of the three references, the one that stood out most was from Mr. Willcutt, the foreman of the vast cattle empire of the Dana Cattle Company. He wrote, "This young couple are good honest folks who are willing to work hard so I think they deserve a chance but I feel fifty head of cattle are not enough to make a living. It is only enough to tie them to a small place where they will starve to death."

The banker knew of some cattle that were being sold. Myron went to look at them and the price was reasonable. Although they were old cows they were young enough to raise a calf or two. Myron reasoned that if he gave them good enough care through the winter he could make a fair profit. Then the next year he could sell them and buy young cattle.

We were thrilled by our first venture into the cattle business and especially proud to be putting our brand, V Bar H, on our cattle. We felt this was one crop that drought, crickets or grasshoppers couldn't destroy. Just as pleasing was the friendship and guidance we were receiving from our fatherly banker.

In February, Myron's stepfather Bill, ran out of hay for his cattle. He reasoned that since spring was close he could put his cattle with Myron's and feed them from Myron's hay as we had more than we needed. If by chance the hay should run out, Bill thought he could buy some and repay "the loan" from next year's crop.

The extreme cold that March was very hard on the cattle. The temperature remained forty below zero that whole month. Consequently, Bill and Myron's cattle both ran out of hay.

Myron said, "Dad, now we are both out of hay and it is up to you to go to your banker and tell him how bad off your cattle are."

When Bill came back he said, "My banker refused to loan me the money because he's already loaned me more money than my cattle are worth. I had to use that money to buy the new car when my other one broke down."

Myron was crestfallen. "Well, where does that leave me and my cattle?" he asked as he walked out the door.

At home he said, "Ellie, I feel so stupid to have left myself wide open so Dad could do that to me again. He's been doing things like that to me since I was a child. Looks like I'd learn. The hard part is to go to our banker and tell him what happened. He's been good to me and he won't appreciate my letting that happen, but what else could I have done? Those cows were all heavy with calf and I couldn't let them die."

When Myron went to his bank the banker said, "Well, what can I do for you?" Myron blurted out the whole sordid story, and he felt sheepish as he told it.

The banker was a very kind man, but this made him so angry that he said, "If what you tell me is true, I'll call in the bank's lawyer, and we'll sue your father."

It all sounded so cold that Myron said, "I can't bring myself to sue my stepfather because it will hurt my mother too much. Not only that, but a suit would be the talk of the country and of course it will go down on my record and that would be something I would have to carry the rest of my life."

As the banker leaned back in his chair he scowled, "I can understand how you feel. Now I'll tell you how the bank feels." He sighed, put his folded hands under his chin and closed his eyes for a moment. "Okay, I'll give you enough money to buy hay which should see you through until you have enough spring pasture. Then when fall comes, we expect you to sell the cows and calves. This bank doesn't deal with that kind of people."

All spring and summer we had hoped for a good wheat crop and it was beautiful until the grasshoppers. Now we owed the bank, the garage where we bought the tractor gas on time, and the grocery store.

When fall came, Myron and the banker picked a day to ship the cattle. That day the market was down, so we ended up owing the bank $800 with interest accumulating until we could find a way of paying off that great big debt.

Our only ray of hope was the hay Myron had put up, and our alfalfa seed crop looked good, but it was a gamble. As Myron said, "Whatever money we are lucky enough to get off the hay and seed, hopefully will take care of our debts."

Little white house, Lodge Grass.

7
HAPPY ANTICIPATION

◆

In everyone's life there are the good times and the bad times. Well, I've been telling you about some of our bad times, but now I want to tell you about our happy anticipation. Although we had problems establishing ourselves financially, our home gave us happiness and Stan gave us joy. Now we were looking forward to another child due the last part of May or the first part of June.

We were pleased to learn that our good friends Doris and Frank Greenough from the Tschirgi Ranch were expecting their first child about the same time. Every now and then Doris and I would get together to compare small problems with our pregnancies or to share expectant mothers' conversation in general.

Another happy coincidence occurred when we learned that my brother Arnold and his wife Evelyn, who lived in Billings, were expecting their first child at about the same time we were. So when I came to Billings for my check up, I'd see and hear what expectant mother news she had.

During the latter part of May, Myron decided it would be best for me to stay in Billings until the baby arrived because he didn't want to make a fast run after my pains started. I was dreading the time away because I would have to leave Stan with relatives and I'd miss him and my home so much. However, the doctor thought the baby would be born about June 4th so probably it wouldn't be too long a stay.

I was glad to learn that Doris would be in Billings early, too. Since Frank was the cow foreman for the Tschirgi Ranch and had to be out with the roundup wagon, they felt she might as well be in Billings near the doctor.

Each of us visited everyone we knew and went to many picture shows. Myron and Frank had worked out a deal that if Frank came to town he was to take both of us to the picture show, and if Myron came, he was to take us. One man escorting two pregnant women provided us with many laughs. One time, Myron decided to take us to the show. To be extra nice, he took us to the Fox

Theater and bought us the most comfortable seats in the house loge. That meant stairs, and stairs for Doris were difficult to climb without becoming short of breath, so we would have to stop and rest.

Myron tried to apologize saying, "Doris, I'm sorry. I just didn't realize you had trouble climbing stairs."

As Doris leaned against the railing resting, I noticed a glint in her eye as she said, "Oh, yes you did. Remember, you told me you'd get even with me?"

Myron chuckled, "Well, now what do you want me to do? Get behind and push?"

"You do and I'll kick you right in the chin."

We all laughed when Myron said, "Doris, you can't lift your leg that high."

Another evening it was just dusk when Doris and I were on our way to a movie. The evening was cool, so we were wearing our big coats and were just strolling along as if we had all the time in the world. We were walking by a hedge when a car pulled up and two young men looking for female company eyed us. When we drew even with them, they realized we definitely were pregnant. They spun plenty of rubber off their tires as they fled.

Doris and I just stood there and laughed.

On June 6th, I checked in with the doctor. He said that everything was normal but I'd have to wait a little longer. I was despondent because I was homesick and wanted to have the baby so I could go home.

As long as I had to stay, I decided to buy my sister-in-law a baby gift and go for a visit because she had longer to wait that I did. But when I rang the door bell, I was surprised. It was her sister, Helen, who answered.

Cheerfully I said, "I've come to visit Evelyn."

Helen looked surprised. "Haven't you heard? Evelyn is in the hospital. She gave birth to a baby girl last night, and that's why I was so slow answering the door. I didn't get much sleep so I was trying to catch up on it this morning."

I apologized to Helen for waking her up and went on my way. I was happy for Arnie and Evelyn, but darn it, it wasn't fair. She got to have her baby way early, and I had to go over time.

By June 8th I was way over time, and Doris was too, so we both went to see our doctor and told him that we were getting awfully tired of waiting. He laughed as he looked at our charts. "Well, your babies are full term now, and if you really want me to do something to hurry them up, I can give each of you a prescription for Castor Oil and Quinine." We looked at him to see if he was joking, but he was very serious and was writing out our prescriptions. We made our way to the druggist who didn't seem to think that much Castor Oil was unusual, so we were willing to try it.

As we walked down the street I said, "Gee! That's an awful lot of Castor Oil to drink. It's such icky tasting stuff." Doris said, "Well, let's do it the easy way."

I chuckled, "What do you mean, easy way? Have you ever in your life taken that much Castor Oil?"

She laughed. "Well no, I haven't, but what I meant when I said "easy" is to take it with orange juice. Oh! There's the store. Let's get our oranges."

That evening, as we tried to drink that bottle of Castor Oil, we found there was no easy way. It was awful, but the oranges did help. With a lot of wise cracking and giggling we finally consumed it.

It was late and neither of us felt very good, so Doris decided to go to her room. I started to go to bed, but my cramps convinced me the baby would be coming sometime during the night, so I went to the hospital. I hadn't been there long when Doris came. Since we had planned to share a room, I was glad that she was there to keep me company. At six o'clock on the morning of June 9th, Doris gave birth to her son, who looked just like his dad. She was very happy because she had wanted a son. I was happy for her, but I was most uncomfortable. However, later that morning, at nine o'clock, our dear little blond girl was born. I was elated. Now I had my dark haired son, who looked like his dad, and the sweet blond baby girl I'd longed for. When Myron came, we named our baby Christine, after my mother.

While we were convalescing, we visited a friend of Doris' who was just across the hall. She loved to play bridge, so we played with her. Often we'd walk to the nursery and look through the window at the many babies, or we'd walk down the hall to visit my sister-in-law. Every day during visiting hours we had a great deal of company, and the ten days went by rather fast. My happiness was complete when Myron and Stan came to take the baby and me home. It was great to be a family again.

8
IT WAS DESTINY

◆

The defeats farmers were facing at this time were mighty depressing. They would give their all and it wasn't enough. Not only were we having problems with grasshoppers, crickets and drought, but anything that we did raise brought very low prices, and sometimes we couldn't sell it at all—like our hay. Yet we had all our regular living expenses, and as a result, we got deeper and deeper in debt.

It was a worrisome problem to me, especially since Myron, who had always been able to see a bright side, now could see none. Stan and baby Christine were such a joy to us but represented an awesome responsibility to Myron.

One fall morning, he said, "Ellie, this is the first time conditions have gotten so bad I just don't know what to do. Jobs are impossible to get, and even big outfits like Dana aren't able to pay wages to their labor and are only furnishing groceries until the time comes when they are able to give them their back pay."

I tried to think of something to say that might lift his spirits, but all I could think of was, "Really, we have a lot to be thankful for, like the children and each other, and we are fortunate that we live in this great country. We'll make it somehow." As I was saying these things, I realized that was exactly what he was worrying about.

Myron got up from the table. As he put on his jacket he said, "I'm going after the mail, but I'm not going to drive the car unless I have to because I don't want to ask for credit. I'll saddle Deacon and ride him. I probably won't be right back so don't worry about me."

I was watching out the window as Myron rode down the lane. The fall day was chilly and the wind was blowing the dry leaves around. As I stood there and watched, I was feeling great concern about Myron's depression and perhaps greater concern about our great nation. But for me, more importantly and immediately, I was worried about what was going to happen to our little family.

The baby's cry brought me back from worrying about the future to my immediate concern which was to feed my two precious children and see that they had their baths and clean clothes.

When that was done, I put the baby down for her morning nap while Stan was off playing in his room. I had done the dishes, punched down the bread and took the ashes out. I was just getting the kitchen straightened up when I glanced out and saw Myron hurry to the house.

He burst through the door and said, "Ellie, listen to this letter. It is from Mr. Willcutt. I want to see what you think of it."

Dear Myron,

Mr. Warren and I are starting a sheep outfit and we wondered if you and your wife would consider running it for us?

At present we have one band of sheep and would like to add to them. Hopefully, we can build a good sheep outfit.

You will live in the dugout cabin on Woody Creek.

We will furnish everything, your pay will be $50.00 a month and 10% of what the company makes.

If you are interested, let me know as soon as possible.

Sincerely,

Harve

Without hesitation I said, "That really seems to be a ray of hope. What do you think of it?"

He smiled a big smile and said, "I think it is what we'd better do. Besides, I think it is the answer to prayer." Quickly he changed his clothes and walked down the lane, hoping to catch a ride to Hardin with a neighboring rancher who we knew was going to town that day.

When they arrived in town, Myron went to the hotel where Harve stayed, told him we wanted the job, and asked when he wanted us to start.

Harve said, "We'd like you to come as quickly as you can, because there is a lot to do. These sheep and some equipment are collateral that banker Warren had to take on a foreclosure, and the only other thing he has is an old truck. I have horses, so I can let you have a good team to use, and of course I have saddle horses. Now that we have you for our foreman and your wife for a cook, we'll order a new pickup for the company and gather up everything else we need."

Myron came home a different man, very enthusiastic now that he had hope and some action was underway. Mr. Willcutt even advanced Myron some money to move with.

HOME IN THE WOODY CAMP

It was difficult to break up the nice little home we loved so much, but we couldn't look back—we could only go forward and enjoy our new adventure.

Woody Camp was a one room cabin, so we had to get rid of some of our things. We took our bed, a cot for Stan, Christine's bassinet and high chair, my sewing machine, a chest of drawers. The cabin had built-in cupboards and a work space, and there was a good cook stove that also heated the cabin.

We arrived on a gloomy day that threatened rain. Myron and a friend who had hauled the furniture on his pickup unloaded quickly because they were afraid of the dirt roads turning to mud. Myron wanted to go out to the sheep camp to get acquainted with the herder but felt he ought to stay and help me. I knew that he was depressed about moving us into that drab cabin so I said, "You go on out to see the herder, and I'll straighten this place up so that it will look like home. The fire you built already makes it more cheerful."

I cleaned the floor and with the beds already set up it didn't take long to make them up. I scattered the rag rugs, put a table cloth on the table, washed the windows sparkling clean and had a stew cooking when Myron came home. "I didn't think this place would ever seem like home but it does," he said.

Dana had a cow camp a few miles away, and the cowboys came often and usually ate with us. I always had fresh homemade bread, and often I would serve roast beef, gravy, mashed potatoes, slaw and cream pie. They thought it great and called it a Sunday dinner. The day I first cooked a pot roast and noodles I thought one man in particular would be sick from overeating. The

Home at Woody Camp as drawn by Eleanor Lynde.

others joked about it but he said, "This is the first time I've had noodles for a coon's age. As you well know, roundup cooks fry most of the food, and in the line camps none of us take time to cook food like this."

More than anything else, the cowboys seemed to enjoy the children. They appreciated the little kindnesses and the attention I gave them for the brief time they were at our home. Always they showed me deep respect. Whenever they butchered, they always brought us fresh meat, which was their way of saying "thank you" for the kindnesses we showed them.

The thing I liked most about this camp was that it had been built on a side of a hill which meant we were able to see a great distance. This was a tremendous help when Myron had to be gone tending the sheep camps because I could keep an eye on the "hospital bunch." These were sheep that were crippled or weren't well enough to keep up with the big bunch on the range and were given extra care.

Lady, our female Shepherd dog, was bred to raise working dogs for the Willcutt and Warren Sheep Company. She had a nice disposition and was very gentle with the children. I appreciated her because she didn't bark when someone was coming; she'd just growl enough to let me know. The only time she barked was when she'd been sent after the sheep and then it was just a yip now and then. Most importantly, she stayed just outside the door on the sunny side of the house to keep an eye on the goings on around the place.

She kept her eye on the sheep, and if they went too far she'd whine. Then I'd step outside the door and say, "Go get em Lady," and she'd be off to bring them back to where they belonged.

When Myron needed to use the old company truck, he discovered that someone had let the radiator freeze. The block was cracked, so he had to take our car. When he got home he said, "I had a flat tire today so first thing in the morning I'll take it to the garage and get it fixed. If you need some groceries, make out a list and I'll get them. I'll see the boss and let him know about the truck."

The next morning as he washed up for breakfast he glanced out the window. "Well! What do you know. Every tire on the car is flat."

I hurried to the window. "Why should all of them go flat?" He looked at me as if I wasn't very bright, and said, "These tires are only four-ply tires. They are okay on highways and even around Lodge Grass, but here in all this cactus it's a must to have six-ply tires."

The car had always made me feel secure because it was there if we needed it. I said, "That car is our only transportation. What are we going to do?"

"For now, I'll eat my breakfast and then I'll take all of the tires off and when the truck hauling the cow cake out to Grapevine Ranch comes back, I'll be on the road and flag them down and they'll haul them and me into town."

Shortly after, we got the new pickup with the six-ply tires on it. We were really thrilled because it was the first "new" vehicle we ever had. With the six-ply tires we had no more worry about cactus causing flats.

We had reasonable weather until January, when a long cold spell—20 to 40 degrees below zero—made keeping the cabin warm a difficult task. It was just a shell made of studs, siding and tar paper. Part of it sat in the ground, and it had a dirt roof. The frost came right through the walls, causing them to become quite damp.

All of us had bad colds. Baby Christine's turned into pneumonia, and we wanted to take her to town to the doctor, but because of the severe weather and snowy roads, I was afraid to make the long trip. Car heaters in those days were not good. Frost always covered the windshield and the driver had to use his hand to clear a small peep hole so he could see where to drive. With severe cold and a lot of snow, there was always danger of trouble on the lonely road.

My decision to keep the baby at home and doctor her myself was a lonely one. I kept wondering if I'd done the right thing. To compensate, we really gave her the best nursing care. I greased her with camphorated oil and kept her bassinet right by the cook stove with the fire going. At night Myron would bank the fire at our nine o'clock bed time, again at midnight, and then at two o'clock. At five o'clock we were up starting our day.

Naturally, I was saying a continuous prayer. I was doing the best that I could and knew the rest was up to God.

When Myron was hauling hay to a sheep camp he stopped to see an elderly lady who lived ten miles from us. She was a wonderful person everyone called Grandma Swanke. When Myron mentioned our baby was sick with pneumonia, she felt the need to help. Being one of those ladies who knew all of the home remedies, she gave Myron a jar of goose grease for us to use on Christine. By then our baby was getting better, and I was afraid to change remedies. However, I felt good knowing I had a friend like Grandma, for I'd never experienced such lonely, helpless, scared feelings before. I felt the weight of being the one who made the decision to doctor Christine at home. Given that, I really did talk to the Lord and when He brought her through it, I felt so humble and so thankful.

During the baby's illness, I hadn't done the washing because I didn't want more dampness in the cabin. In those days, washing always caused humidity because the wash water had to be heated on top of the stove. In fact, the spring water at the camp was so hard that I always tried to melt snow for wash water. Although the weather was still below zero, and I wasn't over my cold, I felt I just had to wash baby clothes, especially diapers. The method I used was to scrub the clothes on the wash board and wring them by hand. With all the exercise in the warm water, I became very warm and sweaty. When Myron came in he said, "You've got no business going out in the cold to hang up those clothes."

I protested, "I've got to. The baby needs the clothes and you know I can't hang them in the house because it would make the house too damp."

Realizing the logic in my argument Myron said, "Okay, then you stay in the house, and I'll hang them out."

Out he went with a dish pan of baby clothes. In a little while I glanced out to see how he was doing and couldn't believe my eyes. Each diaper I'd wrung out was twisted like a sausage. My method had been to give each diaper a flip before I hung it on the line, securing each one with two clothespins, but Myron was hanging each little sausage with one clothespin. I couldn't believe it. A whole row of little sausages hanging there. I sat down and doubled up with laughter. Stan came over to see what I was laughing about, but I could hardly tell him I was laughing so hard. Then I became concerned. How would they ever dry? I consoled myself by thinking at least they were washed and on the line, so I could bring in a few at a time and dry them on the little line back of the cook stove.

When morning came, we were very surprised to hear water dripping off the roof. The nicest warm Chinook wind was blowing. I looked at the clothes on the line, and the diapers were blowing in the wind, smooth, fluffy and dry. All I needed to do was to get them off the clothesline.

At the breakfast table Myron said, "Well, today I'll have to move Ole Nelson's wagon, so I'll be taking the little bay team that Harve had Sandy bring. They are a dandy team and aren't much bigger than a saddle horse, but boy can they pull. I'm especially glad to have them because in such slush you sure couldn't get around with a pickup. I'll have to be gone all day."

When Myron came home that evening with the team and wagon, he unhitched the horses at the barn and turned them loose so they could go to the water trough. Instead of going back to the barn for their oats after a drink, they began running and playing and soon ran off. Myron came to the house very disgusted and said, "That darn fool team think they are colts. It's too dark to go look for them now, and there's a chance they'll come back to their feed. Man, I sure hope they do because I need them first thing in the morning to move Dan's camp."

After supper we listened to the radio until bed time, trying not to think of those crazy horses.

About midnight, we awoke to the sound of horses hooves on the snow and ice, shorting and blowing. Quickly we jumped up, slipped our heavy coats over our night clothes, stuck our feet in our overshoes, and headed out. I ran down to open the corral gate wide, while Myron herded the horses toward the corral. We held our breath until they went through the gate, heaving a mutual sigh of relief as Myron securely fastened the corral gate behind them. Slowly we walked through the starlit night back to our snug cabin and our comfortable bed to finish our night's sleep.

We had many friends and acquaintances who came to visit but none surprised us as much as long-time family friends, Howard and Hilma Johnson. Their world had been Lodge Grass so many years we never thought they'd drive out to Woody. It was a surprised Myron who greeted them. They came in to have coffee and a brief visit.

Soon Howard said, "You know, there are so many people moving into the

Lodge Grass area it's now more of a farming community than cow outfits like it used to be. I was thinking I'd have to go out of the ranching business or cut down to smaller operations, but the other day I got a letter from Jim Kincade who'd like to sell his ranch on Buster Creek. Hilma has never been in this country and the weather is so nice that we thought it a good idea to come over to see it."

The Johnsons loved children but had none. They made a big fuss over ours and gave Stan special attention. They wanted to take him with them, and he was eager to go. Howard said, "Don't worry about him. We are only going to look at the ranch and will be right back. We plan to get back to Lodge Grass before dark."

Myron was busy with his men, getting the sheep equipment ready to move to Lemon Springs where they would be lambing. The day sped by and soon it was supper time. When Myron came in I said with concern, "Isn't it time for the Johnsons to be getting back with Stan? Surely they wouldn't keep him at Jim's overnight?"

"Damn," he said, " they should have been here by now."

I set supper on the table, but neither of us enjoyed it. All we could think about was the Johnsons, Stan and whatever trouble they must be having. Then Myron said, "Let's go and see what's happened to them." I put the food away and put the dishes in the dish pan, took Christine out of her bed where she was playing, grabbed the diaper bag and away we went.

Jim's ranch was twenty miles from Woody Camp. As soon as we turned off the Corporation Road, we were on a primitive road which was seldom traveled. Myron began to look for car tracks and was sure the Johnsons had only gone toward Jim's place and had not returned over this road. Soon it was dark, and we figured they had to still be at Jim's place.

When we got there, Jim was asleep; but Myron called, waking him up and telling him, "This morning Howard, Hilma and Stan left our place to come up and see you. Have you seen anything of them?"

A surprised Jim said, "No, I haven't seen anyone today. By gosh, I don't know where they could be. They sure as hell didn't get anywhere around here or I'd have seen them."

Now all we could do was backtrack and see where they could have gotten off the road. Myron turned off in to the Cashen Ranch to see if anyone had seen the Johnsons. They had not, so we went back towards home.

Completely baffled, Myron said, "I don't know what to do now. Howard might have known of some kind of cut off and that is how we missed them."

By now we were nearly home and the baby was tired and cranky so we took her home. I undressed her and put her to bed where she dropped off to sleep, but Myron and I kept wondering just where we could have missed them. Finally I said, "You know those creeks that we have to ford? Do they ever have to make a new crossing?"

Myron jumped from his chair and almost shouted, "That's it! Way back when Howard was there the road used to cross Muddy Creek above where it crosses now. The new crossing was made because the old one was so badly eroded. Now the only time it is used is to cross with livestock."

We decided that I should stay home with the tired baby and he would go back. As he left he said, "I know that is where I'll find them. Thank heaven I've got a good strong tow chain and all the equipment I'll need. We'll be back as soon as possible."

When Myron found the old road crossing, they were there, badly stuck in Muddy Creek, and it called for a joint effort to get their car out. It was daylight when they arrived back at our camp. I was surely happy to see all of them back, but especially to see that Stan had taken it quite well. I asked him if he'd gotten hungry during their "adventure."

He sighed, "No. They had lots of food so we had two picnics and I slept a lot."

I smiled at him, thinking, "He'll never know how worried we were about him."

While we were eating breakfast, Hilma said, "We sure don't want to ranch in country that sparsely populated, especially at our age." The Johnsons went right on back to Lodge Grass to get some sleep, but Myron had to go to work without any. I could only feel a deep thankfulness that it turned out so well because I'd been thinking they might have turned the car over or had some kind of serious wreck. Also, I had thought about those awful soap holes where anything that got in them soon sank out of sight.

Lambing season.

9
LAMBING AT LEMON SPRINGS

◆

After we left Lodge Grass, we had no use for our first cutting of hay because we'd sold our cows. However, Myron saw John Heigus, who owned the saw mill in the Wolf Mountains and they made a trade, hay for rough lumber.

Myron then sold the lumber to the Willcutt and Warren Sheep Company for the sheep panels they would need for lambing. They also needed a large shed for lambing, but it would have to be one that could be moved because they wouldn't be on their permanent range. Myron drew a plan for building solid panels that would overlap. They could be set up against tall posts that had been set deeply in the ground and in some places be wired to be more stable. The rest of the solid panels would be the roof.

The bosses were pleased with his idea, so Myron hired two carpenters, Bill Footit and Bill Crosby, who drove from Lodge Grass to Woody to build the panels. Myron and his men were over at Lemon Springs setting posts and getting ready to lamb because the time had nearly arrived.

Next, the used trailer house was delivered to Woody. It was to become our bedroom, so we put everything in it that we would need and stored our furniture. The Lemon Springs cabin was to be used as kitchen and dining room.

Sandy Ruthford was a cowboy from Texas who came to Montana with a trail herd as a young man. I didn't know him when the boss sent him to our camp on Woody Creek with several head of horses for the men to use during lambing at Lemon Springs. He put them in the corral, but I didn't see him. Neither had I seen our dog Lady for a while. Usually she was out in plain sight and I wondered about her, so I stepped out the door and was greatly surprised to see a man sitting in the shade of the coal bin petting Lady.

He quickly got to his feet and took off his hat. My first thought was what a homely man he was, but he had the nicest brown eyes and smile.

I said, "So you are Sandy. Myron said you'd be bringing the horses, but I wasn't expecting you so soon. Come in. I'm just fixing our dinner."

He smiled a warm smile and said, "Myron sent me ahead. He'll be along shortly so I'll wait here in the shade with my friend." He continued petting the dog.

That explained why Lady didn't bark when Sandy came. I soon learned that Sandy had a gift in understanding animals, and that is why he was such a good hand. He was a quiet man and got along with everyone.

Christine was still in need of a play pen, but we felt that a crib would be more practical. As we weren't able to buy just what we wanted we asked my young brother Sheridan to build a crib with a solid bottom like a play pen, with legs and castors, yet narrow enough that it could be rolled through doorways. This proved to be very practical and was used for many years.

During the day we had the baby crib in the cabin where I could watch her as I went about my work. When it was nice weather, I'd roll the crib just outside the door in the fresh air. Christine loved it, and five year old Stan could watch his ten month old sister as he played his imaginative games. She loved watching him, and if she grew tired she could go to sleep. I was able to glance out the door, keeping an eye on them as I went about my work.

Sandy's sheep were closest to the camp, so he was able to come in a little earlier than the other men. He'd been working for the Dana Cattle Company; now he was working with sheep. He had a great love for children, but in his kind of work had not spent much time around them. Now that he was around us, he was really enjoying our children. About the first thing he'd do when his sheep were on water and resting was to come to the cabin and take the baby out of her crib to a nice grassy spot under a shade tree near the cabin. He would let her play there while he watched her. He liked to tease me by saying, "Mrs., I'm going to take the baby out to the shade tree where she can sit in the grass and eat bugs and worms and stuff like that."

Stan was a great help to me. Our water came from a spring that was located a short distance from the cabin. Without refrigeration, we had a wooden chest which was set down into the cold water, and in it we kept our butter and other perishables. It was Stan's job to go after a small pail of water if I ran out before the men got in. He really didn't like this chore because of the many water snakes along the path and boardwalk over the spongy ground to the spring. There were many rattle snakes nearby, too, so we taught him to watch out for them. If he saw one, he was supposed to come and tell us.

One beautiful day I had the baby's crib sitting out in the shade of the cabin while I was getting supper ready. Stan rushed to the door and called, "Mother! Mother! There's a great big rattlesnake wrapped around the leg of Christine's bed just looking at her. Come quick or he will be in bed with her!"

I ran out the door. Stan was right—the snake was just looking at Christine, and she was staring back, fascinated. All the excitement caused the snake to crawl down and slither closer to the cabin door. As calmly as I could, I grabbed a shovel and killed the snake. I didn't bury it because it was nearly time for the men to come in to eat and they could do that.

Soon Myron came in with the crew. Stan rushed out to meet him, calling, "Dad, Mama killed a rattlesnake that was trying to get in Christine's bed."

Still shaken but quite proud of myself, I went out to show Myron where it was. He looked at it, and then at me. "Why that's only a bull snake. It wouldn't harm anyone. In fact, they're good to have around because they kill mice and are natural enemies of rattlesnakes, so you seldom see rattlers where they are."

My spirits fell. Instead of being proud of myself, I felt ashamed for having killed a friend. But I justified myself by thinking that not even a friendly snake had any business getting into my baby's bed!

MYRON AND STAN WENT TO SEE DAN

The sheep range was in the vast unsettled area west of the Big Horn River, forty five miles from Hardin. Therefore, our main entertainment was to ride with Myron as he tended the sheep camps. Since such outings broke the monotony and the scenery was beautiful, we all enjoyed it. When I was cooking for the lambing crew and had no time to go, Stan often rode with his father.

One time, one of the bands of sheep was watering in the Big Horn River. Myron wanted to give Dan, the herder, instructions about moving his sheep closer to the camp as they would be the next bunch to lamb. It was the hot part of the day, and the sheep were on water. The spot wasn't so far, but the only way to get there was by foot, down a very steep trail.

Myron knew that he could make the trip much faster alone and told Stan to wait in the pickup until he got back.

When Myron caught up with Dan at the river and gave him the instructions, Dan said, "Say, I need you to help me a minute. See that ewe over there? She has a wire wrapped around her foot and it's crippling her. It's going to take the two of us to catch her."

This delayed Myron for a while, and he hurried up the cliff where he'd left the pickup and Stan. When he got there, five-year-old Stan was gone. Myron scanned the big open country, but Stan was nowhere to be seen. Fighting panic, he looked for his tracks and found them going right down the imprint that the pickup tires had made. Myron carefully followed them back in the direction they had come, stopping now and then to be sure he was still following the small tracks over the hills. Finally a relieved Myron caught up with Stan. His dirty little face was streaked with tears and in his hand he held a wilted bouquet of wild flowers.

Myron hugged his son to him. Still sobbing, and rubbing his tears away with his grubby hand, Stan said, "Dad, I waited and waited, and when you didn't come, I thought you fell in the river and I'd better go home to tell Mama."

When his father asked him, "What were you going to do with the flowers," he looked at his father with his big eyes and tear stained face.

"Well, I knew that Mama would feel bad, and I thought the flowers would help."

SHEARING ON BEAUVAIS

After lambing, the grass around Lemon Springs was used up, so the boss decided that we should move to Beauvais Creek for shearing. I was surprised and asked, "How can we shear on Beauvais when there are no buildings and not even a cabin to cook in?"

Both the boss and Myron looked at me as if they thought I was more knowledgeable than that. Then they smiled and the boss explained. "Well, Myron said that he could move his portable sheep shed over there and set it up for a sweat shed where we can keep the sheep dry while we are shearing. We also have a large mess tent, and there is a roundup stove you can cook on. There is a work table, some cupboards, and then we have the table and benches that you used at Woody and Lemon Springs, and I guess that about does it."

Though we had the trailer for our bedroom, the main problem was where to keep Christine. She really needed something bigger than the crib to play in. To solve this, Myron backed the trailer close to the cook tent and built a fence across the double bed. Here Christine could play and look out the window and watch me work while Stan would be the go-between.

Our neighbor Bob Shibley helped us with the shearing, and we hired his wife to help me with the cooking. This I truly appreciated, because now I had twelve men to feed.

Again Sandy came in early when he could and would take the baby out in the sunshine. He wasn't always so clean about himself, but he wanted the baby to be spotless. It didn't matter how busy I was, he thought I should drop everything and put clean clothes on her. Often I was annoyed, but I truly appreciated his kindness when I was too busy to take Christine outside myself.

Dan Cooper also had been a cowboy all his life, but now was herding sheep for us. Because of all the rain we'd been having, we couldn't get his band of sheep sheared, so he was around camp quite a lot. He seemed to enjoy Stan and gave him attention. Stan had a rope, and Dan taught him how to lasso. Stan loved to play cowboy, and he had a stick horse, which he galloped all around.

When Dan was around, he encouraged Stan as he played his imaginary games. He'd say, "See that steer way out there by that bush? We don't want him to go that way, head him off." Stan would gallop out and head off the imaginary steer and "ride" back for more orders from Dan.

Lambing and shearing camp on Beauvais.

Next Stan would be a sheriff after some bad guy. Dan would say, "See that choke cherry bush? Well, that's Black Bart hiding back of it. He's real mean. Be careful because he is armed, so sneak out there carefully. Don't let him see you. He's slick and will get away if he sees you." Carefully, Stan would sneak up to the imaginary bad guy. They'd have an imaginary shoot out and, of course, Stan always won. If Stan was wounded by falling down, Dan would tell him that he was tough and tough guys didn't cry. In fact they didn't even hurt. For that matter, they didn't even bleed they were so tough.

Bob and Lill were our neighbors in this vast country. As we needed help for shearing, we were pleased to be able to hire them. One day Lill and I were busy in the cook tent. The baby was taking her morning nap and Stan was out playing cowboy. The night's rain had turned the road to mud, so we were surprised to see the boss drive up. He greeted us saying, "I'm pleased about this rain. It makes the range grass fresher for the sheep, but I'm especially pleased that we have this nice breeze because it has dried the sheep off enough that we can soon start shearing."

I smiled a big smile and said, "I sure am happy we can shear so we can get the job over with. It never seems fair that the shearers and the wrangling crew can just sit around playing cards, but the cooks have to keep on working, rain or shine."

Suddenly I heard Stan give a sharp cry. It didn't sound natural to me, so I stepped through the fly of the tent while Lill and Mr. Willcutt continued their visiting. Stan was lying near a patch of sagebrush and wasn't getting up. I knew he was hurt. With my heart in my throat I ran out to him. He held up his left arm whimpering, "It hurts Mama, it hurts."

Immediately I saw that it was broken, because it was bent back in an unnatural position. Realizing the importance of remaining calm I said, "I know it hurts, dear, but try to be brave. I'll carry you to the cook tent, and then we'll see what we can do about it."

As I carried him into the tent, I was still struggling to remain calm. Neither the boss or Lill looked up as they were so deep in conversation. I sat him on the table saying, "Stan broke his arm." Still they paid no attention. Annoyed I commanded, "Look! Stan broke his arm." Now I had their attention.

The boss jumped up saying, "By golly he sure did." Quickly he went over to a case of canned milk, and with his knife he stripped a piece of cardboard from the carton, made four slits in it and wrapped it around Stan's arm. Lill being a motherly soul comforted Stan while I hurried to the trailer for gauze and tape to fasten the cardboard splint securely.

The boss hurried to the shearing pens to get Myron. I rushed to the trailer, slipped on a clean dress, and grabbed a clean shirt for Myron. By then he was there. I carried Stan out to the car while Myron changed his shirt on the way. Even though it was still somewhat muddy, we drove the twenty miles into Hardin in record time. When we arrived at Dr. Haverfield's office, he took us right into the examining room.

He looked at Stan's arm and said, "It's broken all right. Green stick fracture." Noticing how tense we were he said, "You two better sit down and relax a few minutes."

Then Doc continued, "You know that a child's bones aren't too difficult to set, but often there is quite a lot of swelling by the time they get them to my office and I have to contend with that. However, you got Stan to my office so quickly that there is practically no swelling. Say, whoever made that splint really knew what he was doing."

After we chatted with Doc a while he said, "Stan is still under the ether. You can take him now, but don't leave town just yet. Take him down to your parents' and put him to bed. He'll sleep quite a while. When he wakes up, if he isn't in any pain, you can take him out to camp."

Myron picked up the sleeping child and carried him out of the office down a long flight of stairs to our pickup. He handed him to me and then leaned against the pickup, slid down to sit on the running board, and put his head down. "Man, oh man!" he said. "The smell of the ether that Doc gave Stan really made me sick. I was afraid for a while I wouldn't be able to make it to the pickup without fainting."

We took Stan to my parents' home, and knowing he'd sleep for a while, left him with them while we hurried up town to order groceries. Then we hurried back to Stan thinking he might be suffering from nausea or pain. When we arrived, we found Stan at the table, calmly cutting pictures out of a catalog. He was using the fingers sticking out of the cast to hold the paper. He had the scissors in his right hand and was doing a good job with a little assistance from his granddad. Grandma said he hadn't suffered any nausea. When he woke up, he had only asked where we had gone.

Soon we were on our way back to camp. Now my only concern was for baby Christine. Had she caused Lill trouble? How had Lill been able to manage alone when the work had been keeping us both busy? Now she had all the work and the baby to take care of.

When we arrived, the supper dishes had just been finished. Of course they all were concerned about Stan. My first question was, "How was the baby?"

Lill was holding the baby and gave her an extra pat, "Oh, she's been just fine. She is such a doll. I had no problems and the men were wonderful. Even though they were tired when they came in from work they pitched right in getting the meals on the table and they even did all the dishes."

I was thankful everything had gone so well, but I was just a bit hurt that they didn't even need me. Soon the men came one by one to the cook tent to see how Stan was. I was so touched; Lill was right. The men truly were wonderful, and they gave me the feeling that they'd really missed us. One man said, "It's just not the same when you're not here." That cheered me and made me feel needed again.

That had been a long, drawn out shearing. The shearers had been with us a week longer than usual because of the rain. Everyone was tired and glad to be through with the job.

RENO CREEK

Myron and his men took down our camp on Beauvais and we all went into Hardin. On our way into town I said to Myron, "I'm so tired and thankful to be getting away from all that cooking. It's so pleasing to know that I won't have to do a lot of cooking for another year, and soon we'll be on our way up that beautiful mountain."

At my parents' home that evening we all had our baths. After the children were asleep, I slid down into the comfortable bed and thought, "These cool clean sheets feel heavenly, and I won't have to get up at five o'clock to cook breakfast for the crew." I dropped off into an exhausted sleep.

I didn't hear Myron when he came to bed. Neither did I hear him when he got up. I didn't hear my mother when she cooked breakfast, when the children woke up, or when Mother came into our room to get them so they could eat. Later she came in again to get the children's clothes out of our suitcase, but I wasn't aware of it and slept on.

Finally through my fog, I began to hear men's voices, Myron's and my dad's. Then Myron came into our room and said, "In case you don't know, it's twelve o'clock and your mother has dinner ready."

That shocked me. I jumped out of bed, put my clothes on as fast as a fireman and hurried out, terribly embarrassed. I had no intention of sleeping THAT late.

At the dinner table Myron said, "I've got some bad news for you." I looked at him, wondering what it could be. "I saw the boss this morning and he tells me that our plans have been changed. Instead of our being on the way to that nice cool mountain as planned, we are going to have to go to Reno Creek to receive a band of sheep that he bought from a sheep man in Forsyth." Myron sighed, "The worst thing about that is they aren't even sheared. I guess he got a real good buy, but now we are going to have to gather up a crew. Thank heavens I ran into Lonny Layton the shearing boss this morning. He said he'd gather up his shearing crew and they'll shear for us."

I sighed because I was extremely disappointed. "Can you gather up a wrangling crew?"

Shaking his head he said, "I hope so. Any men that I can gather up won't be experienced. All the men who worked for us on Beauvais shearing have promised other outfits or have gone home to do their own work. This morning I drove out to Woody to get the equipment we'd stored there and ordered the groceries, the wool sacks and the branding paint. Art Biles is going to help haul supplies and the men out on his pickup. So far, the only wranglers I could get were Sandy Ruthford and Bronc Savage. They have the know-how, but at their age they can't be running after sheep and doing the leg work. I did talk with four young men who were hanging around the depot yard. I guess you'd call them hobos. They're from Detroit, Michigan—came in on a freight train with few possessions looking for work. They have never worked with livestock, but it was the best I could do, so I hired them and said we would board them, and if they would do as they were told they would receive good pay. They are eager to try it. Art Biles will haul a load out on his pickup and hopefully he'll stay."

Quickly I got our two suitcases packed and ready to go; we hooked onto our trailer and met Art Biles on the highway where he and the men were waiting for us. The young hobos climbed up on our load, as we weren't loaded quite as heavily as Art was.

As much as we hated to take on this extra work, we now thought of it as a new experience. I said, "You know I've never been out to Cort's shearing pens on Reno Creek."

Stan spoke up, "You know, I've never been out there either."

We both chuckled and Myron said, "If Willcutt doesn't get some permanent grass soon, we'll have lived on every creek on the Reservation."

When we arrived at the Cort shearing camp, they had a large cook tent ready. I was glad to see that they had a good cook stove, a cupboard, table and benches. Now it was up to me to get the dishes and groceries unpacked and get started on supper. I was thankful for our trailer because it gave us the familiar bedroom with everything just as we left it.

As Myron was unloading the pickup, he realized that the hobos had no beds. He asked, "Why didn't you guys tell me that you didn't have beds?"

They just chuckled, "Ah, we don't need any beds. This is summer time, and we can stretch out on the grass and sleep any place."

Myron started to walk away, smiling to himself because he was sure they didn't know how cold Montana nights could be even in June. Then he turned back to them and said, "Should you get cold in the night you are welcome to use the new wool sacks. However, I only brought enough to pack the shorn wool; when they're full you'll have to sleep in your jackets."

It was four o'clock when we arrived at Reno, a beautiful sunny afternoon. At six o'clock, supper was ready. As the men came in to eat, the sky clouded over, and there were some rain drops. By the time supper was over, the rain had become a cloudburst. The men got up from the table and rushed to their sleeping quarters. Sandy, Bronc and Art sat at the table drinking coffee and chuckling about the hobos using all the wool sacks for their beds tonight.

Suddenly the dogs were barking, announcing the arrival of strangers. Myron looked out but reported that he didn't see any car lights. Soon we were surprised to see a man, his wife and little boy. In the mother's arms was a baby about four months old. They were all sopping wet. They explained that they had been on their way to town with three sacks of wool they had just sheared off their sheep. They were in their old truck which didn't have a top when this cloudburst hit. Now they were stuck so had walked to the closest place which was this camp. They desperately needed help.

Quickly Myron rekindled the fire in the cook stove. I began reheating supper for them, as they gathered around the stove drying themselves as best they could. We visited while they ate and dried out. We were surprised when we noticed it was nine o'clock. Everyone was tired, and I was wondering how we could offer them beds. Our trailer was small, and I hadn't brought any extra bedding. I was greatly relieved when Myron spoke up. "If you ladies and children work out sleeping arrangements in the trailer, the Mr. and I can stay in the cook tent and keep the fire going. That way we'll all be warm and dry."

We hurried to the trailer. I felt that I had to give my guest the best that I had, so I suggested that she and her children sleep in our bed. Christine's bassinet was large enough for her to sleep in it, and Stan had a little bunk for his bed. I would sleep with him even though I wouldn't rest well because of my concern about bumping his broken arm. Besides, his bed wasn't long enough for an adult, but I was thankful that at least I could lie down and needn't spend the night sitting up, keeping a fire going, as Myron and the Mr. would have to.

The next morning was beautiful and sunny. After breakfast Myron and his men went down to where the truck was stuck, pulled it out and put the family on their way to town.

We were having a nice breeze that morning. About noon, when the sheep were dry enough to shear, Myron found the hobos he'd hired were very poor help, but they gave everyone many a laugh. They had never seen a lamb suck. A big lamb running to his mother to get the teat would butt her so hard he'd raise her hind quarters right off the ground. To these hobos this was so funny they would double up, laughing hysterically, and roll on the ground until they were exhausted.

One of the hobos really broke the tension the next night. Our boss always made it plain that the cooks were not to buy canned fruit. He felt they were very lazy if they didn't take the time to cook dried fruit. Knowing how he felt about it, I never did buy any canned until we had to take on this extra shearing job. I was so weary that Myron decided to buy some gallon cans of fruit—which I was plenty happy about. Besides, the boss only dropped in occasionally and wouldn't be staying for a meal.

That afternoon I baked a chocolate cake for supper dessert and decided that pears would go nicely with it, so I opened a gallon can and put it in a very large serving bowl. When the men came in for supper, I was greatly surprised to see the boss with them. He sat at the table beside one of the hobos. I was a bit uncomfortable about serving the canned fruit, but it would be too obvious if I took it off the table.

Soon it was time for dessert. The cake and the pears were passed around and because the regular men knew how the boss felt they glanced at each other and at me, wondering if the boss would say anything about the pears. When the fruit was passed to the hobo, he helped himself and passed it to the boss. The boss said, "No thanks, I wouldn't care for any."

The hobo refused to pass it on, insisting in a loud voice, "Oh, have some! They're really good. Why, we eat them all the time, and it hasn't hurt any of us yet."

This broke the tension and we all had to laugh. I was greatly relieved to see the boss had also seen the humor and laughed with us as he helped himself to the pears.

Soon the shearing was finally over, and all of us could get away from the dust, smell and noise of the shearing pens.

Above, lambing and shearing over. Top right, sheep on their way to the mountains. Bottom right, herder puppies had to be put in the wagon so they couldn't follow their mother when she went to help herd the sheep.

10

SUMMER ON THE MOUNTAIN

◆

At last we were on our way up the Big Horn Mountain, pulling our trailer. The two bands of sheep that were sheared on Beauvais were already up there, and Myron's first job when we arrived would be to get the sheep into Black Canyon to their summer range. The sheep sheared on Reno Creek were to be pastured at the foot of the mountain, on Rotten Grass Creek. Our camp would be located on Rotten Grass Trail which led to Black Canyon.

Pulling the house trailer behind the loaded pickup over the steep mountainous road was slow but relaxing. Every now and then Myron would stop to let the motor cool off, and we would get out to look at the rocks and mountain plants. Myron had often told me of the untouched beauty of the mountains in the spring. I could see what he meant when I viewed the masses of wild flowers that blanketed the terrain. The sight of snow drifts with buttercups blooming at the edge thrilled me. I smiled at the Creator's handiwork, a true reward for all the grief and hard work we had endured. Stan and I were enraptured with the trickles of water coming from the snow drifts, realizing that they were the beginnings of great rivers like the creeks running into the Big Horn River, which runs into the Yellowstone, which empties into the Missouri, which flows into the Mississippi.

When we stopped at the timber line, I was impressed with the way the wind had twisted the trees. I stood there in the mountain wind with my sweater wrapped tightly around me while I gazed at the magnificent view. My eyes feasted on the splash of wild flowers against the backdrop of the evergreen trees. I thanked God for giving me the privilege of being a part of this land for the summer.

While we were stopped, we decided to have a lunch. We went in the trailer and fixed sandwiches. Just after we finished eating, some friends from Hardin caught up with us. I offered to fix them a lunch, but they said they had theirs with them. They thought the mountain was beautiful but lonely. I knew it would be, but I would enjoy some isolation for the summer. We chatted until they had to go on, and we did too, because we still had a way to go before we set up camp.

At the Rotten Grass Trail that leads into the Black Canyon there is a very nice spring. This is where Myron decided to set our camp. Even though there is quite a steep slope, I appreciated having the icy cold water so handy; it would also be our refrigerator. As soon as the trailer was set, I felt that we were home and I began unpacking, getting things shaped up so I could build a fire and start supper. Myron was busy unloading the pickup.

The next day, Myron started the herders and their bands of sheep into the canyon. He had Dan Cooper take his sheep in first because Dan knew the trail so well. He had spent many summers there riding after cattle. He loved it— to him it was home.

The boss had sent George Buster with the bay team and Myron's saddle horse, Sunday. We were glad to see them because they were good pack horses, and Myron had to pack the herders' camp outfits down in the canyon. The sheep would be needing plenty of salt. Everything needed in the canyon had to be packed on these horses, including the stoves the herders would need in their camp. The canyon walls were much too steep to enter with anything but pack horses, so their wagons would sit at our camp until fall.

Soon we began hearing that bears had been tearing up their camps. Dan said, "It was my fault. I neglected to hang my food cache up in the tree as I should have. It serves me right." If a bear would kill a sheep, he would say, "They only kill what they eat, not like a coyote that kills so many just for fun."

The man herding the other band would get terribly upset when anything attacked his sheep, and finally he quit. It was understandable to have natural fear of bear, but it made it difficult for Myron. Each time a man quit, Myron would have to make the long drive into Billings, bring a new herder up on the mountain, and take him down into the canyon. Then he would take the man who quit into Hardin and put him on the bus, so he could go back to Billings. This happened three times in the three months we were up there. All of this took more time than Myron had to spare.

Each week we would drive the pickup down the mountain for supplies and tend Mike Lamey's camp at the foot of the mountain. This was during the dry years of the thirties. Myron had set Mike's wagon in the shade of the trees on Rotten Grass Creek where the sheep watered. There Mike would cook his meals and because the sheep were on water and resting during the hottest part of the day, it was a comfortable place for Mike to stay out of the sun. Late in the afternoon the sheep would graze toward a high hill where Mike had a range tepee. There Mike had his bed and would spend the night, and the sheep would bed down on this high hill around the tepee.

One day, when we came down from the mountain to see how Mike was getting along and to pick up his grocery list, we found him very upset. Mormon crickets had all but eaten up his tepee. Myron had to make a thirty five mile trip to see if he could borrow an extra sheep wagon from Tschirgi's. They loaned him one, so he had to slowly tow the iron wheel wagon, pick up the groceries and salt at Lodge Grass, and tow the wagon back to Mike so his bed would be off the ground away from the crickets.

As much as I enjoyed seeing people on our trips to town, I rather dreaded these hot dusty trips which always took two days out of the week. It was hard on baby Christine because she didn't like the heat. Neither did she like being held. It was hot with the four of us in the pickup cab, but Stan was a good traveler and accepted everything as it came. He took along his rubber Disney characters and played with them as we drove along.

Now that Christine was a year old, she was walking and did very well on even surfaces, but our trailer was on a slope so when she was out of doors, which she loved so much, she was either walking up hill or down hill and consequently had many falls. This never discouraged her, and she begged to go out to be with the puppies.

Stan really had a fascination with books now, especially comic books, and he loved playing his imaginative games. Although Christine was a bit too young to join in, this was the summer that they became aware of each other as individuals. Stan no longer thought of her as a nuisance. He found that she adored him and wanted to play with him as best she could.

We seldom had company even though there were other sheep men and their families. Esps and Berlands spent much of their summer on the mountain, but they were as busy as Myron which left little time for visiting.

The Indian game warden, Francis LaForge, who lived at Aspen Grove not far from our camp, stopped every now and then. Though we didn't see much of our neighbors, it was good to know that they were there and we could go to them should we have a need.

One day Myron took the children and me for a ride, as I longed to see more of the mountain. Myron knew of a mountain cave and thought it would be fun to look inside it. As we hadn't planned to do this, we hadn't brought a flashlight or lantern with us. All we had was Myron's pocket full of wooden matches, and he needed both hands to light them. I carried Christine on one arm and was leading Stan with the other hand. The cave was so dark that Christine laid her head on my shoulder, and Stan clung to my hand a little tighter.

After we'd gone a good distance I got to thinking of drop-offs in the cave. Myron remarked, "This cave sure has a strong bear smell." We both thought of how helpless we'd be if anything happened, so we left quickly, vowing that we'd get lanterns and come back again. However, with our busy schedule, we never found the time.

Every week Myron had to make two trips into the canyon. He took supplies to the herders, making one trip the day after we'd driven down the mountain to get groceries. The next trip was mainly to haul sheep salt, and many times he stopped to fish. Along toward evening, when he started out of the canyon,

Christine at the cabin on the Forks of Grapevine, age 2.

he would turn the packhorses loose and they'd hurry up the trail to our camp. I could always hear them coming up the rocky trail, so I'd hurry out and open the corral gate and have their oats ready for them. Then I'd go into the trailer to start supper, knowing Myron on his saddle horse would be along soon.

Every time I watched him and his pack horses disappear into the canyon, I'd have a lonely feeling, and I often wondered what I would do if one day something happened and he couldn't return home. I knew I wouldn't be able to go down in the canyon because I couldn't take our young children. Neither could I leave them by themselves. I'd console myself by thinking that at least our pickup was there. I could go for help, but there was that treacherous hill that I wasn't sure I could drive over. If the brakes should fail, that canyon was a long ways down.

One evening Myron was much later coming home than usual. I was becoming more and more concerned when I heard the pack horses scrambling up the trail. It was as though the devil himself was after them. I hurried out, but they were so scared that they ran right past the camp. I was shocked to see Myron's riderless horse with them.

What had happened? I couldn't let myself think he was hurt; I kept trying to convince myself that somehow the horses had gotten away from him, and he'd be walking home shortly. But could he? What in the world could have scared those tired, gentle horses so badly, and what should I do? Should I start down the canyon trail? I couldn't leave the children. Should I try to drive us all someplace to get help?

Soon it was dark, and then it was too late to do anything but wait and pray. I was glad the children could sleep, for I surely could not. I was imagining everything. I tried to read, but I couldn't even do that.

At nine thirty I heard someone on the rocky trail. I hurried to the door. It was Myron! "I started out of the canyon after a long hard day," he explained. "I hadn't thought of turning the packhorses loose, so they were still tied to my saddle horse. When we trailed past a familiar patch of timber I paid little attention. We'd gotten almost past it when the pack horses suddenly spied a mother bear and her cub. The packhorses were badly scared; they reared and thrashed around, getting my saddle horse badly off balance. He fell and got tangled up, and then they all rolled down a steep hill. I'd been thrown clear, but the horses fled up the mountain trail. The commotion scared the mother bear who scampered off with her cub right behind her. I was left alone, somewhat skinned up, but at least able to walk the long, dark trail home."

11
STAN STARTS SCHOOL

◆

I had thoroughly enjoyed our summer on the mountain, but it was nearly over, and I realized how much I had been dreading the fall. Six year old Stan would have to leave home to start school, and I wasn't at all ready to have our little family split up.

Every time I thought of it, my heart would nearly break. Then I'd argue with myself: "Maybe we should keep Stan out another year...but he is such an intelligent child, it wouldn't be fair to him...he needs other children for playmates, something he has never had because we live so far out in the country. Then, too, he loves his aunt and uncle very much, and they would be good to him. His aunt is a school teacher in Lodge Grass and she thinks he definitely is ready for school. I want what is best for him."

The day we brought Stan down off the mountain was a beautiful sunny day. I tried to be happy for him because he was so very precious to us. At his aunt's home, we took his suitcase in and didn't tarry as we said our good-byes. Quickly we got back in the pickup which Myron already had started. He put it in gear and just as we started off I looked back. Stan and his aunt were on the porch, waving good-bye. My tears were coming so fast I turned my head to the window and fought them. What I really wanted was to cry long and hard, but that would scare the baby so I just held her close, thankful that I still had her.

All the way up the mountain, little things reminded me of Stan and there would be more unshed tears—and many that overflowed. The sun had been shining all the way up the mountain, at the top the weather changed. Our camp was engulfed in fog, which made it about the gloomiest place that I had ever been in.

We ate a light lunch and Myron said, "It's early enough that I can pack some sheep salt into the canyon." I wanted to protest but what would I say? Myron was lonely, too, and he was doing the only sensible thing, because he knew work was always good when one hurts. It's surprising how many ailments work cures.

As soon as Myron was on his way down the canyon, I put the baby down for her nap, washed the dishes, and sat down for a real good cry. I felt better and told myself this was something I was going to have to live with all of my life. Stan was God's child and it was up to God to mold him into the kind of person most useful to Him.

I sat there and thought, "I can cry my head off, but it will not change a thing." Then I took out a piece of material and started to make the baby a new dress.

12
MOVING OFF THE MOUNTAIN

◆

Now it was October, and already we'd had a foot of snow on the mountain, but it had melted off. Other sheep people had moved down to their lower range, but our boss still hadn't gotten the grass lease he wanted on the west side of the Big Horn River. He was sure that he would get it, so we would just have to be patient a while longer.

Finally the boss came to tell us he'd gotten the lease. The new range was big open country, and the cabin we would be living in was at the forks of Grapevine. I was pleased because it was a nice cabin with two rooms, forty miles from Hardin.

First we would have to bring the sheep out of Black Canyon and get them started down the mountain. The sheep would graze slowly down the mountain, but now the herders would have their wagons to live in—a welcome change for men who had spent the summer in tents.

After we got the sheep and their herders out of the canyon and started down, we had to pull the trailer from where it had been parked up the steep hill. It had been so easy to pull it down when we arrived, and the boss had been sarcastic about Myron setting it there. He said, "You'll probably have to burn the damn thing because you'll never be able pull it out of there."

Myron was determined he'd pull it out somehow. He hitched the trailer behind the pickup, hitched the dependable little bay team in front of the pickup, and said, "Ellie, you drive the pickup while I drive the team. I've put the chains on but there is one place where we are going to have to give it all we've got or we'll not make it."

Carefully and cautiously we moved forward. Myron called, "Now give it all it's got!" That is exactly what that fine team did. I gassed the pickup as I was supposed to, and out it came. Soon we were on top of the mountain and Myron tied the team to the side of the pickup and took over the driving. I was relieved because I didn't want to be responsible for towing that heavy trailer over the narrow, twisting road down the mountain.

Everything seemed to be proceeding as well as we had hoped, but there the team seemed spooked by the trailer. They kept looking back at it.

Suddenly the rope broke, and they were free. They stayed a considerable distance from us. I wanted to stop and see if we could catch them, but Myron said, "We'll just keep an eye on them and as long as they are going the same direction and down the mountain, I'm happy."

Soon it began spitting rain. The clouds were so low that it was hard to see the horses but I kept straining my eyes. Out of the haze, a cowboy in a yellow slicker appeared and rode right up to us. It was George Buster, who had worked for the Dana Cattle Company and whom we knew quite well.

He greeted us with a wave and a smile. "The boss told me to come up here to see if you needed any help."

"Well, George, I'm real glad to see you." Myron greeted him with a relieved expression. "That little bay team are a couple of dandy horses. They sure helped us out of a bad spot on Rotten Grass Trail as we were climbing out. Right now they don't want a darn thing to do with us, especially the trailer. I'd sure appreciate it if you'd take them to the ranch on War Man and later we can swim them over to the Grapevine Ranch."

Relieved that George had come after the horses, we now began to enjoy our trip down the mountain. There was some rain, but every now and then the clouds would part and the sun would peek through. It was breathtakingly beautiful, and we were the only humans for miles, which made us feel very so close to our Maker.

We were pleased as we neared St. Xavier to be closer to people and, more importantly, on gravel road. The sun was out, the clouds held no rain, and everything was going well. Baby Christine was asleep in my arms. We felt we had left the worst behind us, and soon we'd be getting to Hardin.

We were rolling right along, about fifteen miles from St. Xavier, when suddenly the pickup began rocking. It seemed as if a giant's hand picked us up and turned us around like a toy. The trailer turned over because it had blown a tire and was on its side in the ditch. Both of us were badly shaken and the sleeping baby was now wide awake, screaming. Myron's first concern was whether we were hurt.

When he was sure we were okay, he climbed out to look at the mess. He reported back that the trailer was packed so well that it had not suffered much damage or disarray. No one came along, so Myron worked until he got the trailer unhitched. Then I suggested that we drive into St. Xavier and call the garage in Hardin to bring out the wrecker.

Myron kept studying the situation and finally he said, "You know, I believe that if I hook the two tow chains on each end of the frame and put the pickup on the road crosswise, by shifting into low gear I can get that trailer up on its wheels again."

Myron did just that, and then cleaned the trailer a little. I fixed lunch and we drove into St. Xavier and called the Hardin garage, asking them to bring out a tire and wheel. This accomplished, Myron pulled the trailer to Lodge Grass where Christine and I could spend the next few days with Stan, because Myron would be busy shipping the lambs at the Rawly Stockyards and getting the sheep camps set on the west side of the Big Horn River.

Soon Stan was back in school, and we had to move to the Forks of Grapevine camp. I was looking forward to living in the pleasant two room cabin. When we got back to Hardin, we loaded up with groceries and other supplies and drove up the gravel road, turning off onto the Two Leggin Creek road which would take us to Grapevine.

Myron looked at the threatening sky. "It's going to rain for sure. Man, this is something we truly don't need."

As we slowly drove up the road I kept hoping the clouds would blow over, but I consoled myself. We had all of our possessions with us, including our bed, dresser and the few belongings we'd left at Woody which we picked up on our way. Now the pickup and trailer were packed full.

13
MOVING TO THE FORKS

◆

The threatening clouds didn't blow over as I had hoped and it had begun to sprinkle while we were at Woody Creek. By the time we hit the Beauvais Bridge, it was raining pretty hard; yet we were able to move along in low gear, stopping every so often to let the motor cool. When noon came we let the motor cool again and I climbed in the trailer—over all of the stuff—and fixed a cold lunch. We'd decided that we didn't want a fire in our wood stove because we'd have to take out the ashes and allow the stove to cool before we could move on. We didn't need anything like a fire; we had more than enough other troubles!

All afternoon we went in low gear, stopping every so often to cool the motor. About six o'clock we stopped again and had another cold lunch. Our active sixteen-month-old baby appreciated these rest periods as much as we did, although she was always good about going along with whatever was necessary.

As we started off again, Myron remarked, "With all of this mud it will be at least nine o'clock when we get to our cabin at the Forks."

I tried to be cheerful. "Well, at least it will be wonderful when we can stop moving. One thing about it, if you get too tired we could spend the night in the trailer."

"Ellie, you know how packed that trailer is. I don't know where we could sleep."

Again I tried to say something cheerful about all of this. "Well, I'm glad it wasn't raining too hard at the Woody camp when we loaded the furniture. Christine can have her crib again, and we can have our comfortable bed."

We stopped just before dusk, and Myron put gas in the pickup again. "Damn," he said, "its taking an awful lot of gas to pull the trailer through this mud in low gear. I'm sure thankful we have this barrel of gas with us."

Finally the pickup lights shone through the darkness and rain on the gloomy cabin that was to be our home. I was thankful that we'd finally arrived safely and that we wouldn't be as crowded as we had been in the trailer. Myron lit the lantern and started into the forlorn cabin. I followed carrying Christine. He held up the lantern as we walked toward the sagging door.

Disgruntled he said, "Oh! Man, oh man! Sure! Just what we need is a door with only one hinge." Upon examining it he said, "I guess it won't be too hard to fix; the screws are gone but the hinges are here."

The cabin was cold and very dirty. Mice had been having free reign of the place for a long time. Both of us were tired, but we tried to make the best of it. We decided to unload Christine's crib first, so she could sleep while I cleaned.

Myron brought in the crib, and I took off Christine's coat and pulled off her shoes and socks. She slid happily under the covers and went sound asleep.

I grabbed the broom and started sweeping as Myron built a fire in both the kitchen stove and the one in the bedroom. Now we had both lamps lit and the lantern, so I could see to sweep better. As each place was swept, Myron would set some furniture there. He set up our bed, and I helped him carry in the springs and mattress. Then he carried in the tall dresser and put the drawers back in. Groceries were so well boxed, he set most of them on the floor.

When we had some order established, we washed up and fell into bed. I was happy to be able to stretch out in my nice, comfortable bed. I was particularly thankful for the two cases of bread I wouldn't have to bake until I had the cabin thoroughly cleaned.

Sometime later I was aroused from my sleep. Something was rattling the bread wrappers. I tried to rouse Myron. "Wake up, there's mice in the bread."

He answered drowsily, "Oh, Ellie. Go to sleep. They won't eat any more than they want." He went right back to sleep, but I lay there thinking about it. At least one box of bread was way up on the tall dresser. They probably wouldn't bother it.

When morning came, I cleaned the kitchen well enough to start breakfast. Then I went to get bread for toast. Every loaf was completely gone except for one slice in the very bottom of each wax paper wrapper. The empty bags were still standing. I wondered how they could get the bread out without wrecking the bread wrappers. Now all there was to do was to stir up hot cakes.

Myron had been outside trying to get things organized. He had to get supplies out to the sheep camps and the pickup needed servicing. When he came in for breakfast, I said, "Come here and see what those darn mice did to our bread last night."

When he looked, he had the most surprised expression on his face. He said, "That wasn't mice. That could only have been pack rats." He stood there, sort of scratching his head. "I guess I'd better go down to the Grapevine Ranch to see if they have a trap I can borrow. Also, I'll see if I can locate a pane of glass. I think Dan had some in his wagon that will be the right size. I'm sure that broken window is where they got in."

After breakfast, Myron carried several buckets of water to fill the reservoir, then chopped enough wood to last until he got back. I heated plenty of water, got my cleaning supplies, especially my scrub brush, and began scrubbing the bedroom so Christine could have free run of that room; there was a lot to be done in the kitchen, and I didn't want her out there.

I had already mixed up bread dough and wanted to get as much cleaning done as possible before I had to give it more attention. Finally, when I had the walls and floor clean and everything as free from dirt as I could get it, I started putting the canned food in the cupboard.

Suddenly I glanced toward the window. There sat the pack rat on the window ledge, his beady little eyes looking all around as if he were wondering what I was doing in his house.

I made a noise, hoping it would scare him and he'd leave, but instead he jumped up on some shelves near the window. I grabbed the broom to hit at him, but he ran up on top of the door casing, then jumped down on the floor and scampered around the wall behind the stove and back of the cupboard. A cold chill went down my back as I wondered what to do. Then I realized that I had not pushed the cumbersome home made cupboard as tightly against the wall as I should have, or he could not have gotten back of it. I grabbed the cupboard and gave it a quick hard shove.

Oh! Aach...I crushed the rat.

I leaned against the wall, waves of nausea coming over me. I felt ill, but I couldn't just leave the rat back there so I pulled and tugged until I got the cupboard away from the wall again. With the aid of my broom and dust pan I removed the crushed rat from my kitchen. I was glad it was dead, but now I'd have a time scrubbing up that awful bloody mess back of the cupboard.

When Myron came home he said, "I didn't get over to the Grapevine Ranch to get the trap, so I'll set a coyote trap."

Very pleased with myself I said, "Oh, that's all right. We won't need it now. I killed the rat."

Surprised, he looked at me. "You did? How?"

Sure that our troubles were over, I proudly told my story. Myron leaned back in his chair and said, "Well, I'll be darned. But they always live in pairs. Its mate is around here somewhere. I'll go right out and put a coyote trap under the window where they've been going in and out. We'll see what that does."

Sure enough, the next morning the mate was in the trap. Myron fixed the window and repaired the door, and we had no more trouble with rats.

14
SNAKE BITE

◆

    Our little cabin home was located against a rocky rim with large boulders all around it. Pine trees grew among the rocks and the lively creek flowed by the cabin. We loved the place, but every now and then someone would mention seeing a rattlesnake. Myron saw two when he was digging the cellar, and just after that I saw one on my way to the root cellar. Of course, our concern was for our children. Christine was still too young to know fear and was fascinated by everything she saw, but we did our best to keep a sharp eye on her.

    Stan was home for a break from school but wasn't up when Myron left to tend his sheep camps. Before he left, he reminded me that he would be gone all day and cautioned me to keep a careful watch on the children. I promised I would, knowing that if anything happened, we'd be alone until evening without a car. We lived forty miles from town and had no telephone.

    About two o'clock, I was surprised to hear Myron returning in his pickup. He hobbled into the cabin. "I've been bitten by a rattlesnake. Get the kids so we can get into town before I get too bad."

    With distances so great, I generally served as doctor to our family and crew. Fear ran strong. "Let me see; maybe I should give you first aid." Painfully, he pulled up the leg of his Levis. "It is so badly swollen you might have to cut off my boot." He pointed to the leather top, "See, that's where he struck me." Sure enough, there was the mark of the fangs.

    Carefully I pulled off his boot and sock saying, "It sure doesn't look swollen to me and there isn't a mark where he hit you."

    He carefully studied his leg, surprise registering on his face. There were no punctures. Again we examined the boot. The fangs had not gone through the leather.

    Relieved, we both sat there and laughed. Rather sheepishly he said, "I wouldn't have believed that my imagination could play that bad a trick on me." Then sighing he said, "Well, if I'm going to get Dan's camp moved, I'd better get back there and finish my job."

A BAD COUGH

Before Thanksgiving, we drove to Lodge Grass to see how Stan was. He was getting along well in school with good grades and was enjoying his friends, but he looked pale. His aunt told us that he had a bad cough. She said she'd been doctoring him, doing everything she knew to do, but the cough persisted.

We decided to take him home with us, as it was almost Thanksgiving vacation. I felt if I kept him indoors he would get well faster and could return to school the next week. As we drove toward Hardin, Stan's cough was so bad that Myron said, "When we get to town, we'll just take him right up to Dr. Haverfield's office and have him looked over."

The doctor examined him and said, "I believe Stan just has a bad cold. If there was whooping cough around, I'd say that is what he has, but I haven't heard of a case. I'll prescribe some good cough medicine. Keep him in and keep him warm."

I did just what the doctor told me to do, but soon we knew it was whooping cough. Stan couldn't keep food down. The medicine was a help, but anytime he got the least bit active, he would cough and cough until he was blue in the face.

There was no way to keep eighteen-month-old Christine away from Stan because she had missed him and was thrilled to have him home. In a short time she had whooping cough and couldn't keep food down either. I racked my brain trying to think of a food they could keep in their stomachs. Finally Myron said, "Let's try an eggnog." I gave him a questioning look wondering why he thought of that. He grinned. "Well, I've watched cowboys coming out of town after too much celebrating. They'd beat a raw egg in their milk because it was the only food they could keep down."

It worked. They kept their eggnogs down and started gaining strength to fight the illness. Every dose of medicine lasted about two hours before one of the children would start to cough, waking the other one. I kept the medicine bottle near and dosed each of them with their spoonful of medicine around the clock.

Lack of sleep was taking its toll; I was weary, but I still had to cook for Bill Mills who was herding the bucks and George Buster who was helping Myron.

One day, when I was preparing dinner, two men rode in bringing a freshly killed deer. They told me that they were riding the grub line. They were nice young men, but I didn't feel like company. They went out to the bunkhouse, and I hurried around, though I wasn't feeling up to par. When it was nearly time for the five men to come in to eat, I became dizzy and sick to my stomach, and I vomited, so I had to go to bed. I realized I might be coming down with whooping cough, but really suspected exhaustion.

When Myron came in he was very concerned but I said, "I'll be okay. I just need some rest." He put the dinner on the table and the men came in to eat. I lay there thinking, "I'm glad that I had the whole dinner ready, even the pies." I soon fell into a deep sleep and didn't hear a thing, not even the children coughing or Myron taking care of them.

The first noise that woke me came from Myron fixing supper for the men. I felt like a slacker and offered to get up, but Myron said, "No, don't get up. I want you to stay in bed and sleep through the night. Don't worry about the kids. I'll take care of them. Tonight I'll get up and give them their medicine."

He did a fine job. At eight o'clock he got the children ready for bed and gave them their prescribed spoonful of medicine. But at ten o'clock, when they woke up coughing, Myron was sleeping so soundly he didn't hear them. I got up and measured out their precious medicine. I felt okay by then. The extra sleep and rest I'd had was enough. I was glad that come morning I could go about my regular work. There was bread to bake. I was sure the herders were out, as it was time for Myron to tend their camps. They did so appreciate light bread as it was difficult for them to make it in their wagons because of the yeast freezing and their having to be gone all day.

Before we knew it, the first of December had arrived. Christmas didn't look too promising, because ever since Thanksgiving, snow had been piling up. The huge sheep shed Myron built when he first got to the Forks was used to store sheep cake, salt and coal. He'd even put the pickup in the shed, because the snow was too deep to drive to the sheep camps, and he was using horses to get around.

It seemed harder to keep the children quiet. It wasn't so bad with Christine because she still took two naps a day and liked to play with her dolls, but with Stan it was different. He missed school, his friends, and playing out of doors which, of course, he couldn't do. He loved to play Superman, or pretend to be the sheriff going after bad guys—anything with action. But when he raced around he'd go into a fit of coughing so hard he'd get blue in the face. I taxed my brain trying to think of things that weren't active but would amuse him, like drawing, coloring and reading.

Santa Claus was reading letters over our battery-powered radio and Stan loved to listen to them. One afternoon he decided to write a letter to Santa to be mailed the first chance we got. I was all for it, because it would keep him quiet for a while. He got out the catalog and chose toys for himself and Christine. Each evening Stan remembered to turn on the radio to listen to Santa read letters he'd received. Santa always signed off with the reminder that there were only so many more shopping days until Christmas.

Each day we eyed the little bottle of cough medicine which had been prescribed for only one child. It kept going down until it was dangerously low, and both of them still needed it every two hours. Also, we were getting short of groceries; often I had to substitute in my cooking, and the herders complained because they were out of their favorite foods.

One day Myron came in very depressed over the snow. "You know, Ellie, it doesn't seem to be getting any better. Everyone is low on groceries and the kids are nearly out of cough medicine." He sighed as he looked out of the window, watching the wind blow the snow. "The only thing I can say about this eternal wind is that it's moving the snow off the hills—and, of course, it's piling up in the coulees. Right now I'm going out and dig a tunnel to the shed to get the pickup out. Tomorrow I'll go into town if I have to shovel all the way."

15

A TRIP AFTER COUGH MEDICINE

◆

Early the next morning, right after breakfast, Myron bundled into his sheep skin coat, tied his black silk scarf around his neck, put on his hat and buckled his overshoes. I handed him the mail, letters the herders had written, those I'd written to family members, Stan's precious letter to Santa, and of course the very important catalog order.

Myron said good-bye at the door. The elderly Bill Mills walked out with him. They talked a bit and Myron slid into the driver's seat and skillfully drove out the gate. It was six o'clock and just breaking day, and I felt good about him getting the early start. I stood at the window, watching him maneuver through the snow drifts until he was out of sight. I felt great love, pride and admiration, that he was willing to tackle this difficult trip for his family.

He told me not to worry, but how could I help it unless I kept myself busy? I washed clothes, baked bread, did some sewing, read to the children and cooked a nice supper.

Bill Mills had taken a lunch as he had to be out in the hills with the bucks, but he came in at six o'clock for supper. Both of us were worried about Myron and had hoped he'd be able to make it home by supper time. He hadn't, but I was determined to make pleasant conversation. The first words that rolled off my tongue gave me away, though: "I wonder if Myron made it to town okay?"

The same thing was on Bill's mind, and he answered quickly, "Oh! Mine (his way of saying Myron) is a real good driver. He'll make it if anyone can...but in all of this snow, I don't see how anyone could make it. The worst part is that the road goes through those deep coulees. They're blown full of snow, and when it crusts like it is now, a pickup could drive out on it and drop through then really be stuck. You know, my horse couldn't waller through it."

Supper was finally over and dear, kind Bill went to his bunkhouse. As I was picking up the dishes, I paused at the darkened window, hoping to see the pickup lights. I said some prayers for Myron and then felt better. That night, each time I got up to give the children their cough medicine, I'd look out; at twelve o'clock, it wasn't snowing. The wind wasn't blowing like it had been and the stars were shining. I wondered if it was a good omen.

The clear weather was more cheerful, but I knew that Myron could still be in trouble. I decided that if he hadn't returned by the next day, I'd have Bill ride down to the Grapevine Ranch and ask the cowboys to start searching the country.

I got up early for the usual six o'clock breakfast, but Myron still wasn't back. As I looked out the window, I was reminded that the children would be needing fresh underwear so I hurried out to the line and got a handful of clothes to dry back of the cook stove. While I was out, I thought I saw a pickup on top of a high hill which was nowhere near the road. I couldn't imagine who would be up there among those boulders. I hoped it was Myron, although I knew he wouldn't be driving up there. But who else could it be? And if it was Myron, why was he so far off the road? Was he lost, sick, injured? I could hardly wait for Bill to come in, and I could hardly prepare breakfast for looking out the window every few minutes.

My vigil was finally rewarded by the sight of our truck pulling into the yard. Myron had been stuck so many times on his way to Hardin that he didn't get there until six o'clock at night. He went right to the druggist and got a large bottle of cough medicine, and fortunately our grocer was willing to stay open until Myron's large order was boxed up and loaded.

Stan, hearing his dad's voice, scurried into the kitchen. "Dad, Dad! Did you get my letter mailed to Santa?"

Myron grinned. "I sure did Son. I had a lot of trouble, but I got to the Post Office and put the letter to Santa right in the mail slot."

Wearily he leaned back in his chair and talked about the past twenty-four hours. "As soon as I got gas and everything was loaded, I started back, hoping my tracks weren't badly blown in. It was dark by then. Some of the road was okay because I could see the tracks, but there were plenty of times I got stuck and had to dig out. On my way to town I noticed the wind had blown snow off the top of the hills and when I couldn't go through a coulee I'd try to go around it by going up in the hills. I made my own roads whenever possible, even though I knew that I could run into a boulder and tear up the pickup. That is why I was on the hill near here. Ellie, I sure was glad when I saw you out to the clothesline so early. I figured that the kids weren't too bad or you wouldn't be out there. You know, the cabin with the smoke coming out the chimney and you out to the clothesline was a beautiful sight. I knew everything was normal. These hotcakes are a mighty welcome sight, too. Let's eat."

Yes, everything was normal. Myron was home safely, a big bottle of cough medicine sat on the shelf, and a two month's supply of groceries was stowed in the cupboards and cellar. I said a prayer of gratitude.

CHRISTMAS

More snow fell and wind continued to blow as Christmas neared. Myron cut a cedar tree and made a base for it. The children were thrilled as our tree made Christmas seem closer. We decorated it with the few ornaments we had, then to give Stan something to do, I popped some popcorn for him to string, and he made paper chains which we used to trim the tree.

We enjoyed that tree. Stan would sit on his bed and look at it as he listened to Santa Claus read the letters from children on our little battery-powered radio. That was a special time. Once, as we sat there listening I noticed a mouse had sneaked in, climbed up in the tree, and was eating the popcorn. Annoyed, I hurried to set a trap under the tree.

Then one evening Stan turned on the radio to get his Santa Claus program, and we were all listening when Santa read Stan's letter. Oh, the thrill of having Santa Claus read your very own letter when you have whooping cough, are snow bound and only six years old! He read off the gifts Stan and his little sister wanted. Santa said he was sorry Stan and his sister Christine had whooping cough. Stan sat there with stars in his eyes. We were so happy for him.

Each day we hoped the trucker, who was supposed to bring our mail order and more coal and cotton seed cake for the sheep, would get through the deep snow to our camp. We figured the truck could get through the drifts better than the pickup and that the driver would bring one or two men to help shovel.

Each day we prayed this would be "delivery" day—right up until Christmas Eve. Then I knew I couldn't put if off any longer, and with heavy heart I said, "Stan, because of all of this snow Santa can't make it to our place tonight."

He looked at me with annoyance. "That's silly Mama. Everyone knows Santa has a sleigh and reindeer and he can fly through the air."

I tried again. "Well, he may not be able to find us since we've moved."

The child looked at me as if I weren't very bright. "Mama, Santa knows because he got my letter and he read it on the radio."

Feebly I tried again, "Last year we were at Grandma's, and he might leave our gifts there."

He refused to be convinced, "Santa knows everything. He even knows I have the whooping cough cause I wrote it in my letter and he read it on the radio."

Myron had been in the bunkhouse with Bill and he only heard the last of the conversation. I went to the kitchen door where he was taking off his overshoes and said, "I didn't get anywhere. He still wants to believe Santa will come."

Quietly Myron said, "Don't worry. He won't know that tomorrow is Christmas. Every day out here seems alike."

"That won't work," I said. "He knows. Santa said this is the last shopping day before Christmas, and tonight Santa even said, `Merry Christmas' as he signed off." We decided that our best course was to tell Stan as gently as possible that there is a Christmas spirit, but the parents furnish the gifts. We explained that all the gifts he and Christine wanted were at the Post Office, but they wouldn't arrive until the roads opened up and Bob could get through with the truck.

I thought we'd handled it well, as Stan didn't seem too disappointed. But early Christmas morning, he jumped out of bed and hurried to the tree. After a quick glance, he looked at us sadly. "Some Christmas. Nothing under the tree but a mouse trap." We laughed and agreed—but it wasn't funny.

New Years arrived and everything changed. A Chinook had come and the coal truck made it through. We had our Christmas a week late and opened our many gifts, but it wasn't the same, and for Stan it never would be.

Our whooping cough quarantine was over, and Stan could go back to school. He'd be happy, but the rest of the family would start missing him all over again.

16
LAMBING AT POINT CREEK FALLS

◆

When spring came, our boss told us we would be lambing and shearing at Point Creek Falls. I couldn't understand why. "But there are no buildings at the Falls."

Myron looked at me, frowning. "There were no buildings at Beauvais Creek and we sheared there."

I brightened as if a light had been turned on. "Oooh! A tent."

They laughed and Mr. Willcutt smiled his funny little smile. "Well, I figured Myron would move his portable shed over there, and we can use one of the Dana roundup mess tents to cook in and a bed tent for the bunk house."

I was sad to be leaving the Forks of Grapevine camp, but now it was time to move to Point Creek Falls. Again the trailer was to be our bedroom and was set at the end of the cook tent. A sheet of canvas called a fly was stretched from the cook tent to the trailer, creating a "porch," and I could go back and forth during the rainy times without getting wet.

The mess tent was handy, and the stove burned exceptionally well. Meals were served roundup style: everyone helped themselves and there was no setting or cleaning up tables. The plates and food were set on a serving table right by the stove where the men filled their plates and got their coffee. On nice days, they went outdoors to eat, and on rainy days, they squatted around on the earth floor of the cook tent.

After eating, they cleaned and stacked their plates. I washed them, took care of the leftovers, and started getting ready for the next meal. I didn't have real "housework," but my job of cooking for twelve men and caring for Christine was never-ending. Often the baby proved to be almost too much. Men squatting down eating their meals were fascinating to her, and she tried eating the same way—but always spilled her food.

I tried putting her in her high chair and serving her before the men came in, but she refused to eat. When the men came in she made a big fuss, and because I wanted the men to enjoy their meal, I'd let her down and tell her to go to her dad, but that wasn't fun. Myron expected her to behave, but Sandy, who thought Christine was the sweetest thing ever, would say, "Come over here, baby." Sandy was her pal, so she'd hurry right over. "Are you hungry, baby? Have some noodles." She'd pick one noodle at a time off his plate to eat with her fingers. The other men took the cue from Sandy and some did the same. The more it bothered me, the funnier it was to them. Finally I just gave up, but I wondered what kind of manners this child would have when she grew up.

In this vast unsettled country, I watched her as well as I could, but there were times when she got away from me. I'd panic because I wouldn't know which direction she'd gone. Myron came up with an idea to solve the problem of Christine's disappearances. "I'll build a chicken wire fence from the trailer to the tent, and you'll be able to keep an eye on her."

This worked only a little while before she discovered she could crawl under the trailer and escape. I complained, but Myron was not to be bested by this child. He had the men chop a lot of wood and stack it under the trailer. It worked. Then she discovered she could wiggle though the other opening in the tent, even though it was securely tied. I was busy with my cooking and didn't notice that she was gone until one of the men found her, set her on his horse and led it to the cook tent. This just made her more eager than ever to run away.

The situation seemed impossible, but Myron wasn't giving up. He asked one of the men, who was a carpenter, to build shelves across the back of the cook tent to close off that opening. The men packed a month's supply of cases of canned food on those shelves, and Christine spent hours arranging and rearranging the bright labeled cans. One day she fell asleep during her arranging process, and it looked as though we finally had our problem solved.

However, another day when I was preparing dinner and Christine was very quiet, I was sure she'd gone to sleep. When I looked, she wasn't there. She'd wiggled out back of the cupboard and through the securely tied opening.

I stepped out, hoping to see one of the men. In scanning the terrain, I noticed a red spot. "Oh! Lord, that's my baby in her red coat. She's a long ways away and moving over the top of the hill!" It was ten minutes to twelve, but I couldn't wait for the men to show up. I dashed back in the cook tent, pulled all the food off the stove and took off running. The little red speck would soon be out of sight. I ran faster than I thought I could and was gaining on her when she looked back, saw me and picked up speed. I caught her, spanked and scolded her, picked her up and started back to camp. She put her arms tightly around my neck and laid her head on my shoulder as we hurried to see about my dinner.

The next day it was raining. Christine didn't go out in the mud but played in the passageway under the big canvas sheet stretched between tent and trailer. This was not exciting enough for our little girl, though, so she stood at the edge and let the cold rain drip down on her curly blond head.

We missed Stan and looked forward to the end of school so he could be with us again. I also looked forward to Christine wanting to be with him—which would mean I wouldn't have to keep such a sharp eye on her all of the time.

At this time, I was cooking for eighteen men. They liked my cooking and especially desserts, as they were their only source of sweets. They all loved pies, especially cream pies, so I made them about every noon. Because we had no refrigeration, I always made just the right amount—one piece for each person. If someone dropped in at meal time, Myron or I would let the guest have ours. If we knew soon enough I'd cut the pies in six pieces instead of five.

All of the food was put on the serving table and the men served themselves meat, potatoes, gravy, vegetables and salad. They were welcome to come back for as much as they wanted of the main course. Then they would go back for their piece of pie. Soon we noticed that we were always short one piece of pie and began to wonder what could have happened to it. It became quite a mystery: "Who took an extra piece of pie?" This went on for some time.

One day, when the rest of the crew all went back to work, Sandy went to the wood pile. He stood there with his hands in his pockets, grinning like a kid with a secret and said, "I know who's been taking the pie."

Surprised, I asked, "Really, Sandy? Who could be doing it without any of us seeing him?"

Pleased with his detective work, he said, "It's Jim, Jim Kincade."

I stood there with my hands on my hips, "Oh! Sandy! How could he do it? He always eats with all of you men around him."

Sandy continued to stand there with his hands in his pockets and a grin on his face, very satisfied with himself. He chuckled, "Well, you know he always eats more and faster than anyone else. After he finishes his first plate, he goes back for a second helping. Then he takes his pie, covering it with meat, potatoes and gravy. After he wolfs that down he goes back with the rest of us and gets another piece of pie for himself and sits down to enjoy it like the rest of us."

For a moment I was stupefied. Finally I said, "Oh, Sandy! Not the cream pie with meringue on it!"

Still chuckling he answered, "Yes! Even the cream pie with meringue on it." We stood there and laughed.

The spring of 1938 was one of the wettest that I remember. Much of the time I had to wear overshoes because of water running under the tent making the floor muddy. It was particularly difficult for the men, as they had to work with the sheep in the rain and try to save all the lambs possible.

One day it was cold, and Bronc Savage came into the cook tent and said, "It's too cold and wet out there for me. My horse is shivering. I can't see how a lamb coming out of its mother's warm womb into this icy cold rain can survive, but most of them do."

Lee Shocky made himself a raincoat out of tarpaper and used a rope for a belt. The men made smart remarks about his coat, but that didn't faze Shocky. "Go ahead and laugh, you bastards. I wasn't hired to sit around the fire; I was hired to herd sheep. I'm doing my job and I'm keeping dry. How about the rest of you?"

Howard Pickard came down with pneumonia. The roads were terrible, but Myron offered to take him to the doctor. Howard wheezed, "No sir. I'd rather stay out here in my bed in this tent and die than to travel over these awful, muddy roads. Anyway, it doesn't take much for me to come down with pneumonia. I've had it many times. I'll come out of it fine if I stay in my soogans. My roundup bed is warm. Bronc's good enough to keep the fire going and Sandy is good about bringing me what food I can eat."

I valued these men and hated to leave when word was brought to us that Myron's mother was in Sheridan, Wyoming, being operated on for cancer and wanted to see him. Each of the men had their job to do, and Myron felt they were dependable. We would only be gone until the operation was over. But who would do the cooking?

When we talked it over, Myron said, "We all know that Dan is a fine cook, but he is in charge of herding the drop band and that's time-consuming. He is doing a good job, so I'll leave him right where he is. Bronc's ewes and lambs are closest to the camp, so I'll ask him."

Bronc was surprised. "My Lord, Myron! I've been asked to do a lot of things in my time, but nobody ever thought of me as a cook and that is because I'm not. In no way am I any kind of a cook."

Myron was desperate. "Well, Bronc, I'm in one hell of a spot, and I don't know what else to do. I'm short handed with Howard sick and now this outfit is short a cook and a boss. Couldn't you just make coffee and open some cans?" Bronc agreed to give it his best.

We hurried off to Sheridan early that morning. The operation was performed, and his mother came through just fine. The next morning, the doctor told Myron, "Go back to your sheep where you are needed."

Back in Hardin, we got groceries and other needed supplies. Myron hired two men, Wayne and Curly. Wayne had a car of his own which meant help if we had trouble on the road.

When we got back, the sheep and the camp looked good, but Bronc met us at the cook tent. "Man, am I glad you're back. Everything is an awful mess."

Myron was startled. "Why, what's happened? The sheep looked okay as we drove in."

Bronc took off his hat and scratched his head. "Yea! Well, everything else went wrong. I told you I was no cook. Then Dan proceeded to show me I didn't know a damn thing. He stole all the can openers so I used a butcher knife to open the cans. Then he stole all of the butcher knives. He stole the oranges you gave Howard because he was sick. He turned all the horses loose—every one of 'em. A few of the men were able to catch their horses, but only heaven knows where the rest went. The whole crew is mad enough to quit, including me. But I'll be damned if I'll give Dan the satisfaction of making me quit."

It was nearly noon, so I cooked steaks and had a nice dinner for the men, knowing there would be fireworks when Myron talked to Dan. Then Myron would have to soothe the hurts of the other men to get them to stay, and I thought a good dinner would help. Myron was really disgusted with Dan for not cooperating during a time of emergency. That was bad enough, but to deliberately cause trouble was just too much. The men coming in for dinner were happy to see us. You'd have thought we'd been gone for months instead of a couple of days.

The men calmed down and enjoyed their dinner, but it was easy to see they thought Dan should go. Myron walked out and met Dan before he got to the mess tent. All he said was, "Dan, as soon as you eat I'll take you into town so roll up your bed, and we'll take off."

With the two new men there was enough help. Curly was a good cook and would take over until I got back. Bronc would take care of Sandy's sheep along with his own while Sandy went after the lost horses. Wayne would take care of Shocky's sheep. Shocky would herd the drop band which had been Dan's job.

Again we were off to town in the mud with Dan. Most of the time, when we reached a muddy spot, Myron would have the pickup revved up enough that he had the momentum to splash to the drier spots, but at Muddy Creek there was a narrow bridge, and you had to slow down enough to hit it just right. We got across but hit some bad ruts and the rear end went out of the pickup.

All we could do was walk. There was a road crew trying to build a better road about ten miles closer to Hardin and that's where we headed. Myron had me put Christine down the back of his jacket to make carrying her easier and Dan carried the suitcase. Myron was an exceptionally fast walker and he'd outdistance Dan and me. When he got far enough ahead, he'd sit down in the sun to rest and let the baby play on a grassy spot while Dan and I were trudging along, trying to catch up. What made matters worse was I'd put heels on that morning and had forgotten to take my flats along.

Dan and I would drag ourselves to Myron's resting spot and flop ourselves down, hoping for a nice long rest; but before we'd even get our breath, Myron would jump up. "Well, let's get going. We've got a long ways to go before night. " We'd trudge on.

We finally got to the road camp, but the only person there was the caretaker and he didn't have a car. There was a two-way radio, but he didn't know how to work it and said he didn't have authority to let anyone else try. We were hungry and appreciated it when the caretaker offered us coffee and a lunch.

Knowing there was slim chance of anyone coming to this camp, Myron said, "The only thing to do is to leave you folks here. I'll walk to Camp Four. Surely there is someone there who'll take us into town."

I sat on the wood pile and let the baby play in the sunshine. As she played, I fell asleep. Before Myron got to Camp Four, he hailed a man in a pickup who was on his way to town. The driver agreed to take us into town, and we were soon on our way—again.

We had hoped to get back to camp that night, but a mechanic had to come out with spare parts to put the pickup back together, so we had to wait until morning. Before daybreak, the mechanic drove us out to our camp. They dropped the baby and me off and hurried back to fix the pickup. It didn't take long, and soon Myron was back among the men to straighten out anything that had gone wrong in his absence and get everything back to normal.

Muddy roads could really hamper driving.

Top left, docking's going smoothly. Left middle, docking's nearly over. Bottom left, lambs wait to be docked. Top right, Myron stopped for a smoke. Bottom right, the tails still have to be counted to get an accurate count. Also, the male lambs are castrated at this time.

17
GOLD HILL

♦

We welcomed the beautiful weather because it was time to dock the lambs. Male lambs were to be castrated and tails were cut off all the lambs. Then Myron counted the tails because lambs are so frisky that counting the cut off tails is about the only way to get an accurate count. Everyone was cheerful after the count because there had been fewer losses than we thought during our terribly stormy lambing weather.

The good weather continued during the shearing. Everything went well, and we were soon finished. Stan was out of school, and because he was home, two year old Christine was no problem while I was cooking for the big crew.

The boss was at our camp during shearing and told Myron that he wanted us to set up our summer quarters at Gold Hill. We were pleased because it was a good place to camp. Myron looked forward to the excellent spring water which could be hauled to the herders. I was pleased because the icy cold water would be used for refrigeration which was badly needed through the hot summer months.

Myron pulled the trailer house close to the spring, so it wouldn't be far to carry our water. The trailer was hot and confining, so Myron decided that we should use it for the kitchen. He would use the wooden panels from the sheep shed to construct a floor and sides for a combination living room and bedroom. He built a frame of ridge pole and rafters to drape the bed tent over and then put screen above the panels. The tent sides could be raised or lowered depending on the weather, and our "house" was complete with a screen door. When it was finished, he set up our bed, Stan's cot and Christine's crib.

I happily made up the beds and scattered my hand-made rugs. It was roomy and comfortable, and I was even able to have my rocking chair. The room was cool, too, because the floor panels were laid over soil made damp by the springs.

That first night the children eagerly went off to bed, happy to be in the big room. There was enough room that each child could have their own toy box, and we all welcomed the roominess that allowed us to have the large chest of drawers, where each of us could have our own drawer.

When it began to get dark, Myron and I went to bed. It was pleasant to have the cool fresh air waft over us—and no mosquitoes! Stretching out between clean sheets in my comfortable bed, I thought, "This is heavenly."

Myron was dozing off when I felt something crawling on me. I hit at it, trying not to wake Myron. Then there was another one crawling on me and another and another. I hoped I was killing whatever they were but soon noticed a strange odor. Granddaddy Long Leg spiders were everywhere. I was so unnerved I woke Myron up. "There're spiders in this bed! Get up so we can fumigate. Let's take the bed apart and do a good job."

Weary and annoyed he said, "Oh Ellie, go to sleep. They are only Granddaddy Long Legs. They won't hurt you." He turned over and went back to sleep. I was offended because he didn't share my concern, but as I thought about it I realized that were times when he had to roll out his bed on the ground and put up with various kinds of insects. He'd put in a long, hard day and tomorrow would be another, starting at 5:00 AM.

Nothing was said about the spiders at breakfast, but I vowed that as soon as the children were up, I'd see what I could do. The next night wasn't as bad and each night after that there were fewer night "visitors." Finally they decided they didn't like our company either, and that was the end of our spider invasion.

HAPPY TRIP TO DETROIT

Myron always liked to tend his own sheep camps instead of having camp tenders. He liked being close enough to the herders that he heard of their problems right away, because that was the best way to keep them satisfied. In this way, the sheep received the best care. If anything went wrong, he'd be right there, correcting the situation before it worsened.

Because his time was limited, he used the pickup instead of the slower team of horses and trap wagon. At that time, all of the sheep wagons were iron wheeled and definitely needed to be pulled slowly.

That didn't keep Myron from longing for a pickup with a fourth low steady gear so the wagons could be pulled slow and steady, yet have the power to pull a hill without making a run at it.

One day, Myron talked with Dick Warren, the Ford dealer in Hardin. Dick said, "You know they make trucks that way, but not pickups. However, I'll call the Ford factory in Detroit and see if they'll make a special order for the sheep company."

Mr. Willcutt and Mr. Warren really liked Myron's idea. As they also were very pleased with the money the company was making, they decided that we deserved a vacation. If we wanted to go to Detroit, they would pay our expenses. Mr. Willcutt said he would look after the sheep and herders until we got back.

This was truly good news to us. My sister said that she'd take care of our children...and my parents would be driving to Sturgeon Bay, Wisconsin, to visit relatives, and we could ride that far with them. That worked out very well. After a brief visit in Sturgeon Bay, we decided to take one of the large boats that ferried loaded railroad train cars, automobiles, etc., across Lake Michigan. Then we'd take the bus from Luddington to Detroit. My teenage brother, Sheridan, went with us.

The three of us were awestruck at the vastness of the Great Lakes. Up until then, the most water we'd seen was rivers and, of course, Yellowstone Lake in the Park.

When we arrived at the Ford factory, we found that they hadn't yet built our special order. Myron was mighty unhappy, so we went to the Factory Manager. He apologized. "I'm damn sorry. We were building pickups yesterday and somehow they missed your special order. Today we are building cars, but we will make your pickup with the fourth gear while you wait. We have a fine museum and the Greenfield Village that you can wander around in until we get your pickup ready. You're also welcome to go through the factory and watch the cars being built."

We wandered around and then went to the factory where the cars were being made. We watched the gigantic electromagnet carry great piles of steel sheets clear across that monstrous building. Then we watched them shape the sheets into car bodies which were sent down the assembly line, each man doing his special job.

True to the manager's word, there was a pickup being made amongst the many, many cars. When the pickup got to the painting department the workers painted it black just as we ordered. Finally it was finished. With a turn of the key, it started right off. This truly was a thrill of a lifetime for ranch kids from Montana.

Just as we were ready to leave the factory, Myron was told how fast to drive for the first miles on the road. Afterwards, he could drive it as fast as he wanted to.

City driving and the many signs confused us because we were from the wide open spaces. We got lost and found we were driving back to Detroit instead of away from it. Luckily, we made it back to the boat on time.

In Wisconsin, we left Sheridan to visit for a while longer, and we came back to Hardin, got the children and returned to Gold Hill, to our wonderful camp—our home.

FIRE AT GOLD HILL

The weather had been hot and the Campbell Farming Corporation's wheat was nearly ready to harvest. It was so very dry that all of us were concerned about range fires starting. It was much too dry as we drove into our place, and I was again thankful that our headquarters was where the springs kept the earth damp and green. Our outdoor living and sleeping quarters had been a joy, and we were safe from range fires.

One beautiful morning, I fixed the children's breakfast in the trailer and sent them back to the "bedroom" to get dressed while I did some cleaning.

Soon I had everything ship shape and went to see if the children had found the clothes they were supposed to put on. Then it was time to make up the beds and tidy up.

I heard the pickup and glanced out. Myron was pulling in the sheep wagon which had just been recanvased. It needed new paint, linoleum and a general overhaul to make it livable. I hoped he wasn't planning to bring it in close to our living quarters, because there really wasn't room to park it and the pickup too.

Next time I glanced out, I noticed he'd parked the wagon just off the road coming in. I continued to keep busy. Stan was outside watching Myron. Christine was with me, trying to help make the beds.

Again I glanced out where Myron was and noticed a tiny flame just starting on the dry grass. Soon it was growing rapidly. Myron grabbed a gunny sack and tried to smother the fire, but it was burning so rapidly I knew that he needed help.

I picked up Christine and put her in her crib. "I want you to stay in your bed where you can see Daddy. I'm going out to help him fight the fire."

Stan came running in to tell me about the fire. "Stay in here with Christine, and I'll go out and help Dad," I told him.

I grabbed four gunny sacks, poked them down in the water trough, hurried out to where Myron was, and gave him two. With the wet sacks and both of us working, we felt confident that we'd be able to put the fire out. Then a breeze fanned the flames and the fire really took off. We followed it, each of us working as hard as we could.

Finally I was about to give up. I was nearly exhausted, but I knew that Myron was tired and wouldn't be able to handle it alone. I was so afraid the flames would reach in the Campbell's wheat, but I was too spent to be of any help. Then we heard the fire truck loaded with men coming from the Corporation. That really cheered us both.

Myron stayed with the men and they worked on. I hurried back toward camp, somewhat concerned for the children. I tried to hurry, but at times I felt that I couldn't go on. We had fought the fire much farther than I realized.

However, as I grew nearer the camp I could hear both of the children crying loudly as though something had terrified them. My fear gave me a second wind, and I ran faster than I thought I could.

When I burst into our living quarters, both children were crying great heart broken sobs...I wanted to gather my darlings into my arms. But when they looked at me, they pulled away. They didn't seem to know me and they continued to sob.

I soon realized they weren't hurt, only scared. I was so covered with soot, I really wasn't the mother they knew. I said, "Look kids, it's me. Now stop crying. Dad will be back soon. Right now I'm going into the trailer and take a bath."

They calmed down, and after I bathed and dressed in clean clothes, with my hair wrapped in a towel, I went out to the children. Then they snuggled in my arms. "Now," I said, "tell me why you were crying so hard."

Stan looked up at me, his big eyes very sincere. "Well, Mom, when you grabbed the sacks and went out there in all that smoke, we thought that both you and Daddy burned up and we were all alone."

No wonder the poor darlings cried so hard. A big lump came up in my throat. As I thought about how frightened and alone they must have felt, I wanted to cry, too, but that would really have scared them.

I swallowed the lump and forced a cheerful tone. "You know something? I sure don't like to fight fires, but I had to help Daddy until the men came with the fire truck. Come on, let's get the tears washed off your faces so you'll look nice when Dad comes back. Then it'll be his turn to get cleaned up, won't it?"

18
EAGLE SPRINGS RANCH

◆

At Gold Hill we had a lot of company—town people who had driven out to visit us, partly because our camp was near the road and easy to find. I appreciated their thinking of us, but visitors meant a lot of extra cooking for me. I wasn't having the relaxing summer I had hoped for.

Now Mr. Willcutt came to us with the news that he had gotten the lease on the Eagle Springs Ranch. I greeted his announcement with mixed feelings. Eagle Springs was a pleasant old ranch only twelve miles from Hardin which meant Stan could go to school in Hardin, and we could have him home every weekend—but it also meant I'd have a lot more people to cook for. With a ranch that close to town, you would never know when you prepared a meal how many extras would be there to eat.

Our boss was anxious for us to move before the fall rains set in, as there was a lot of work to be done to get the place fixed up before winter. We didn't want to move until the present occupants moved out, but Myron tore down our camp and moved everything to Eagle Springs except our trailer house. He moved that to a hay coulee not far from where the sheep camps were set. It was a relaxing time for us.

Each time the boss came, we'd ask him if the ranch occupants had moved yet. Finally he said, "I've talked to them many times, and they say they will, but they don't. I think the only way we can get them to move is to set the trailer near the ranch buildings. That way you can get started on some of your ranch projects, and they can see how much we need the ranch."

We put Stan in school in Hardin. He was living with my sister and her family and had many children to play with. He liked his new school and teacher. The people moved off the ranch and Mr. Willcutt hired Ray Prine, a good carpenter, to remodel the house. It took some time, but we were able to live in one bedroom and the kitchen. Then the painters took over and the paint smells were awful. It was cold weather, so as difficult as it was to put up with the smell, it was too cold to have the house opened up.

Next there were all those windows to wash and curtains to be purchased and hung. Along with all our other work, we had to go to Billings to buy furniture and linoleum for the living room and bedrooms. The kitchen and dining area had hardwood floors. I scattered a few homemade rag rugs around the kitchen, but my greatest thrill was having a real kitchen sink with hot and cold running water.

It was nearly Thanksgiving before we were really settled. Myron had a great deal of work which needed doing before winter set in, so we decided not to accept an invitation from either family for Thanksgiving Dinner. The boss wasn't going any place so we suggested he eat with us, as I would be fixing dinner for two hired men. The day before Thanksgiving, I baked chickens and dressing, cranberries, pumpkin pies and fresh bread for the herders. Even though they would be alone, they could enjoy a special meal.

Early that morning I had the food all boxed up, ready to go, when Myron came in for it. "I only have to take this food out to the herders and move Ole's wagon which won't take long. Be ready to go to town right after lunch. Mr. Swindle, at the meat market, is holding a turkey for our Thanksgiving dinner, so we'll pick that up, and you can get whatever else you need."

Noon came—no Myron. I decided he'd had some problem so the rest of us ate. I put Christine down for a nap, hoping she'd be fresh later in the afternoon while I was hurrying around doing my errands in town.

Supper time came. Still no Myron. I thought he'd be home soon, but we wouldn't have time to go into town. Instead of turkey dinner, I'd be serving baked ham and sweet potatoes.

Bed time came. Still no Myron. Bill Mills came in to help me worry. "I know Mine's all right, but surely he's had trouble or he'd be home. You know how it is out there. Anything could happen and there's no one to help him."

I was having plenty of negative thoughts, and I sure didn't need to hear more, but I couldn't help appreciating his concern for Myron. Bill loved Myron like a son, and before long I found myself comforting Bill saying, "Even if he's had trouble he's probably walked to one of the camps. When morning comes, we'll see what can be done. Hopefully Mr. Willcutt will come early." Satisfied, Bill went back to the bunkhouse. I went to bed, but my sleep was fitful. Each time I woke up, I'd say a prayer for Myron's safe return.

Breakfast came. No Myron. The men came in to eat and each wondered what to do. Neither one of them had a car, and they had to care for their sheep and do their chores. We had high hopes that whatever problem Myron had run into was overcome, and he'd be arriving soon.

About nine o'clock Bill came back to the house, again trying to cheer me. He said, "You know Mrs., I know Mine is all right but he could have run off a cutbank way out there and nobody would ever find him. I know he's all right but there's those soap holes out there. When cattle get into them they sink out of sight and nobody knows what's happened to them."

Just then some acquaintances from Hardin stopped at the ranch to ask if they could hunt geese. I told them our trouble and asked them to take me to our neighbor on Woody, because he'd helped Myron move the camps, so he knew where they were. Then we could follow Myron's pickup tracks.

These Hardin folks were eager to help, so the children and I got in their car and started off. About five miles from home, we met Myron. His pickup was covered with mud except for a little place on the windshield he'd cleaned off to see to drive. He was driving fast and didn't recognize the unfamiliar car. He didn't even slow up enough to see that we were in the back seat. We turned around and followed him back to the ranch. He'd rushed into the house, found no one there, and became concerned, thinking something must have happened to one of the children, and I'd taken them to town.

We were happy to see him, and he was happy to see us. He explained his delay. "I got the dinners delivered and decided to take the cut across. I told you about the pontoon bridge I'd fixed so I could save about twenty miles. Well, this time I was a little reckless, too much in a hurry, and slipped off. I carried sagebrush and everything else I could find to put under the wheels trying to get out. I spent the night there, and then this morning I discovered two fellows from the Ford garage who were hunting geese. I heard the shooting and hurried up the highest hill, took off my jacket and waved it like crazy. They saw me and they pulled me out. Man, I sure was glad to see them."

Myron had just finished cleaning up when the boss arrived for Thanksgiving dinner. We were very thankful that Myron was safe, and the dinner was nice—in spite of the fact I really hadn't had my mind on it.

The Eagle Springs Ranch house was big and roomy and I enjoyed it. When the weather was bad, Christine could ride her tricycle inside the house. However, she liked being outdoors best. We had a good fenced yard, but she loved being with people and liked being where the men were working. They were good to her and thought everything she did and said was the cutest thing ever.

We still had the mother dog, Lady, and some pups. Two-year-old Christine thought it was up to her to feed the dogs and, of course, they became her good friends and protected her. Because we were having trouble with coyotes killing sheep, we bought some wolf hounds who were trained to catch and kill coyotes.

When Myron tended the sheep camps, he always saw coyotes, but now he took the hounds with him and they killed many coyotes. This was good news to the sheep owners and to anyone who ever saw coyotes tear up sheep just for fun.

At the ranch, Christine wanted to take care of the hounds just as she did the sheep dogs, not realizing there was a difference and that the hounds had to be penned up except when they were needed. She hated to see them locked up and was always wanting someone to turn them out. There was a real bond between the little child and the hounds, and she even called these vicious dogs sweet names. There was Sugar Boy, Honey Boy and Johnny Boy. The pup with the crooked tail was logically called Crooked Tail. Blue was an excellent hunter. He could kill a coyote with one snap of his sharp teeth, yet seemed to be pleasant around the children.

I didn't like having Christine around the hounds, but she was always with them when they were in the yard. When they were resting, she'd sit on their backs and bounce up and down, which was bad enough, but the time she took food out of one's mouth, gave me a real scare. After that, I made her stay in the house until they'd finished eating, and I tried to make her understand that you never, never take food out of a dog's mouth.

If the hounds were around, they wouldn't let me punish her. If she'd yell or cry when I was trying to do something with her, they'd growl and look at me as if they were going to attack. I quickly learned to take her in the house if she had any punishment coming.

Since Mr. Willcutt was an old time cowman, cowboys who were out of work, usually men who had worked for him in the past, were welcome to stay at the ranch for the winter, providing they worked for him in the spring. Now that the sheep company was running the Eagle Springs Ranch, these men were welcome to stay providing they wanted to work with the sheep in the spring.

The cowboys who stayed with us were good lambing hands and liked being part of our family. They also liked my cooking, so all winter we had four extra men except for the short periods of time they spent in town on sprees. I got awfully tired of cooking three meals a day. There were extra men riding the grub line who stayed for a day or two. The wolfer, a man hired to take the hounds out to catch the coyotes on the sheep range, stayed with us through the winter and spring months.

Whenever Myron was going out to the camps, the wolfer liked to ride along. They'd put the dogs inside the stock rack in the back of the pickup. One morning, they drove across a big flat and spotted a coyote. They let the dogs out, and the dogs raced after it. Then the men in the pickup raced along after the dogs. They were watching the chase so intently that they sailed into a washout and came to an abrupt halt. After the dust settled, they decided that neither of them were hurt and the pickup could still be driven even if all four springs were broken.

Two very thankful men came driving into the ranch for dinner. Myron suggested that Christine and I go into town with him, because he might have to stay all night to get the repairs done.

Christine and I climbed into the pickup, happy for a change in our routine, but it rode like a lumber wagon as we crept along. In a jiggling voice I asked, "What in the world makes this pickup so rough?"

Myron's voice jiggled back: "I broke all four of the springs on it."

I looked at him, disgusted. "Well, why didn't you tell me before we left the ranch?"

He grinned at me. "You wouldn't have come to town with me if you'd known, would you?" So we continued down the corduroyed gravel road all the twelve miles to the Ford garage.

MEASLES

All of Stan's early years we lived far out in the country, and because he was not around children he had none of the childhood diseases. The year he came down with measles, we brought him out to the ranch where I could take care of him. It was in January, when we had a crew to wool blind and tag the sheep, so I put Stan in our bedroom, right off the kitchen. There, it would be easy to keep an eye on him as I was cooking. He was lonely, and his eyes were sensitive to the light. He wanted me to read to him. I'd go in the bedroom as often as I could to be with him and to read, but it was hard with all my other work. Myron tried to take care of Christine as much as he could, but that was difficult, too. There was always the chance that she would run off or get hurt with the busy schedule he had.

I was exhausted and concerned about how long I could keep up with all the demands on my time without getting sick myself. One morning, I got breakfast over with and had just gotten Christine bathed, dressed and had started to comb her hair when a woman's voice called. "Ellie, it's me, Lottie."

Quickly I went to the door to greet her, "Well hello, Lottie. Where are you headed this early in the morning?"

"Oh, you know me. I just got tired of my job at Warman and decided to go to Sheridan and look for another one. Say, I heard that Stan has the measles. Now you go in there and take care of him, and I'll do your cooking until he gets to feeling better. Go right in there and stay with him."

I couldn't believe this woman coming into my home and taking over! I said, "Okay, Lottie, okay. I'll go just as soon as I finish Christine's hair."

Lottie put her hands on her hips and scolded. "Ellie, I know all about curling little girls' hair. Remember? I had a little girl once. She was just Stan's age when she was killed."

I was sorry I reminded her of that sad time, but I knew it was never far from her thoughts. Just then Myron came in the door. He and Lottie always had fun razzing each other, because he'd known Lottie and Len since he was a child.

When she told him she was going to stay and take over while Stan was sick, he greeted her with enthusiasm. "Lottie, that is mighty good of you. I'll see that the boss pays you for it too."

She answered quickly, "Oh Myron, don't be dumb. I'm doing this for you and your family because they need me right now. Ellie is a mighty tired young lady, and Stan is sick and needs his mother. I'm glad to take over for all of you. Now you get on out of here and do your work. I'm going to take care of Christine and dinner will be ready on time."

Take over she did! She wouldn't let me do anything. About the only time she'd let me come out of the room was to eat, but rest proved to be exactly what I needed. I'd read until Stan went to sleep, and then I'd sleep too. The second day, Stan was badly broken out and no longer had a fever.

Soon Lottie and Len decided they had to get on to Sheridan. I was feeling fine and anxious to get back to my work. But I was oh so thankful for that fine woman and her wonderful, helpful spirit.

Stan wasn't long getting over his measles and was able to go back to school, but then Christine came down with them. She had a high fever and couldn't seem to break out. We put her bed in the living room by the heater and kept her very warm, but she was so sick and wanted me to hold her and rock her. Myron wanted to help, but she didn't want anything to do with him. When he came into the room, she'd turn her face to the wall.

Bill and Sandy were just as concerned as we were. They would come in and peek at her, but she'd turn her face away.

Finally Myron could stand it no longer. He went to Dr. Haverfield's office and asked him to come to the ranch.

After a careful examination, Doc looked at us. "Well folks, there is little for me to do. You are already doing what I would prescribe. Main thing is to keep her warm as you are doing. Hold her and rock her as she wants you to. She'll break out in the next couple of days."

Each day the ranch hands quietly came in to ask how she was. Each man seemed to feel a genuine concern while we waited for a special little girl to break out with the measles. Finally she broke out, and the tension was over. She still didn't want anyone but me to see her, and when anyone came in, she rolled over with her face to the wall and wouldn't let anyone look at her until the measles were gone—not even her dad.

Top photo, drop band (1,500-2,000 sheep) ready to lamb, night man ready to take over. Middle left, early morning – looking to see which sheep should be turned out after lambing. Bottom left, Tim Hargrove, left, pick up man (picks out sheep ready to lamb), and Alec MacLennon, herder. Middle right, Myron feeding a jailer's lamb (an orphan).

19
LAMBING AT EAGLE SPRINGS

◆

The weather was beautiful. Myron considered himself lucky to have gathered up a crew of good, experienced lambers. Several came from Big Timber where there were many sheep outfits. They had learned about lambing when they were youngsters. The atmosphere around the ranch was very positive; everyone knew what to do and was happy doing his job.

We had a neighbor, Ed Kopac, who farmed large acreage. He decided that, because he had plenty of pasture and hired many men, he should go into the sheep business, even though he wasn't experienced. In the winter he did fine, because he'd hired a good herder, but lambing was a different story.

When Ed began to have trouble, he asked our boss, Mr. Willcutt, if he could get Myron to help. The boss grinned his funny grin and said, "I don't know. You'll have to ask Myron."

For several days, Ed came to the Eagle Springs Ranch for dinner, and we all wondered what he wanted. Finally he said, "I asked Mr. Willcutt if it was okay if you came over to my place. He said I'd have to ask you. Will you come?" Myron was very hesitant, as he had all the work he wanted with his lambing, but Ed, being highly excitable, said, "Will you come? I've got lambs a running and ewes a running and a crew of men and none of us knows what to do."

Myron answered after a moment. "Ed, I don't want to leave my lambing operation because everything is going smoothly, and I want to keep it that way, but I will take the time to go over to see if I can make some suggestions."

As soon as Myron got there, he could see there were too many men. They were chasing the ewes, trying to make them have their lambs, but the ewes were so nervous they didn't know what the men were trying to do.

Ed was nervous himself. "What would you do?"

Finally Myron said, "Well Ed, if it were me, I'd load up all those men and take them to the ranch and keep the sheep out here in this good pasture. They know more about mothering up than humans do. You've hired a good herder, so let him take care of the sheep. He'll know what to expect."

That was what Ed did, and he had a pretty good lambing. In the fall, when he sold his lambs, he got top price. He also sold his ewes and made money from everything.

SANDY

Coyotes were always bad around sheep, but they were especially bad at lambing time, even though the men cared for the ewes and young lambs. The men would ride into the ranch for their meals, but at night they slept in their range tepees because human smell discouraged the wily coyote. If coyotes did get in the sheep, a man could hear the commotion and get a shot at them. The noise and gun powder drove them off.

Sandy was very good with twin bunches. He always knew which twins belonged together and knew the mothers. His sheep range was not far off the highway, so it was easy to get to him. Myron had debated which herder to locate there and had decided on Sandy because he wasn't alcoholic and wouldn't leave his sheep to catch a ride into town to get liquor.

One evening Sandy didn't come to the ranch for supper. I wasn't concerned because I supposed he didn't feel like eating. Next morning when he didn't come in for his early morning coffee I became concerned, but thought something had delayed him. However, later that morning when Myron found time to stop at the ranch I asked, "Have you seen anything of Sandy? He hasn't come in for breakfast—not even for his early morning coffee, and you know how he likes that. Do you suppose he's sick or something's happened to him?"

Myron looked surprised. "Well, I just came by there. He was riding his horse, the dog was with him, his sheep were quiet and everything appeared to be okay so I didn't stop. However, that isn't like Sandy. He hasn't missed one meal since he's been with us, and his coffee means so much to him. I just can't believe he'd miss supper and breakfast. As soon as I can get to it, I'll go and see why he hasn't come in."

Puzzled, Myron finally went to see Sandy. He stood there leaning against the pickup waiting for Sandy to come out of his tepee. When he finally came out Myron said, "Sandy, the cook has been wondering why you haven't been coming to the ranch for meals."

Sandy stood on one foot and then the other, pulling his hat a bit lower on his forehead. Looking off in the distance he said, "Well, the saloon owner, Jake, brought me out a girl. Yes, he brought Marian out."

Myron stood there dumbfounded. He'd run into all kinds of problems, but this was the first time a bar owner ever brought out a prostitute. Sandy continued, "Yesterday afternoon he brought Marian out and she is staying with me in the tepee...and a...she brought some liquor and coffee and stuff to eat. She's still sleeping."

Myron was fuming. Angrily he got in the pickup and drove right into town, got hold of Jake and said, "Jake, the last time you brought liquor to one of our men, I told you it's against company rules to bring liquor to men on the ranch. Now you not only bring liquor, but one of your prostitutes. I'm telling you right now, you get in your car, drive out to Eagle Springs and get your girl and her liquor back to town. Don't you ever let me catch you or anything that belongs to you out there again."

Lambing time for me was a grind with steady cooking for a crew of ten to twelve men for six weeks with no break. My day started at five o'clock with cooking breakfast so the men could eat at six. I seldom got rest during the day, and it was always ten o'clock before I got into bed.

After three weeks of that, I got sick and had to go to bed. It was just before supper, so Myron put the meal on the table and the men did the dishes. I went to sleep and wasn't aware of anything—not even my child. I knew Myron would take care of her.

But about nine o'clock, Myron shook me awake. "Ellie, Ellie. Clyde's wife came all the way from Lovell to see him. It's too late for her and their little boy to drive all the way back to Hardin when we can bed them down here. Will you get up and see that they are taken care of?"

I dragged myself out of bed, slipped on a few clothes and ran a comb through my hair. Myron sounded helpless, and I could empathize with the young wife and mother in a strange country in a stranger's home. I felt better as I went out to meet my guest.

She was a charming young lady. I liked her and we had a pleasant visit. She seemed grateful for a place to stay, and next morning she was right out in the kitchen helping with breakfast. We worked together beautifully. Our children played together, and her overnight visit lengthened into a week. I hated to see her go.

At shearing time, we hired a young boy to help me in the kitchen. He was good help, but he didn't like the work. Whenever he wasn't needed in the kitchen, he'd hurry out to be with the men.

Now that school was out, Stan was great help, and I had no more trouble with Christine running away. The latest imaginative game he liked to play was Lone Ranger and his horse Silver. Little blond Christine was Tonto and her make-believe horse was Blackie. There was a hill near the house where Stan liked to ride up and down calling out, "High ho Silver, away." Christine would call, "High ho Blackie, away." It was wonderful seeing them have such a good time.

Myron was pleased with the good sheep outfit he'd built up. His ability to keep it running smoothly gained him a good reputation with the older sheepmen.

A neighbor, Carol Clark, who was also a sheepman, became very ill right when it was time to shear his sheep. He sent for Myron and asked, "I know that you are busy, but along with your own work could you manage my outfit, tend my sheep camps, move them into the shearing pens and then get them sheared for me? I can't get out of bed, but if you take over, I know you'll treat my outfit like it was your own."

Of course Myron took over, and I did the cooking. Things weren't as handy at his camp as they were at Eagle Springs Ranch, but the weather cooperated so we were soon finished and I was glad to get back home.

When we were shearing, our banker Mr. Warren asked, "How much wool will each sheep shear?"

Myron pushed his hat back on his head, looked up at him and said, "These sheep have had good feed so each fleece will weigh ten pounds."

He looked at Myron over his glasses and said skeptically, "I doubt it. I never knew of a sheep shearing that well."

A bit annoyed, Myron answered the banker's doubt. "Well, there is an old hand scale in the barn. I'll get it and we can weigh a fleece."

They weighed several fleece, each one weighing right at ten pounds. The banker found it so difficult to believe, that he took a spare wool sack, spread it in the trunk of his car, put three fleece in it and took them into town to weigh them on a reliable scale at the hardware store. Each weighed ten pounds. He even called in some of his cronies to show them how heavy these fleece were. Myron and Mr. Willcutt really chuckled when they heard about that.

Many of our acquaintances drove out to Eagle Springs to watch the shearing. Generally they went right to the shearing pens, but some came to the house to visit a while.

The shearers always ate first. There were ten of them, and it worked out fine as I could seat ten at our table. After they ate, they went back out to the shearing pens to sharpen their shears so they'd be ready to start the next day. I would quickly wash up the dishes and reset the table for the wranglers. These were the ten men that took care of the sheep, seeing that the ewes and lambs got back together, "mothered up" and back to their home range. I was never sure just how long it would take for them to finish and arrive for their meal, but I'd have the food all ready so the tired, hungry men could eat as soon as they got in, generally about seven o'clock.

One particular evening, we had cold roast beef. While I was slicing it, I realized it was much more meat than the men could eat, but I put it on the huge platter anyway so I could get the roaster washed. I had just placed the platter on the table when I heard a knock. Thinking it was the men I called, "Come in." I was shocked to see the Indian Eagle, his squaw and three children at the door. He didn't speak English, and I didn't understand his language. He used sign language to show me they wished to eat. I nodded my consent and pointed to the end of the table. He motioned for his wife and children and they seated themselves around the freshly set table.

Mr. Willcutt had made it plain to me that any time Eagle came to the ranch it was important to feed him. That was the agreement written in his lease, so I hurried to get the hot food, hoping they'd be finished before the ten man crew arrived.

Eagle and his family ate their supper. I hurried to serve them dessert and Eagle leisurely drank another cup of coffee. I kept looking at the clock, glancing out the window, wishing that my guests would leave, so I could reset the table and the weary hands wouldn't have to wait.

Finally, Eagle got up from the table and patted his stomach, showing me that he'd had enough and had enjoyed his supper. His family went out the door to their car. Then Eagle walked over to the wood box and pointed to a stack of newspapers I used to start my cooking fires. Thinking he wanted them for the same purpose I picked them all up and started to hand them to him, but he shook his head and held up one finger. I gave him the one paper, glad that he was leaving.

Eagle had other ideas. He unfolded his newspaper, spread it out on the table, picked up the huge platter of roast beef, dumped all of it on the paper, wrapped it carefully and walked out the door.

I stared after him, dumbfounded, and leaned against the door, trying to overcome my state of shock. Then I heard the men arriving in the truck, ready for supper. I rushed to the pantry and began searching for canned meat. Corned beef! I quickly opened a number of cans, sliced it and put it on the table.

When they were all gathered around the table, I explained why I was again serving canned meat. I expected them to complain, but they didn't. They thought it was funny, but from then on, whenever I served corned beef, one of them would tease, "Has Eagle been here again?"

20
I QUIT

♦

The boss was helping Curly and his young wife get a start in the sheep business. They had about 500 head of ewes on their lease about eight miles from the Eagle Springs Ranch, and he spent a good deal of time advising them. He wanted Myron to put Curly to work whenever he needed extra help, but Curly wasn't really interested in ranching. Myron thought and acted quickly, and Curly was slow, which caused problems when they had to work together.

Now that it was time for Curly's operation to shear, they decided to bring their sheep to Eagle Springs instead of shearing them at their place. Everything was moving at a rapid pace. The shearers were shearing as fast as they could, and Myron was overseeing the whole operation, making sure the men kept the shearers' pens full, checking on the wool tramper, and seeing that everything went smoothly, as we were anxious to get through and get the sheep up on Little Mountain.

The boss drove up and came over to Myron. "Curly just got here with his sheep and is ready to shear."

Myron was disgusted and didn't try to hide his feelings. "I told Curly to bring them in the morning. The shearers won't be finished with this band until evening, so all we can do is to corral his sheep until morning."

Next morning when Curly's sheep were sheared there were ten head missing. They accused Myron of stealing them. Very annoyed Myron told the boss, "I'm busy and I'm tired. You just see that Curly and his wife go home. I don't have time to argue with them. I'm not about to steal ten head of Curly's sheep. I've got all I can do to get your sheep sheared and up to the mountain."

It was a big relief to be done with shearing and all of its problems, but now it was time for Myron to move the six bands of sheep up the mountain. He pulled and set each of the wagons himself so was under a lot of tension. Right in the middle of the preparations, the boss came to Myron and asked, "Could you spare a little time to go over to Curly's, and show him how to build a corral that will keep his sheep in?"

Myron had reached the boiling point and exploded. "Harve, I've built you up a good sheep outfit. It takes all my time and energy to run it, but I still don't seem to be doing enough to suit you, because you want me to wait on Curly and his outfit. I've had it. I quit. I'll stay until the lambs are shipped. By then you'd better have a foreman because I'm leaving."

Mr. Willcutt didn't say anything. He just got in his car and drove off. In town Myron was told the boss had decided to take a trip to Arizona. No one seemed to know when he'd be back, so Myron ran the sheep outfit like it was his own and the banker continued to pay the bills.

We had a busy summer and still had people from town come out to visit. At the ranch, we had the two steady ranch hands, and the two men Myron hired to build the reservoirs which had been planned and were badly needed. When I wanted to go up on the mountain with Myron, I'd put a roast in the oven. At noon, when the men got in, they would have the roast and fix what they wanted. I always had homemade bread and a cake, which they loved enough that they didn't mind the cook being gone.

It was early fall when Mr. Willcutt got back from his vacation. He was happy to be back and told us all about his trip. He said, "Say, Myron, I'm looking for someone to put up the hay on my Grapevine Ranch. Do you know of anyone?"

Myron looked at Harve, "I think you are making a mistake to cut that alfalfa for hay when you've got hay left over from last year and all the first cutting of this year. Why not let it go to seed and then cut it? That seed will make you some money. The last time I was there, the seed was really setting on."

Harve said, "But I don't know anything about seed. I'm a livestock man not a farmer."

Smiling, Myron put his hand on his hip and pushed his hat back, "Yes, I know, but around Lodge Grass everyone raises seed, and on the Grapevine you seldom get the early frosts that they get at Lodge Grass. Let's drive over to Grapevine and look at those meadows. Then we'll know."

When they got there Myron was amazed. He had never seen a crop like it. "Why that is a thousand bushel crop if I'm any kind of a judge!" he told Willcutt.

Mr. Willcutt was skeptical. "Ah, Myron. You couldn't get that much off one crop."

Myron was very enthusiastic. "Why that is the best I've ever seen. If I had money to bet I'd bet $500."

Now Harve was caught up in Myron's excitement. "I'll tell you what I'll do. You keep your eye on it, tell my men at the ranch when it is ready, and they will mow and bunch it. If it makes a thousand bushel, I'll give you $500."

When it was time Myron said, "Harve, have you hired a man with a thrashing machine?"

He looked surprised, "No, I haven't. I don't know anyone who owns a machine. Do you?"

Taking a deep breath, Myron said, "The only ones that I know of are over at Lodge Grass, and all of them are busy at this time of year. Most won't want to drive their slow moving machines this far."

Harve calculated the distance. "Yes, forty five miles to Hardin over rough roads and thirty miles to Lodge Grass. My god, that's 150 miles round trip. But why don't you go over to Lodge Grass and see if you can't hire one of them as long as you know them so well."

On our way to Lodge Grass, Myron thought about his options. "The only thrasher I can think of who might consider going to Grapevine is Denver Sherman on Rotten Grass Creek."

When we got to Sherman's ranch, Myron said, "Denver, I see you got your seed thrashed. Have you got another job lined up?" Sherman shook his head, and Myron continued. "Well I know of a good big job over at Grapevine. How about coming over there to thrash?"

Denver chuckled. "The only way I'd go over there is if I could ford the Big Horn River." He laughed and slapped his leg. Myron perked up. "Say, that's the answer! There's a darn good ford at the Spotted Rabbit crossing."

Sherman crossed the river and did the thrashing—and Myron's prediction of a thousand bushel crop turned out to be 1,040 bushels. Mr. Willcutt had the seed hauled to Sheridan, Wyoming, and sold it to a seed company. When Harve got back, he came right out to Eagle Springs to show us his check for $25,000. He was elated. "You know, this will finish paying for the Grapevine Ranch."

We were happy for him—and pretty elated ourselves when he wrote Myron a check for the promised $500.

21
MOVING SHEEP DOWN THE MOUNTAIN

◆

It was a beautiful day, and I felt like getting away from the ranch and its many duties. Myron suggested the children and I go for a ride with him, as he had to move two sheep camps and would appreciate the company. We were pleased to go. Fresh air and a change of scenery were refreshing.

When Myron had set Ole's wagon, he'd taken it down a steep hill because that part of the range had choice grass that hadn't been grazed. He drove into a pretty little canyon. The slope was covered with rocks and cedar trees and there was a small creek at the bottom. I marveled at it, hidden in this little canyon. But now it was time to pull the wagon out.

Myron chuckled. "The boss told me, `The only way you can ever get that wagon out of there is to burn it up,' but I know I can get it out all right. I'll have to do everything just right. A mistake could make a difference."

Myron checked the wagon to see that Ole had everything packed and then loaded the heavy water barrels and wood. I stood there in the mountain breeze and gazed at the breath-taking scenery. He backed the pickup to the wagon tongue, and I helped him hook them together.

Slowly and carefully, we started back to the little canyon. I was to watch out the rear window to see that the wagon was traveling okay. We drove around the side of the hill and I realized how sidling it was. The top-heavy, cumbersome wagon had the two wheels on the one side much higher up the hill than the other two. It was scary the way it was leaning, and I wanted to say something but was afraid to distract Myron.

I was relieved when we got around the hill and started down into the steep little canyon. Myron said, "Now I want everyone to really hang on, because I'll have to hit the bottom pretty hard. I don't want anyone to say a word. Everyone be really quiet." As he was easing the pickup into the little creek I noticed he hadn't shifted it into the low, low gear; it was in neutral. I didn't think that was right, but he was an exceptionally good driver and had done this many times. Besides, he warned us to be quiet.

At the bottom he stepped on the gas to climb up the other side but discovered he had no power. We were stuck. He used some choice words. Quietly I said, "I noticed that you didn't have it in compound."

"Well why didn't you say something?" he demanded. I felt bad, yet a little pleased, because I wasn't the only one who did dumb things. We were miles from help, so I sent up some silent prayers to the Lord.

Myron had to do the jacking, blocking and digging, and I did what little I could to help. He put the on the chains and was finally able to back out of the little creek. "Ellie, you take the kids up on the hill to those bushes and wait. I'm really going to have to gas this outfit, and that means I'll have to hit that creek hard if we're going to get out of this place."

Dutifully the three of us climbed to the top of the hill. I stood there praying as we watched the pickup and wagon slowly climbing up the long steep hill. The wagon swayed and bounced, but it came right along.

When Myron got to where we were standing he stopped and said in a hushed, anxious voice, "Oh, my God! Ellie, don't move or let the kids move. There is a big rattlesnake right behind you." We stood there petrified as the snake slithered away. Then we climbed in the pickup, thankful and relieved.

Finally we got the wagon to its new location, but now we were behind schedule so we hurried on to the next camp.

THEN WE MOVED OTTO'S WAGON

It was getting late, and the children were tired and hungry. Myron had told Otto to take his sheep to the new camp and to expect his wagon about dusk. Because of our trouble, we would be late, and Otto would be waiting to cook his supper. Also, his sheep needed their salt. We knew he'd be grouchy, but we hurried to his wagon, loaded the sheep salt, water barrels and wood. Feeling confident that Otto had his wagon all packed and ready to move, we hooked it to the pickup.

As we started out Myron said, "I'm sure we'll be late, but if I take the cut-off I can save a number of miles." When we got to the cut-off, I remarked that it looked awfully steep; but Myron assured me we'd be saving two or three hours. He neglected to tell me that he'd never pulled a wagon down this hill.

Myron put the pickup in compound, and slowly we crept down the hill. It was my job to look back to check on the wagon's progress, and I was shocked to see how awfully steep the grade was. It looked as if the wagon was about to stand on its nose. I winced at every bump and rock we bounced over, realizing there was nothing I could do but pray.

When finally we reached our destination it was nearly dark. Myron got out and started to dig down the wagon wheels. Stan and I got in the back of the pickup and began throwing out the firewood. Myron set out the water barrels, salt troughs, kerosene can, etc.; then, in order to see if the wagon was level, he started to climb inside to set a pan of water on the stove.

When he pulled open the door, I heard the language which always signaled a problem. I asked, "What happened?"

His voice rose. "Man, oh man! What a mess! I forgot to check to see if the ashes were emptied. I just assumed that Otto would have done it. There are ashes every place." He started to climb in the wagon. "What is this? It's sticky!" Otto had a gallon can of Karo syrup which hadn't been packed solidly, so it spilled. Thick syrup mixed with ashes had run the full length of the wagon.

We both went to work on the wagon. I grabbed the broom, hoping to sweep the worst out the door. That didn't do anything but gum up the broom. By now, Myron had the lantern lit, and he got a dish pan of water from the water barrel. I tried scrubbing with it, but soon found out you can't clean up syrup with cold water. Myron chopped some wood and built a fire in the stove to heat a dish pan full of water. Hot water worked, and I got the syrup and ashes washed up.

It was getting dark, so it was hard to see what kind of job I did. I felt it should be scrubbed a second time, but I hoped Otto could get his supper and get into bed without getting too sticky. I was just washing out the broom when Otto arrived.

We explained what had happened, afraid he might be disgruntled. But he was pleasant about it and said, "I'll clean it in the morning. It's too hard to see to clean by lantern light."

We were glad to climb into the pickup and start for home with our tired, hungry children. I realized how sticky I was when everything I touched got sticky, even the children.

The darkened ranch house looked beautiful as the pickup lights shone on it. I don't know when I was quite so thankful to walk in that door. Myron lit the lamps, and we were home. It was about ten o'clock before I got everyone fed, bathed and into bed.

MIKE HALCO

Finally, we all had the sheep off the mountain and the lambs shipped. The two herders who would not be with the sheep outfit through the winter were Ole Nelson, who was happy to be returning to his home in Norway, and Mike Halco. Mike had come to work for us in May. He only planned to work through the summer, because he seemed to have plans for the fall. He was a pleasant man to be around, a good herder, a good cook and very clean about himself and his wagon. Myron liked him, and when he had to eat at one of the wagons, he'd work it around so he could eat with Mike.

Mike liked nice things, but he was never extravagant. He took good care of what he had and respected his money as though he was saving for a special purpose. Herding sheep was a good way to save your money.

When Ole came to the house to get his check, he was cleaned up, dressed in the suit he'd worn when he came from Norway. He was very happy to be going home. Then Mike came walking across the yard. My friend Frances and I were standing by the window watching, and I said, "I didn't realize Mike was such a sharp dresser."

She agreed. "Yes! His fashionable hat is tipped at just the right angle. If you saw him in a city, you'd think he was a businessman."

When we arrived in Hardin, Myron helped him unload his bed and suitcase at the Hardin Hotel, which we'd recommended because it was clean and near the depot. Many of the working men stayed there. Mike only wanted a bath and hair cut before he caught the evening train.

Myron took our little family down to my parent's home, and we visited while Mother prepared our lunch. While we were eating, there was a knock at the door. It was Mike Halco asking for Myron. Myron stepped outside the door and they talked. Mike was very upset, as he told Myron, "Right after you left me, I checked into the hotel and went across the street to the bank and cashed my check, so I'd be ready to leave when the evening train came in. I hid my money amid my clothing in my suitcase. While I was taking my bath, Marian, that thieving prostitute, came into my room with a pass key and went through all of my clothing searching for my money. She stole all of my wages for five months. I'm flat broke. I haven't even money to eat with or to pay my hotel room. I can't even buy a train ticket to leave."

Feeling much sympathy, Myron said, "I'll loan you enough money to tide you over until I finish my lunch. Then I'll come uptown and see what I can do. I know the sheriff, so we'll go over and talk to him." That was agreeable with Mike, so Myron gave him ten dollars to eat on and get his hair cut. Mike seemed appreciative, and after he left we finished our noon meal.

Right after lunch, Myron said, "Well, I guess I'd better get uptown and see what I can do for Mike."

When he got to the hotel, many people were gathered around, and there seemed to be a lot of confusion. He asked what had happened.

A fellow standing there said, "Mike Halco just shot Marian and a sheep shearer happened to be near so he got hit. Then Mike went into the coal room and committed suicide."

The ambulance took the wounded man to the hospital. Mike and Marian were taken to the morgue.

22
OUR TEN PERCENT

◆

When the lambs were put in the stockyards, ready to ship, they were beautiful and weighed heavier than the other lambs the buyer had bought. The two partners were happy with the money they brought in. When Myron met with them at the bank, they were figuring up how much money they'd made on the lamb deal. They boasted about how much money they'd made on the wool and the lambs. They talked about how successful they'd been since the banker had to foreclose on that first bunch of sheep. Both men were in a high mood, so Myron thought it a good time to ask about the ten percent promised him when he first went to work for them three years go.

Myron had just gotten the question out of his mouth, when they snapped, "It can't be done, because no one knows what the outfit is worth until we sell out." All there was for Myron to do was get up and walk out.

As he walked down the street, he was mighty glum. On the way to his pickup, he met a friend, Harvy Cort. Cort was a sheep man with a big operation who had always shown a fatherly interest in Myron. Noticing Myron's glum mood he said, "Come on over to my office where we can talk."

At Cort's office, Myron went into detail. "I'm just not making enough here. I'm leaving as soon as I get everything shaped up, but from the looks of things, whether I leave or stay, I won't get my ten percent because they sure aren't going to sell out."

Mr. Cort leaned over his desk and smiled. "I can tell you how you can get your ten percent." Then he leaned back in his chair and chuckled. "Here's how you do it. Get the market price on the two-year-old ewes, the three-year-olds and the four-year-olds, etc., and figure what the grass leases are worth. The hay in the barn is worth $30.00 a ton for the 50 or 60 tons. It's damn good hay you've got there. Also, you'll need to figure the going price for sheep wagons, dogs, horses, saddles and all the sheep supplies and the pickup.

Even the household furniture—everything you can think of. If they try to tell you no one will pay that much, you say you will."

Myron chuckled. "They'll know that's a joke because I was flat broke when I went to work for them, and they know I just finished paying off the Billings bank. With the kind of money I make, I won't have enough money to buy a car to leave the ranch. Why, they'll just laugh me right out of the bank."

Mr. Cort laughed. "That's what makes this funny. They know you haven't got the money or the credit to buy a big sheep outfit like that, but here's the joke. I have. You'll be buying the outfit for me. I'll go to the Security Bank in Billings and tell them that any check that comes in with your name signed to it, no matter how big, take it and withdraw the money from my account. After you've bought their sheep outfit, you and I will settle up."

Myron went to Willcutt and Warren and offered to buy their sheep company. They couldn't believe he had that kind of credit. In times like these, no young couple was about to get credit enough to buy a big sheep outfit. Nevertheless the partners did accept his check of $10,000 down payment. In a state of bewilderment, they immediately got in their car and drove to Billings to see if Myron had given them a bad check. They were sure that it wasn't good.

It was a real shock to them when they found the check was good, and they'd sold their sheep company. Mr. Cort gave Myron the pickup, chickens, milk cow, wolf hounds and all the household furnishings.

We received our ten percent from Willcutt and Warren's company and moved to Lodge Grass. It was good to get back to our little leased home where Stan could be with us and ride the bus to school. Christine could have children to play with, and I was happy because I wouldn't have all that cooking. I was pregnant and our baby was due in March. I was looking forward to a reasonably quiet winter.

In the meantime, Willcutt and Cort began having problems. Mr. Willcutt claimed that he was not allowed to sell his leases. Without that range, Cort would have to sell some of the sheep as he didn't have enough range on Reno Creek to pasture that many more sheep. He started home with his sheep.

Willcutt and Warren decided they wanted to stay in the sheep business, so they caught up with Mr. Cort and his men at Crow Agency. They bought back part of the sheep but Cort was still smarting over not getting the range leases so he sold them everything they wanted at inflated prices. Cort charged them $10.00 a ton more for the hay in the barn than he'd paid for it.

Besides the inflated prices they had to pay, they lost a good foreman, and good foremen were hard to replace. Myron built up the sheep company. He knew all the animals, equipment, the range and the men. One of our big advantages was that the foreman and cook were one unit. The men admired me. We always had a good relationship, and many of them thought of our place as home. Now they had to try one foreman and then another, and finally they decided to go out of the sheep business.

Matt Tschirgi, left, had great faith in Myron's ability. He leased many range land acres then rented them, and in our case, he was our partner. Ralph Cunningham, right, was a lamb buyer and trader.

23
DREAM COME TRUE

◆

There were many things to do in our home on Lodge Grass Creek before we could really feel settled. Myron was putting up the curtain rods when I heard our dog growl. I glanced out the window; a large shiny car was coming up our lane.

Curious, I said, "Myron, there is a big car driving up to our house. I believe it is a Cadillac. Who do you know who drives one?"

By now, Myron was at the window. "Oh, that's Matt Tschirgi. What do you suppose he wants?" Myron hurried out to greet him. When they came to the house, I was pleased to meet this livestock baron. Before this, I'd only had a fleeting glimpse of him.

We made ourselves comfortable in our unsettled living room and made small talk, but Matt surprised us when he asked if we were interested in staying in the sheep business.

Myron answered the question. "Well, I can't think of anything I'd rather do, but I haven't gotten around to see about range or financing yet. I felt I'd better get the family settled first."

Matt leaned back in his chair. Crossing his arms across his chest, he said, "Well I guess you know Ned Randough and Ken McCaughn have been in the sheep business and have been leasing range from me. Now they want to sell out, so I decided to see if you'd be interested in buying their band of 1,200 head of good three year old ewes at a good price."

Myron perked up and they began talking price. "The way things are, we'll have to get financing, because the only money we have right now could barely make a down payment."

Matt seemed pleased and grinned. "I have an interest in the Wyola Bank. They'll loan you enough money for running expenses. I can let you have range for your sheep. Of course I'll expect you to pay the going rate. Anyway, as long as you are interested, come on up to the ranch, and we'll fix up the agreement, and everything else will work out okay."

The offer was almost too good to be true. After Matt left, Myron and I kept talking it over and over. We were walking on air. Next morning, Myron went right to the bank and on up to the Tschirgi Ranch to close the deal.

The grass Matt let Myron lease was on Squaw Creek, Onion Creek and Brush Coulee which is located near Crow Agency. We were pleased, because when Myron tended his camp, most of his travel was on the highway. He gave his sheep the best of care and they came through the winter in good shape.

LOSS AND SADNESS

On March 14, 1940, our third child was born. She was a pretty, blond-haired baby girl with blue eyes, and we named her Marlene Sharon. She lived only one and a half hours because she had a breathing problem. Both Myron and I went through a very bad time. The doctor wouldn't let me out of bed to go to the funeral, so Myron had to make all the funeral arrangements. Fortunately, Pat Woodard, a very dear friend, went with Myron to buy the baby a pretty dress for the funeral. I don't think she ever knew how much she was appreciated for all the kindness she showed us through the years.

On the day of the funeral, families from Hardin and Lodge Grass came. I felt so helpless, because all I could do during the funeral was stay in my hospital bed and cry. After it was over, the families came to the hospital and shared my tears.

In the maternity ward, I found it agonizing to hear the babies cry, especially at feeding time when the nurses brought the mothers their babies. It was a happy time for them, but for me it meant tears. I asked the doctor if I could be moved to another floor, because I thought it would be a little easier. It was, but I still grieved, shed buckets of tears, and wondered, "Why me?"

On second floor, I was put in a ward of four beds, but I was the only one there. I was thankful, because I could have a good cry and not be heard. I also was able to talk to God, trying to understand why this had happened to me and what He wanted of me. It seemed the only answer was to go home and be the best mother I could to our other children.

Just after I had come to that conclusion, a young girl, only sixteen years old, was brought in. Her mother had died when she was quite young, and she was raised by her father on a ranch. She had met a boy, eighteen years old, and they married and moved in with his father because he'd lost his mother too. Now she was six months pregnant and had just gone through an appendectomy. She was scared about her baby and knew little about the facts of life. Truly, she was in need of a woman to talk to.

She asked me many questions about many things, and often we talked into the night. This was good for me, because I now had her problems to think about. I answered as patiently and honestly as I could. She absorbed every word and let me know how appreciative she was of every bit of knowledge I was able to pass on.

The 10th of April was lambing time, and I was still quite despondent. Myron hated to leave me at the ranch alone, so we decided it best for me to go out to lambing camp with him. Christine wasn't quite four years old and she would go with us. Stan would stay with Myron's family as he was in school and was happy with his friends. We felt he wouldn't miss us too much.

We'd be lambing on Nest Creek. There were no buildings so we'd have to use a sheep wagon to cook and live in. It would be confining, but at least I could sit down to do my work. The men slept in a tent and range tepees.

Myron felt he needed shelter for ewes lambing, so he improvised by setting posts on the range and used wire to tie the wooden sheep panels against them. In this way, he formed ten small pens, each just large enough for a ewe and her lamb. Then he put tar paper over the pens, providing a comfortable shelter at little expense. The sheep corral was built of posts and woven wire. This proved to be an efficient lambing camp and could easily be moved off the range as soon as lambing was over. In a short time, there would be no evidence of a camp ever having been there. Lambing was going well and we were fortunate in having two of the lambing hands that had worked for us at Willcutt's.

The day was beautiful. The men were out to the bunches herding them, and Myron was working with the ewes in the improvised shed, making sure they had accepted their lambs before he turned them out.

Suddenly, he looked up and saw a beautiful shiny car driving towards our camp. He called to me in the wagon. "Ellie, company is coming." We watched, wondering who it could be. Out in the hills you seldom see a car, only pickups. As it came closer, Myron said, "Well, I'll be darned. That is Matt Tschirgi and his wife, Bertha!"

Myron greeted them. We asked them in the wagon and found they hadn't had lunch, so I prepared them a quick meal. As they ate we sat and chatted with them. After they'd finished eating, Myron said, "You haven't seen my lambing outfit so come out and see my shed and corral."

They looked everything over. Matt said, "You've got a good range set up and your sheep are in darn good shape for lambing. They have plenty of milk and those lambs are strong and healthy. Man, you've sure got a lot of twins." Both of them chuckled as they watched the lambs run and jump.

This was music to our ears, but Matt went on. "I've been observing your sheep, and I like the way you are handling this 1,200 head of ewes. Would you be interested in a 'partnership' with me? I'd like to buy 3,500 head of yearling ewes."

A big grin spread across Myron's face. That was what he wanted, but he hadn't expected it so soon. Matt had three other partners, Henry Esp, Svere Berland and Bill Prante. They were happy with their sheep companies, and now we could have one too.

All of our crew was happy to have lambing over, but no one was as happy as young Donnie Doherty who had just turned eighteen. He was a good hand with sheep, having grown up with his father's sheep. A likable and conscientious boy, we'd have liked to have kept him with our outfit, but he'd made it plain that he would only work through lambing. When he came to the wagon to get his check, he was elated because he was off to join the Navy. Now he had enough money to see him through. Donnie's big dream was to complete basic training and be assigned to duty aboard the USS Arizona with his brother who had been writing about how much he enjoyed life aboard ship. We felt sad; he was of small stature and so pitifully young he looked like a school boy.

I was tired when lambing was over, but cheered to learn that all the Tschirgi partners took their sheep to the shearing pens on Shoulder Blade Creek and hired a man cook. That meant none of the women had to worry about cooking for a shearing crew.

The other partners had leased grass on top of the Big Horn Mountains for the summer, and they'd be taking their sheep there as soon as they were sheared. Myron was disappointed, because he couldn't take his sheep to the mountain, but Matt said he could run his sheep on the Flat Iron range. It was good range, but our lambs probably wouldn't be as heavy as the mountain lambs.

When fall came, all the partners sold their lambs to the same lamb buyer. Everyone was surprised when Myron's lambs weighed nearly as much as the mountain lambs—and we hadn't suffered the losses they had.

There was a lot of camaraderie around the stockyards as the men weighed their lambs and received their checks. Then one by one they left. As Myron and his men were about to leave, they realized the lamb buyer didn't have all the lambs loaded in the stock cars, and there were many things still to be done before he could leave. Myron's crew stayed and helped until everything was finished. It was after dark when the engine came to hook onto the stock car, but all was ready and Myron and his men came home to their supper.

Thirty years later, we met up with the lamb buyer, and he talked on and on about how he appreciated Myron and his men staying to help, and he repeated how pitch black the night was. We were impressed with how many years the man remembered that good deed.

Myron still had the farming leases and put up quite a lot of hay which he usually sold. That fall, Matt let us have the Nest Creek range for our permanent range. We were very pleased because it was nearer to Lodge Grass, but there were no sheds for lambing. Myron talked with his friend John at the sawmill on the Wolf Mountains, who he said he'd like to trade lumber for hay. It took a lot of hay for his work horses, and he needed his horses badly to snake out the trees.

Two carpenters were hired to build the sheds at Nest Creek, and they managed to get the sheds finished before the snow and cold weather set in.

Our lives were busy with friends and community: we were enjoying our home, we were attending church, Stan was in Scouts, I belonged to a club, and we had lots of company.

Early in 1941, Myron was concerned because he needed to get the cookshack and bunkhouse finished even if the weather was bad. Lambing time would be here before we knew it. Finally it was decided to have the lumber hauled and stacked just off the highway on the other side of the railroad tracks. There, the carpenters built the cook house and bunkhouse on skids. When they were finished, Myron borrowed a Caterpillar tractor, hooked onto one at a time and dragged them out to Nest Creek range. We were prepared for lambing season.

The Randough ewes were bred to lamb in March. We surely welcomed the beautiful weather we were having, even though we'd be lambing them at the ranch. I was happy to get to do the cooking in my own kitchen, and Stan was with us, riding the bus to school.

Everything went well, and we were able to take the ewes and lambs to the Nest Creek range. The yearlings were to start lambing in April, and we were getting ready to move to the cookshack. The crew had already moved out with the sheep, planning to batch for a day or two until we could get there, when a terrible snow storm hit. It was impossible to drive out with the pickup, so Myron again borrowed the Caterpillar tractor, hooked it to the pickup which we'd loaded with groceries, and pulled four-year-old Christine and me out there.

The men were very glad when we showed up, because they were having all kinds of trouble. The yearlings ewes began lambing heavily. The snow was rather fluffy, so when a young, inexperienced ewe dropped her warm lamb, it would just melt down into the snow—and she would run off. Others couldn't see or smell their lambs and ran around looking for them. Much confusion and commotion resulted.

When Myron and I got to the cookhouse, he quickly started a fire in the big old cook stove. One of the men helped Myron unload our beds and all the groceries. I hurried to get everything in order so I could start dinner, but first I fixed a pan of soapy water and wiped off the cupboards and table. Then I cooked the men a good dinner which truly was appreciated. Being so busy with the sheep, they hadn't had time to cook meals for themselves.

It was impossible to get around with the pickup, so everyone had to ride horses. But if a ewe was having trouble, there was no way to haul her to the shed. Myron said, "I guess the only thing to do is ride over to Charlie Long's ranch, and see if he can loan me a wagon and team."

When he got there and told Charlie his problem, Charlie said, "The best I have for that kind of situation is my team of mules and my buggy." Soon Myron came riding into camp in the buggy, driving the team of mules, his saddle horse tied behind. I wished I could have taken a picture of him, but I'd left home in such a hurry I'd forgotten my camera.

That team of mules was a god-send. They really helped us through a difficult time. Soon the snow melted and the mud dried up enough for Myron to take the mules back.

Now we were having beautiful weather; the sun was shining and the grass was getting green. I enjoyed watching the birds making their nests and wild flowers were everywhere. We saw baby skunks, a baby badger and a baby coyote. And there were baby puppies, plus the many, many baby lambs. Yes, Spring was surely here.

Four-year-old Christine was happy, as she no longer had to be cooped up in the cookhouse. Now she could ride in the pickup with her dad and be around the sheep and the men caring for them.

One day, Myron found a ewe having trouble giving birth to her lamb. He jumped out of the pickup, leaving Christine there. He had hold of the lamb and was gently tugging when he became aware of his little girl standing just back of him, very concerned. "Daddy, how'd he get in there? Daddy, how'd he get in there?"

The confused Myron didn't know what to say, but answered, "Go ask your mother."

She wasn't going to wait that long. She had figured it out. "I guess he just fell in."

After shearing that year, Myron could take his sheep to his lease on the mountain. He loved the mountain. His sheep could have greener pasture and much cooler air. There was the fresh running water and snow they liked to nibble on. Also, there was the huge array of wild flowers, a real delicacy to them.

Often, when Myron went up to tend the camps, the children and I went along. We'd all get so hungry in that mountain air that it was great fun to climb in a cozy sheep wagon, drink some of the herder's coffee and have some kind of lunch. Often it was just bread and butter and strawberry jam, but oh, how good it tasted.

When Myron was getting wood for the herders, we'd all join in and help in whatever way we could. One of the herders wanted wood that he could split. There was some down timber, so Myron brought a big cross-cut saw. As the herder wasn't near by Myron said, "Ellie, you grab the other end of the saw and sorta help guide it." We sawed quite a pile of wood.

While we were sawing, Svere Berland, one of the sheep partners, happened to come by. He got out of his pickup, stood there and laughed and laughed. "You sure got things worked out," he said to Myron. "Now your wife has to cut the wood. What kind of work you got the kids doing?"

On each trip we made up the mountain, the children were eager to see the wildlife. We saw deer, elk, bear and buffalo.

One time, some of our sheep got mixed with some of Henry Esp's. Myron and I left the children with family, because we knew we'd be gone all night in order to sort the sheep early in the morning. We stayed in a sheep wagon, and when Myron got up to start the fire so we could get breakfast, he quietly said, "Ellie, look out the window." I looked, and bedded all around the wagon was a bunch of buffalo who had spent the night there. It truly was a beautiful sight. We just stood there and watched the buffalo, until they got up and went away.

24
WAR BREAKS OUT

◆

It was a beautiful fall, but a busy one for Myron. He brought the sheep down off the mountain, cut off the lambs and shipped them. Each of the herders wanted a vacation before winter set in which meant bringing out relief herders—and that accounted for several trips to Billings. Because of his busy schedule, he decided to cut and stack the alfalfa seed and thrash it at a later time.

The first part of December, we had a spell of good weather. Myron gathered a crew of men, and they began thrashing the seed from the stacks. Of course, I was cooking for the crew. While I was busy in the kitchen, I had our battery powered radio turned on to get the news. Suddenly over the radio an excited voice announced, "The Japanese attacked Pearl Harbor." I was stunned. I stood rooted to the floor, listening carefully.

Soon the men came hurrying home. A friend passing by was sure they hadn't heard the news, so stopped at the thrashing machine to tell them of the attack. They quickly shut the machine down and hurried home to listen to the news. They sat around, listening to every word; it was a sobering experience. When announcers talked of the USS Arizona being sunk with all men aboard, we thought of Donnie Doherty who had worked for us and had become almost like family. Both he and his brother were good boys and so young. Then we began to think of all the other families we knew who had lost sons at Pearl Harbor, and each man began to think about what he could do to help the war effort. At meal time there was no bantering or joking. Everyone was listening to the radio.

Soon men began leaving Lodge Grass. Young men were enlisting and older men and their wives were going to the coast to work in defense plants. There was a shortage of teachers, and many elderly, retired teachers began teaching again.

Everyone's conversation was "WAR." Every sheep herder had a battery powered radio and listened carefully to the news. Often, they informed Myron of news he hadn't heard. Rationing caused us problems. When the herders went to town, they would trade a bartender or a lady-of-the-evening their sugar stamps or sometimes their shoe stamps. Back at camp, they'd complain about not being able to live without sugar or to herd sheep without sturdy shoes. Myron would have to find a way to get the needed item, or whichever herder was complaining would quit. They had the boss in a difficult spot. However, older men who'd been good hands often asked for jobs.

The day Bill Gardner asked for a job herding sheep, Myron thought he was joking. Bill was a long time friend of the Lynde family and had been and still was a good cowboy. He had lost a leg, yet no horse was too difficult for him to ride. He was tough enough that no man was willing to challenge him, yet he was a very gentle man. Ladies and children appreciated his kindness.

In Lodge Grass, he had met a fine lady, and they had a good marriage. He bought the old livery barn and used part of it for a garage and also delivered bulk gas to the service stations. Virgie, his wife, took in lady boarders who were mostly teachers. Bill's kindness and fatherly advice made them feel at home.

No one had any idea how much Bill longed for the wide open spaces of the range until he asked Myron for a job. Myron wondered if he was serious. When he asked Virgie about it, she smiled. "Yes, he'd really like a job with you. I'd be pleased as I know you'd look out for him."

Bill was good with livestock and very dependable. The war caused a real shortage of "good" men, and Myron was thankful that Bill could start work lambing. As soon as he hired on, Myron took him to the bunch of sheep he'd be herding and to the wagon that would be his home. He gave Bill a brown pinto horse called Prunes and a young brown and white spotted dog called Chief. They got along well and Bill was content. Virgie baked him good things to eat and brought them out to his camp when she visited him.

Later in the spring, Myron was going out to tend his camps. He stopped at Virgie's to see if she had mail or anything she wanted to send to Bill. She said, "Yes. I want you to take out his clean laundry and this cake I baked him." However, when Myron got to Bill's camp, he couldn't find him or his sheep. He stopped at Bill's wagon to leave the groceries he'd ordered, his clean laundry and his cake.

When he climbed into Bill's wagon, he noticed the clock had stopped. Myron wondered about that. Herders always kept their clocks wound. Then he realized the wagon was cold. He felt the stove; it was cold which meant that Bill hadn't cooked breakfast. It had rained the day before but there were no muddy tracks around the wagon and it was very clean inside.

Now Myron was concerned. He wasn't sure what direction Bill had taken, but he got in the pickup and started out. As he drove up on a hill, he could see Bill's dog, Chief, about a mile away sitting on another hill. He was sure Bill would be right there because the dog wouldn't have left him. Myron drove over as quickly as he could. There Bill was, stretched out on the ground in his yellow slicker.

When Myron stopped the pickup, Chief came right over to him as if he wanted help. There was a wind and Bill's slicker was flopping. For a moment Myron thought Bill was alive, but when he squatted down and felt his cheek, it was cold. There was no pulse. Bill was dead and Myron had to hurry to town to report it.

All the way he worried how to tell Virgie. He saw her minister walking up the street and asked him to help break the news but there was no need. When Myron stopped at her home and carried Bill's laundry and cake in with him, Virgie said, "Myron, when I saw you come back with the things I sent out to camp I knew Bill was gone. I am so grateful that his last days were the life he'd longed for."

The war news was not good. There was a certain restlessness among those left at home, and even Myron was talking of joining the Army. When Matt heard about it, he came right over to see Myron and give him a talking to. He said, "Myron, now more than ever our country needs wool. Every soldier, sailor and marine needs to be outfitted with wool. It takes the wool off of at least 20 head of sheep to outfit one man. You'll be more help to the war effort if you stay here and grow meat and wool. You know these younger men can carry guns just as well as you can and maybe better, but how many men do you know that could run a sheep outfit as well as you can, or even has the opportunity?"

When we lambed at our camp on Nest Creek, the weather was beautiful so all went well. Now the sheep were on the cool mountain, but without rain, the range grass was dry. Everyone was concerned about range fires, which meant men were needed to plow fire guards. Most of the men who could drive a Caterpillar tractor had gone to the service or to the Sea-Bees and were overseas or in Alaska building roads, or involved in some other war effort.

Again, Matt came to Myron. "This country is so damn dry, a spark could burn up the whole country, and there are hardly enough men to fight a fire. The mechanic at the ranch said that he would plow the day shift, and he has a man who will handle the grader. Will you take the night shift and pick up a man for the grader?"

Myron pushed his hat on the back of his head and looked off in the distance. "Well, I can but I'll have to find a man to tend my sheep camps on the mountain." All the time, he was wondering where in the world he could find a good reliable man who could be responsible enough to leave up on the mountain without a vehicle to drive. He would have to know how to drive a four horse team, which was needed to move the wagons up some of those steep mountain trails.

Just when he was most concerned, a man came looking for Myron. He truly was an answer to prayer. He was a bachelor about Myron's age, very capable of any task set before him. Sid Harvey had worked for different outfits and certainly knew about horses and sheep. He was good at shoeing horses, which was badly needed on those rocky mountain trails.

Now Myron had to find someone who could handle a grader. He located a young Indian boy about sixteen who wanted a job. Johnny Sun Goes Slow was a good worker and very smart. Myron explained the working of a grader which Johnny caught easily. While they were on the flat land, he did fine and he could even handle most hills. All seemed to go okay, but when Myron started up an incline that was steeper than he realized. Johnny got excited and put the grader in the ground too deep, which stalled the tractor. There was nothing to hold the Caterpillar tractor back until Myron could crank it again, so both started to roll down the steep hill.

Myron hollered, "Jump, Johnny, jump!" They both jumped and watched the outfit roll down into a gully. Once he realized that they were both okay, Myron's thoughts turned to the awful damage that probably had been done and how nearly impossible it was to get new parts. Machinery companies were building tanks and other machinery for fighting the war.

Quickly the two men climbed down into the steep gully. Anxiously and carefully Myron looked over the Caterpillar and surprisingly no harm had been done, but the grader stood at a strange angle. Johnny said, "Hey, Myron! All that got broke was that big iron tongue that hooks it to the cat."

Relieved, Myron said, "Man, oh man!. We are two lucky guys. No one hurt and our outfit escaped real damage, but now I guess we've got a long walk back to the pickup."

They hadn't gotten far when they looked up and saw Bill Prante slowly driving along side of the plowed furrow. He was bringing gas to them. He greeted them and said, "When I didn't see you guys up on that high divide where I thought you'd be, I just followed the furrow and knew that I'd find you at the end of it."

Myron took Prante to the trouble spot and explained what happened. "All that broke was that thick iron tongue and it can be welded."

Bill had been scared looking for them. Greatly relieved, he began to laugh. "By golly, Hitler never heard of you or he'd give you a pair of pliers and send you out to wreck the whole British Navy!" He laughed at his joke, but Myron couldn't appreciate Bill's humor.

When the fire guards were finished, Myron hurried up the mountain with groceries, kerosene and any supplies the herders might need. He was quite concerned, because there often were problems between the herders and the camp tender. But Sid had a problem he hadn't expected: "Joyce, the older one of the black team, dropped dead of a heart attack so instead of the four horse team I had only three horses. I took it upon myself to ride over to the Tschirgi roundup wagon where they were branding calves and talked to Frank Greenough, their foreman, and told him my troubles. He said he could let me have a bronc as they didn't have anything gentle, so now I'm breaking him to work."

Feeling thankful that Sid had gotten along okay, Myron went to talk to the herders. Each one had some gripes, but they were getting the war news. They were patriotic and willing to do what they could to get the war over with.

One herder named Fred was from Scotland and had fought in World War I. Myron asked him, "Are you getting the war news on your radio?"

"You bet I am," he said. "That Hitler, he's crazy. He don't even make sense."

Myron asked, "Oh, what's that all about? I haven't heard the latest news."

Fred sat on the bench in the sheep wagon, pouring tobacco in his pipe and packing it down; he lit it, puffed on it until he got it going, and finally answered. "Well, its bad enough the way them Germans have been bombing in England, but they didn't have to bomb Scotland."

Shaking his head as he poked a stick of wood in the stove, he continued. "Now they've done it—the very worst. I tell ya boy, 'twas the worst."

Myron was really concerned. "What happened, Fred? Did some of your family get killed or suffer serious damage?"

Again he was shaking his head. "Yea, boy, 'twas awful and I don't know what to do about it." He paused to relight his pipe and gave it a few more puffs. Then, with much bitter hatred, he said, "Twas sad," and he shook his head again. "They bombed my oatmeal mine."

It took Myron a second to realize what he said; then he caught onto the joke and they both began to laugh.

25

MOVE SHEEP TO WEST SIDE OF BIG HORN RIVER

◆

It was almost time to bring the sheep down from the mountain, when Matt came to Myron and asked, "How would you like to run your sheep on the west side of the Big Horn River with your headquarters on Beauvais Creek? Right now we have only our cows in all that country."

Myron gave it some thought. "Yes, that is damn good sheep country. I liked it when I was working for Willcutt and Warren, but I understand your daughter and her husband Bob have their sheep on part of it."

Matt pulled his hat a bit lower. "Yea, I know. But if you'll take that range, you can run as many sheep as you want. I'll bring my family to my ranch in Wyola. There the children can ride the bus to school, and they can run their sheep on the Nest Creek range. Bob isn't a livestock man. I may have them sell their sheep and buy cows that can be run with mine. How about it? Will you take it?"

"It sounds good to me," Myron said, "but I'll have to talk it over with my wife."

Eagerly Myron told me all about his conversation with Matt. I listened carefully and appreciated his enthusiasm, but the offer threw me into a real gloom. "I know it is a great opportunity, but I want to live where the kids can stay at home while they are going to school. Christine starts school this fall."

To him this was an opportunity of a lifetime, and he wasn't going to let it slip away. "You and the kids can stay here while I go back and forth. Sid Harvey will stay over there with the sheep and be our camp tender."

Frowning, because I didn't like to see the family broken up and couldn't see how it would work, I said, "If I stay, what will you do for a cook?"

He grinned. "I've thought about that, too. I'm sure I can hire a man cook."

I still had my doubts, especially with the shortage of hired help, but he was enthused. "I know you want this range, and I know our country needs what the sheep can produce. Let's pray about it for a day or two," I suggested.

He agreed with me, but added, "Matt wants to know as soon as possible."

We were praying about it, but our conversation and our thoughts were on that big roomy country: the beautiful loneliness of it; the advantage of sagebrush for livestock and the smell of it; the bitterroots, sago lilies, the blooming cactus and other wild flowers. We felt close to nature out there.

I brought up the violent way the wind blew out there, but he quickly answered that objection. "Yes, but that's what makes it a good livestock country. The wind blows the snow off the grass, so you don't have to feed so much hay."

It wasn't long before we'd convinced ourselves that the move to Beauvais was what we wanted to do.

At the foot of the mountain, Myron cut the lambs off the ewes and hauled them to the stockyards to be shipped. The herders with the ewes took them the shortest way to the Big Horn River, so they could cross on the Two Leggin Bridge. Sid brought the horses and trap wagon to our ranch on Lodge Grass Creek.

Early next morning, right after breakfast, Sid hitched the four horse team to the new sheep wagon, which was well supplied with groceries. The wagon would be his home in the Beauvais country. Right behind the sheep wagon was hooked the trap wagon; Sid's saddle horse was tied behind.

I went out and said, "Well Sid, have a good trip. We'll be seeing you out to Beauvais." As Myron and I stood there watching him leave, we both had a real nostalgic feeling as he went down the lane and on up Lodge Grass Creek Road.

"That is a sight we probably will never see again," Myron remarked. "Few men know how to hitch up a team, let alone drive a four horse team." We continued to watch until he was out of sight.

The next day, Matt and Myron drove over to the Beauvais country, so Matt could show him boundary lines of the range he was to have. There was a big sheep shed, shearing pens, a large wool shed and a cookhouse on Beauvais Creek. Where Buster Creek runs into Beauvais was the Cashen Ranch which would be our headquarters. The log house had four rooms, but they were large, and the kitchen had a sink with hot and cold running water. There was a big log barn and a large cellar, a blacksmith shop and a bunkhouse. Once it had been a fine ranch, but now it was old and neglected. The apple trees hadn't been cared for but still produced a few apples.

Myron was anxious to get started on the Beauvais Ranch right away, but the other folks weren't moved off yet. For now, he would have to set his sheep headquarters on Big Woody Creek near the reservoir. Our company was to be called the Beauvais Sheep Company.

When Sid got to the reservoir he parked his wagons, and he and Myron went to work building a corral for his horses. Myron bought a big used army hospital tent to store enough sheep cake for the winter. We hired a trucker to haul hay and oats from the Lodge Grass Ranch for the horses.

Both men were proud of their camp. Here Sid would spend the winter and Myron would be bringing groceries and mail when he'd check the herders and the sheep to see that all were okay. Myron had never been so happy, and the herders were also in good spirits. They now had plenty of room for their sheep, and the sheep were doing very well in the Farming Corporation stubble fields. Eating the wheat heads that were scattered about caused them to produce more twin lambs and grow better wool.

At lambing time, Myron had to spend all of his time on Beauvais except for coming after the mail, groceries and other supplies. I enjoyed the quietness with just the children, but we did miss Myron. I also missed doing the cooking and being part of the lambing crew. However, pregnant now with our fourth child, I was glad I didn't have to cook for them, because I really didn't feel up to it.

Myron had hired Harry Sharp who had been a roundup cook for different cow outfits. He was getting up in years, so didn't want to go out on the roundup, but said he would cook for the lambing crew in the cook shack.

That spring we had a very good lambing. The only calamity was when Beauvais Creek flooded the cook shack and the bed tents. Fortunately Myron had purchased used Army hospital cots, so the crew's beds didn't get wet, because they were high off the ground.

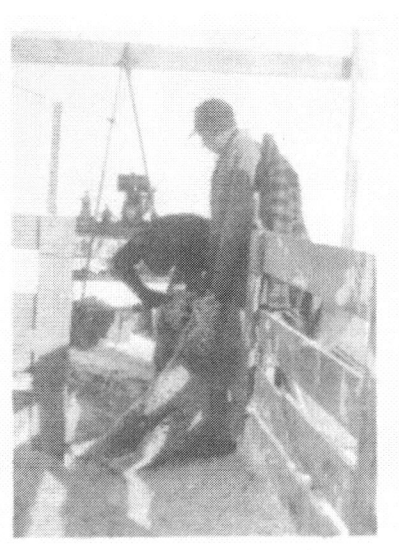

When our young men were busy fighting the war, Mexicans came and helped with the shearing.

26
STORM AT SHEARING TIME

◆

When school was out, Myron came after the children and me. The ranch house was vacant by then, and we could stay there. It was only a mile from the shearing pen and cook shack, so the drive back and forth would be easy.

We were thankful that we could get the Jess Portor shearing crew, because they were top shearers who sheared their way from Texas to Montana. At that time a good shearer could shear 150 head a day, but Jess was a top shearer who could shear 220 head a day.

June 2nd was a balmy day, and we were all pleased to see the Jess Portor shearing crew arrive. There was bantering and joking as we greeted each other. The Portors were a nice family. There was Mr. and Mrs. Portor, three of their sons, and the other shearers who were just like family. It was a large crew of twelve shearers, and they brought their families in campers, tents and trailers which made our lambing camp look like a village.

Right after they arrived, they went to the shearing shed to set up their hangers and sharpen their cutters and combs so they would be ready to start at 8:00 AM. This could be easily done with a large sheep shed. The sheep were put in the shed overnight, so their wool was protected from the early morning dew.

We were glad to be first on Portor's list, as we were anxious to get the sheep up on Little Mountain where the fresh grass was covered with wild spring flowers. But more importantly, we were having this exceptionally nice weather. When it rained, we couldn't shear, and 45 miles of gumbo roads were impossible to travel. Everyone got restless and despondent. The cook in particular got grouchy, because he was the only one who had to work.

There was a great shortage of labor, so many men having gone to war. Myron was concerned, as we always needed eight or ten extra men, called wranglers, who would keep enough sheep ready for the shearers. Then he learned that Mexican Nationalists were brought into Hardin to hoe beets for the beet farmers. There were extra men, so Myron hired three of them. These men had never worked with sheep, but they were willing workers, and Myron felt they could learn. Only one spoke limited English and he interpreted for the others.

Coming from a warm climate, these young men from Mexico weren't dressed warmly enough and had only sandals. We'd have liked to have bought them sturdy work shoes, but with rationing we couldn't. God willing, the nice weather would hold.

The first day everything went well; the shearers got one band of sheep sheared by noon. They sheared the second band in the afternoon and shut down at 5:00 PM. When Jess Portor was putting on his jacket he said, "Myron, you've got a beautiful set of two year old ewes there, but never in my life have I seen any sheep fight like they did when we were shearing them." The two men stood there chatting, wondering why those ewes should fight worse than other sheep.

At 6:00 PM, when the shearers came in to eat their supper, they remarked about the weather having turned colder. We wondered what was coming. (This was before weather reports on the radio.)

Soon a big black cloud came over the ridge. It looked bad. Then a violent, driving, freezing rain lashed at men and animals alike. The men hurried for slickers and shelter and the frightened freshly shorn ewes ran. The lambs ran after them, bleating for their mothers, following as best they could.

Myron and the herders knew they were in for real trouble. Myron called to the herder, "Bill, put your sheep in the shed." Quickly he put his 1,200 head of ewes and lambs in the shed, filling the shed to its very limit.

Through the driving wind and sleet Myron shouted, "Alex, you keep your sheep moving. As soon as Bill's sheep warm up a while, I'll have him bring them out and put yours in the shed. We'll keep rotating them until the storm is over."

However, when it was time to put Alex's sheep in, Bill's sheep would not go out the door. The men and dogs worked hard trying everything they could think of to get them to move, but always they balked at the door. Some of the men tried to man-handle the sheep, but when they did they'd fight so hard they'd get away and run back to the wall of sheep standing at the door and plunge until they got in.

Icy rain continued to blow and Alex's cold ewes began to die from shock. They developed a high fever and died. The men tried covering the shivering sheep with hay for warmth; still they died. They tried making a shelter of the dead sheep for the ones who were yet alive, but they died too. Nothing anyone could think of helped.

The crew and shearers worked all night; the cook was also out there. Everyone was doing what they could in the cold and slush. In the cookhouse, I kept the coffee pot hot and chili on the back of the stove in case anyone wanted it, but food was far from their thoughts.

When morning came the men could see the devastation. Twelve hundred head of ewes were dead. There were tears of compassion. The ewes were lying in their natural position with lambs snuggling close, wondering why their mothers didn't nuzzle them. Hungry lambs, bleating pitifully, wondered why their mothers didn't rise so they could suck.

It was losses like these which inspired the shearers to invent combs that left more wool on the sheep. Now they can be shorn much earlier.

That morning I cooked breakfast; the men came in and ate a very quiet meal. It had been a terrible night for everyone, but it was worse for Myron, as it had been his decision to shear at that time. He wasn't much comforted by what everyone told him. "No one could have known we'd have that kind of storm the first of June. We'd been having such beautiful weather!"

Myron had many more decisions to make. The 1,200 ewes had to be buried, but what about 1,400 lambs that couldn't live without their mothers? Now they needed bottle milk substitute. As soon as the other sheep dried off, they still had to be sheared. The most important thing to do now was for Myron to report this to his partner Matt Tschirgi.

In the morning, without sleep, Myron issued orders to his men. The road was muddy, but he felt he could make it to the gravel of the St. Xavier Highway. He took a pickup load of lambs with him, stopping at ranchers who had asked for bum lambs and telling them to pass the word.

When he reached Hardin, he contacted Father Owens and told him of his trouble. "If the St. Xavier School has ever thought of going into the sheep business now is the time." Father Owens liked the idea.

When Myron called Matt he said, "I'll meet you in Hardin as soon as I can get there." While he waited for Matt, Myron worried about what he would say about the horrendous loss.

Upon Matt's arrival they shook hands and Myron got in the car with him. Then he began giving Matt all the details of what had happened, fully expecting him to say he no longer wanted him for a partner. Matt sat and listened. He wasn't critical of Myron nor did he make any suggestions.

Myron could stand it no longer, "Well, Matt. What do you want me to do?"

Matt looked surprised and he turned to look at Myron. "Well, the only thing to do is to buy more sheep to make up your loss."

We expected lots of people who had milk cows to come after the motherless lambs, but nobody braved the muddy roads except a truck load of boys from the St. Xavier Mission School. They did a lot of pushing and shoveling, but they got there. It was a good feeling to see those boys leave with a truck load of lambs and know they would take good care of them.

On their next trip, the road was drier and they had less trouble. The boys got about 100 head of mighty good lambs which started their own bunch of sheep at the school.

As in all tragedies there were beautiful rays that shone through our gloom. Many people, some we didn't even know, offered sympathy and came to let us know they too had suffered much the same kind of tragedy.

One extremely wealthy man told us that, when he was struggling to make a living, he had five bands of sheep and had just gotten them to his mountain range. It was about the first of July when the same kind of storm hit his sheep and all of them died. In one night, he was out of the sheep business, and he still owed money on the dead ones. "All there was to do was start over."

We felt cheered as we walked away from our visit with him. If he came out of a loss like that, then we could too. At least we'd give it a good try.

27
OUR MOVE TO THE CITY

◆

After taking over the cooking during the storm, I continued to cook, as Harry didn't want to. The shearers finished and moved on to their next job, and Sid got the sheep moved up on the mountains. The crew got all of the dead sheep buried and everything cleaned up around the sheds. The groceries were moved to the Beauvais Ranch, where the couple who would be cooking for the haying crew would now take over.

Myron took us into town because it was time for my prenatal check up. The doctor seemed concerned. "Although the baby seems fine, it's low for six and a half months of pregnancy. You say that you have the feeling that you might miscarry? You say you have had difficulty walking? I don't like the sound of that. I think you should move into town where you'll be near a doctor and hospital. You have three more months to go, too."

We rented a furnished house in Billings and Myron went back and forth to the ranch and sheep. I missed the ranch, but the 45 miles of rough roads was out. The children and I settled down to city living, and they quickly became acquainted with the youngsters in the neighborhood. They began attending Sunday School. On Saturdays, the neighbor kids would walk as a group to see a matinee. Movie afternoon gave me time to get caught up on things I needed to do.

Myron came to Billings to buy the ranch groceries and run errands for the sheep herders. He always spent time with us, even though he generally was handling the work of two men. The war was still making it difficult to hire extra help.

I was enjoying the modern conveniences of our Billings rental—and having the mail delivered. I loved chatting on the telephone, renewing old acquaintances, and taking long walks on the city sidewalks, which gave me the opportunity to admire the city people's beautiful flowers. It was fun to walk downtown to shop, but if I got tired, I could catch a bus home.

Soon it was time for school. Stan would be going to Lincoln Junior High which was quite a distance. His friends planned to ride their bicycles, so Myron went to Lodge Grass to get Stan's bike. I made a list of things I wanted him to bring, to be sure the children would have everything they would need.

Stan loved his bike and was always willing to go on errands. One day I was out of change, so I wrote a check and asked him to go to the grocery store to get some cash. On his way home, he passed the filling station and decided to put some air in his tires. A short way down the street a front tire blew out. He got off and wheeled it on home, crushed because tires were hard to come by during war time.

He leaned his bike against the steps and was telling us what happened. We were feeling bad, because we knew how much the bike meant to him when suddenly we heard a loud explosion. We knew what it was and all rushed out. Sure enough, it was the other tire. Even though we were just sick about it, Myron and I burst out laughing and laughed so much that Stan got really disgusted. He couldn't see the humor. To us it was another example of a country boy moving to the city. Now he had learned about free air.

Myron tried to soothe Stan's hurt feelings. "Son, don't let it get you down. You couldn't have known how little air a bicycle tire takes. I'll look around and see if I can find you some tires."

There were none in Billings, but being ranchers, we got out the Montgomery Ward catalog. They had bicycle tires listed. Myron quickly made out an order and took it to the Post Office to mail, hoping to save time. We all began praying Wards would have the tires in stock, so Stan could have his bike before school started. In about a week they arrived. There was plenty of happiness in our little family. Myron and Stan loaded the bike in the pickup and took it to a bike shop to have the tires put on. Now his bike meant more than ever to him.

The day school started we had a wet slushy snow. We hadn't brought the children's overshoes so Myron had to take them to town in the pickup to get some. They were important because Christine had to walk five blocks to Broadwater School.

After she had been in school a brief time, her teacher sent a note asking me to come to school. She wanted to talk with me, which I thought was a bit unusual. I went at the appointed time, just after school, and the teacher showed me some of Christine's work. "I don't know what kind of teacher she had last year," she said. "She isn't at all ready for the second grade. However, she is a very good worker. If you will help her at home, I will work with her here, and in that way we can get her through the second grade."

I was surprised, as she had received good grades in the first grade. However, I was grateful that she now had a teacher who was willing to give her extra time and also glad she had the chance to attend school in Billings.

When it was time for me to go to the hospital, a teenage girl from Lodge Grass, Malena Berland, came to stay with the children. She was a dear and the children enjoyed her. The evening I was to go to the hospital, we had planned a birthday party for Stan, and we had invited all of his neighborhood friends.

He wanted a "watermelon birthday cake," the kind a roundup cook told us about. The batter was colored with red food coloring, had raisins for seeds, and was baked in a metal bowl to make it round. A rather thin white icing covered with a darker green icing made the finished product resemble a watermelon. The cake made quite a hit with Stan's friends.

Everyone was having a great time, when it was time for me to leave for the hospital. Malena took over, and Myron and I hurried off.

Our big strong baby boy was born September 24th. He had blond hair and blue eyes. We named him Casey Jonathan. Again, the ten day wait at the hospital seemed like eternity. When Myron took us home, I nursed the baby at 10:00 PM and put him to bed hoping he would sleep the night. I was weak and very tired. He dozed off and then woke up fussing. It made me nervous, as I didn't know what to do. He had been such a good baby at the hospital.

Finally Myron said, "I believe that baby is hungry."

"I've been nursing him at the hospital, and the nurses never said anything about feeding him extra when they'd take him back to the nursery."

However Casey kept fussing. Finally Myron said, "I don't care what they did or didn't do at the hospital, that is a hungry cry if I ever heard one. I'm going to see if I can find a drug store still open and buy him a bottle and nipple."

He found a drug store open, got the bottle and hurried home. When Myron got the bottle washed and scalded, he took canned milk and mixed it with half water, and we fed the baby. He took six ounces. I was afraid it might make him sick, but he went right to sleep and slept through the night. Next day I called the doctor, and he gave me a formula over the phone. From then on we found that the child was just a big eater.

When Halloween came, Stan's friends decided to go to the picture show, as they were having a special for Halloween. The boys weren't interested in costumes. Christine was invited to a neighbor girl's costume party, so we went to town and looked at the available outfits.

She didn't like any she saw. Finally I said, "Christine, there are a lot of costumes here. It looks like you could find something you wanted to wear."

She looked up at me, "No, Mother. I want to go as a nurse and there aren't any here my size." I could see that going as a nurse meant a lot to her and wondered why.

Then it began to dawn on me. She had been going to picture shows which showed news reels of war casualties with nurses taking care of them. So I said, "Okay, dear. If it means that much to you to go as a nurse, I think I can make a nurse's apron that can be worn over your blue dress. I'm sure I can get a cap done too."

The nurse's uniform and cap took priority over everything. I got them finished, embroidered the red cross on them, and starched them stiff. When ironed, they looked real trim. That night, when she got dressed to go to the party, she was a happy little girl. Just seeing her eyes sparkle made all the effort worthwhile. At the party, she won the prize for best costume. She came home so happy I didn't know who got the greatest thrill, her or me.

When school was out in the spring, we planned to move back to our ranch home on Lodge Grass Creek. Before we were ready to leave, I decided to get the children some clothes. Stan needed jeans, underwear and socks. Christine needed shoes again. She was so hard on them, we had real trouble making them last from ration stamp to ration stamp. As we were leaving town, I wanted to buy a pair ahead which seemed impossible until I remembered we had a ration book for Casey. He wouldn't need his shoe stamp. He could stay in booties until he was ready to walk, so we knew exactly what to do with his ration stamp.

It was a beautiful Saturday as the children and I walked to town. Casey was in his buggy, enjoying the ride as we strolled along. Soon we had our shopping done and started for home. The farther we went, the darker the sky became. A huge cloud hovered over the city. I said, "Kids, we're going to have to hurry. It's going to rain real soon, and we've got seven more blocks to go."

We walked as fast as we could and cut across every street where we could save a few steps. It began to rain huge drops. Quickly I pulled the rain cover over the buggy. The baby was dry but the rest of us were sopping wet and getting wetter as we hurried along.

Christine whimpered, "I wish Daddy would come." She seemed to feel he could perform miracles.

I answered, "Save your breath and hurry. You know he's out to the ranch and won't be home until next week. Let's just cut across this street."

We were starting across the street when a pickup drove up beside us. It was Myron. He happened to be several blocks up the street when he saw us. I took the baby from the buggy and we all climbed into the pickup and Myron put the buggy in the back. In no time, we were home getting into dry clothes.

In many ways I hated to leave Billings, but I loved our little ranch house on Lodge Grass Creek. Of course, I would have to do without the conveniences I'd been enjoying in town. We left Billings on a chilly, cloudy day. The weather mirrored my emotions, but I knew I mustn't look back, just toward the future.

We settled into our familiar ranch home, and it was almost as if we hadn't left. Coal, wood and water, filling lamps with oil, taking out the ashes—I was back to my routine. Even the muddy lane had to be accepted.

One day, when Stan had a sore throat, I decided to have him stay home from school. Christine bravely took her lunch bucket and started off for the school bus as I watched from the window. I was glad there was frost on the ground, so she could get to school without getting muddy.

That evening, I was again at the window when the bus stopped. Christine got off and started up the lane but stopped. I saw her set her lunch bucket down in the mud. I fretted, "What in heavens name is that kid doing fooling around in that awful mud?" As I watched, I became more annoyed. I stepped to the door and hollered, "Christine, quit fooling around and come on home."

I thought she answered, "I can't." More annoyed, I thought, "She could if she wanted to."' I slipped on my boots, grabbed my coat and hurried down the lane on the sod.

When I drew near, she looked up at me, half crying. "Mama, I just can't. I'm stuck."

I grabbed her under the arms so I could lift her to a grassy spot at the side of the lane. I couldn't budge her, so I said, "Hang on to me so we can free one foot at a time." That is the way we had to get her free, and it wasn't easy. Then I took her muddy hand and carried the muddy lunch bucket, and we trudged home on the sod by the side of the lane.

28

LIGHTNING AND ED PETERSON
(Story told by Myron)

◆

It was June and shearing was over. We were moving our sheep to the mountains. Sid Harvey, our camp tender, was pulling the wagons with the team. It was war time, so we only had one pickup to get back and forth for supplies. I was keeping my eyes on all of my men, the sheep and the Beauvais Ranch, spending time with my family on Lodge Grass Creek, and checking our crops that grew on the leases there.

I tried to visit my herders often. If they had a gripe, they could tell me, and I could straighten it out. In that way, their peeves wouldn't grow so big they caused problems which often led herders to quit.

After visiting the other camps, I stopped to visit Ed Peterson, partly to see what he wanted in the grocery line, but mainly to let him know I was going to Lodge Grass and would be gone for a few days. I always liked visiting with him. He was intelligent, knowledgeable and a fine herder. I told him how well I thought his sheep were doing, and he said he was anxious to get them on the fresh mountain feed. After the brief chat, I left his camp on Point Creek Falls and hurried toward home. It looked like rain, and I sure didn't want to get in any mud.

That afternoon there was a violent lightning and thunder storm with a heavy downpour of rain in the Point Creek country. Sid had intended to move Ed's camp first thing in the morning, but he thought they'd better wait for a day or so until it wasn't quite so muddy. He saddled up his horse and rode to Ed's camp to let him know about the change in plans. He didn't understand the eerie feeling that came over him as he neared Ed's wagon.

Sid didn't see Ed, but he could see the sheep with Ed's dog Chief herding them. Just before he got to the wagon, he saw Ed stretched out on the ground. He went to him and was shocked to see that Ed had been struck by lightning and was killed instantly. Sid then went to Prunes, Ed's horse, got Ed's slicker off the saddle and carefully tucked it around his friend. He unsaddled the horse, gave him his oats, and put the saddle under the wagon.

There were no cars at the ranch, and Sid knew that he had to get word to me about Ed's death. He rode his horse fast for the twenty miles down Fly Creek to the highway. He flagged the patrolman and told him what had happened and asked him to contact me in Lodge Grass. Then Sid rode back to be with Ed's body and take care of things at his camp, especially the sheep.

When the message reached me in Lodge Grass, I called Mr. Bullis, the coroner and undertaker. I told him I'd meet him in Hardin at 4:00 AM to show him the way to Point Creek. Going to a rugged country like that, Mr. Bullis always drove his pickup with a body basket strapped in back instead of the hearse.

We drove down the Billings highway until we reached the Fly Creek turn-off. We had twenty miles of muddy roads to cover. We took this trail because it was hilly and covered with sod, but there were bad places like creek crossings that we had to get through. With the heavy rain, the whole country was about as muddy as it could get. Every so often we got stuck, and because I was younger and it was my herder, I felt obligated to dig us out or push when the need arose. Often we had to jack up the pickup and put rocks, wood or brush under the wheels.

Mr. Bullis was unfamiliar with this country, but finally we reached Beauvais Creek and drove over to our shearing camp. George Yoeman's wagon was camped there, waiting to trail his band of sheep up the mountain. We climbed in his wagon and fixed lunch and cooked a pot of coffee. The food and rest felt good.

It was 3:30 when we finally reached Ed's camp. Sid saw us coming and was at the wagon when we arrived. The three of us somberly walked the hundred yards to where Ed's body lay carefully covered with the yellow slicker. I questioned why something like this had to happen to Ed out there, all by himself. He'd been such a fine person and loyal worker, and I wondered how his brother Tom would get along without him; Tom was unstable, and Ed always looked after him.

Mr. Bullis pulled the slicker off Ed's body. It was a shock to see what that huge bolt of lightning had done to this man. I wondered, if I had set his wagon in a different place, could this have been avoided? I finally decided it had to be an act of God. Only God could have prevented it from happening.

It was June and the death odor was bad. Mr. Bullis sprayed the body with formaldehyde, and then we put Ed in the basket, strapping it down in the back of the pickup, and started back to Hardin. Mr. Bullis checked his watch. It was 4:00 P.M., exactly 12 hours since we left Hardin. We wondered how long it would take us to get back.

We had more problems at the creek crossings, but nothing too bad until we got to Big Woody. It had deep ruts, and we couldn't go around them. We knew how bad it was, because we'd been stuck there on our way in. All we could do was give it a try. We got badly stuck again, so we jacked up the wheels, gathered up bark and pieces of wood—anything to fill in the ruts.

When we finally got out, we were both exhausted. I asked Mr. Bullis if I could drive, as I was familiar with the road, and he willingly agreed. It was getting dark, and we still had a long way to go. Whenever we came to the places I knew were bad, I'd really wind up that pickup and fly through. It was only momentum which got us through those bad spots.

It was broad daylight when we drove into Hardin. Mr. Bullis's assistant was at the mortuary and helped us unload Ed's body. They examined it, and I stayed long enough to be a witness. They showed me his clothing. His felt hat was blown to pieces like it had been in an explosion. His sturdy shoes? The soles were blown off and the leather was brittle. His heavy socks were crisp like burned paper. The gold watch and chain in his pocket were welded together in one glob. I could only shake my head when I thought of the mighty force in that bolt of lightning.

Wearily, I left the two morticians with their work and went to the Club Cafe to get some breakfast. With no sleep, I had another long day ahead of me. The cafe workers knew of two herders looking for work, and I located and hired them. I called my wife, got my grocery order filled and we started back to the sheep in my pickup. It had dried some now, but when there was trouble I had TWO husky men to help me.

I drove to Ed's wagon where Sid had everything of Ed's packed. We left groceries that were needed, and the one herder, who was taking Ed's place, immediately started to make friends with the dog, Chief. Sid handed him the horse's reins and showed him where the sheep were. I told him about the range and said that Sid would be back soon to move his wagon closer to the mountain.

Sid and the other herder got in the pickup, and we drove to Tom's camp where I told him what had happened to his brother. The news was a shock to Tom, as Ed had looked after him all of his life. Tom's camp had been just ahead of Ed's, and he kept saying, "From where I was I could see Ed's sheep and everything looked normal. I could see the dog with the sheep, but I never saw Ed." He had trouble accepting his brother's death.

Tom rolled up his bed and got his suitcase, and we drove back to Ed's camp. There Sid got his horse and rode back to where the various other herders were camped to let them know what had happened and that he'd be moving them closer to the mountain.

In Hardin, I took Tom to the mortuary. It was very hard on him. I think he knew it was Ed's body, yet a part of his mind refused to believe the body he was viewing was his brother's. Finally Tom decided to go to the cafe with me. I was hungry and felt the food would help us both. He then decided he wanted to go to Billings.

I knew I was too tired to make the trip, so I called the garage to see if I could find him a ride. A friend was on his way to Billings and said Tom could ride with him. I wrote a check to Tom for his wages, and I wrote Ed's check, made payable to Tom. As soon as I saw Tom off, I got in my pickup and drove home to my family and some rest.

Ed was a veteran of World War I, so he was buried at Custer Battlefield. It was a nice funeral, and Tom was there with about two car loads of people from Billings. My wife and I weren't sure if they were family or friends, but I felt good they were taking care of Tom.

After the funeral, I had to get back to the ranch to see how Sid and the other herders were doing. Sid had to carry so much responsibility, I was thankful that he was a person who could handle it.

About two weeks later, the FBI came looking for me to question me about Ed's death. Tom had told them I murdered Ed. That really was a shock. I told them it would be best if they talked to Mr. Bullis, because he could give them all of the details. I was thankful when that chapter of my sheep career was finally closed.

29
DEEP, DEEP HURT

◆

In 1944, the Beauvais Sheep Company was doing fine. Myron had expanded to 10,000 head of breeding ewes, and we had good dependable help. Myron hired a pilot to fly him over to check on things. Except during lambing, shearing, haying and thrashing alfalfa seed, he would stay at the ranch.

Because he was flying over the Beauvais country, he had more time to spend with the family in Lodge Grass. He had a garden and enjoyed working in it. All of us were enjoying family life.

Casey started walking at nine months, and from then on he seemed to think he was big enough to play with thirteen-year-old Stan and eight-year-old Christine. Often they played the game of "good guys and bad guys," and they were very realistic.

One time they were playing in the yard when pheasant hunters were near. I was quite concerned because those shots sounded too close to the house. Suddenly Christine put her hand up to her chest and called out, "They've got me, Pal," and fell over. It scared me so badly I rushed out. When I got as far as the porch, she jumped up and began chasing Stan.

When the children played this same game in the house, Casey joined in, but when he pretended to be shot, he'd stagger to a comfortable chair or couch and throw himself against it. He didn't want to fall on the hard floor.

In the summer, with the creek so near, I'd let the children swim in a rather shallow part of the water. I'd take Casey, and we'd all have a good time splashing, laughing and playing little games.

However, that summer a young couple who lived on a ranch near Wyola lost their two-year-old daughter, and after a day and night she was found drowned in the creek.

Gloom hung over the community. When Myron came home from helping with the search, he said, "We have a good yard fence, but I'm going to build a better one."

He bought new woven wire and fenced off the front gate. Now we had only the back gate just off the kitchen where I could see anyone who went though it. He even fixed a latch that no child could open saying, "Nothing like that is going to happen to us."

The year before, when the children and I went to pick wild plums, we had Casey in the buggy. This fall he wanted to walk, but we thought he would tire. I offered the buggy, but he got angry and started to cry.

Stan said, "I'll bet he'd ride in the wagon." Casey thought that was a good idea and hurried to the wagon. I agreed, even though it would be a rough ride because the wagon had no springs. We put a blanket in the bottom, hoping to cushion it so if he got sleepy at least he'd have a place to lay down. Christine decided that he needed his pillow and she hurried in the house to get it.

When we finished picking plums, we started home. Myron came along in the pickup when we were about half way. He stopped and Casey and Christine climbed in with him, then he waved to Stan and me as we walked the short distance home.

That evening, Myron and the young man who was working for us started to pump some water to irrigate the garden from the beaver dam right by our house. When Donnie tried to start the pump, it kicked and the crank fell in the beaver dam. Donnie couldn't swim, so Myron dove for it. The family was there watching him. Myron didn't find it right away, so had to dive several times. Casey thought that was the funniest thing. He laughed and laughed. We all laughed because he was laughing. Finally Myron found the crank and the fun was over. The children and I went back to the house.

It was birthday time for Stan and Casey on the 23rd and 24th of September. Stan would be 14 and Casey would be two. Stan again requested on the watermelon cake, so I baked it in the same bowl I used every year. For Casey's cake, I used a small bowl about the size of a tea cup.

That evening at supper, we had a little family birthday party. I set Casey's cake on his highchair tray and lit the candles. We sang, "Happy Birthday, Dear Casey," and told him to blow his candles out. He blew the two candles right out, and then we sang Happy Birthday to Stan, and he blew his candles out.

Casey kept looking at his cake. I handed Stan a large knife and Casey a small one, and Casey whacked away at his cake, giving us all a chuckle when he got icing all over himself.

With Stan and Chris in school all day, Casey would get lonely with just me for company. I mentioned this to Myron, and he bought Casey a puppy for companionship. Casey's favorite place to play was under the porch where there was dirt and rocks to play with. He'd make roads for his little trucks, but he enjoyed his coffee can more than anything. He'd spend long periods of time dropping rocks into the can. I guess he liked the sound. I could always tell what he was doing as I'd hear "plink, plink, plink"; then, maybe he'd come in for a cookie or milk. Sometimes he'd come in and tell me a big story that I couldn't understand. If I was busy I'd say, "yes, yes." Sometimes it was a

Casey Lynde, age 1.

funny story, and he'd laugh, and then I'd laugh and say, "My that sure was a funny story," even though I didn't know what he'd said.

There were times he'd come in and just want me to love him a little. We'd sit in the rocking chair and sing. I was seldom able to understand what he was telling me. He loved to go for walks, too, so we often did that.

It was getting to be fall, the 3rd of October. After breakfast, Myron left for the Beauvais Ranch. I fixed the children's lunches, checked to see if they were neat and clean, had their books or whatever they would need for the day, and then they hurried off to catch the bus.

I got out Casey's clean clothes, fixed his bath water in the dishpan, and he came running. He loved his bath, knowing he could go out in the yard afterwards. I'd rinse out his pajamas, diapers and a few other things and hang them on the line.

Then it was time to wash dishes and listen to the latest war news on the radio. All the time I was aware of Casey under the back porch, as every now and then there was the "plink, plink" of the rocks going in the can. In a bit, Casey came in the kitchen and tried to tell me something I couldn't understand. Thinking it one of his big yarns, I smiled at him, saying, "Yes, yes." Importantly, he walked out the door, and I went on with my dishes.

In fifteen minutes the news was over. I turned off the radio. I didn't hear Casey, so I went out to see what he was doing so quietly.

I looked under the porch—no Casey. I walked around the house calling him. The gate was still fastened; he couldn't have gone out that way. I walked around the house a second time. Then I saw where the puppy had dug under the fence, and Casey must have crawled out too. I became panicky and rushed out the gate scanning the lane where I hoped he'd be. I kept calling. I thought of the creek, my greatest fear, and hurried over to the beaver dam. No sign of him. The slew grass on the edge of the creek wasn't disturbed.

Casey loved to go for walks and especially loved to walk down the lane when his Dad was coming home. Someone always went with him, but this time he must have decided to go alone. I hurried down the lane but there were no tracks. Now I was in a state of panic. I ran back to the house and over to the barn—no sign of him.

I knew I needed help. I began running back down the lane, then slowed a bit. The sky seemed to turn amber with streaks reaching to the ground. I heard a distinct sound, like a large covey of bird's wings, just over my head, but there were no birds, only the amber sky. It was a strange feeling, and I knew the Lord was with me. Quickly I walked down the lane. Just as I reached the road, an electrician, Frank Ball, was coming down the creek road. Seeing me, he stopped and I told him my troubles. There were no telephones nearby, so he quickly drove the mile back to notify Myron's parents. Men working for them came right away.

Many people came to help, and Stan and Christine were brought from school. Frank and some of the men got in the creek and walked along, looking under the slew grass that grew along the banks. Casey was found way back under the slew grass at the beaver dam.

Frank knew CPR and went right to work on him, but it was too late. Soon Myron and a friend arrived and then a doctor, who pronounced him dead. A patrolman also arrived, and we rode to Hardin with him. Myron held Casey wrapped in the warm wool blanket he loved. We left our precious baby and his blanket at the funeral home. He wasn't ours anymore. He belonged to God.

The four of us went to my parent's home. Mother and my sister Ruby had heard the news and hurried to Lodge Grass, but they missed us. Soon they were back and family and friends began arriving. We tried to keep our emotions under control but were glad when we could go to bed. Myron and I spent the night in each other's arms, crying.

The next day was hard. We went to Lodge Grass, and I picked out Casey's clothes for his funeral. Remembering how happy he was, when we bought his new shoes, brought a flood of tears.

Oh! There were so many tears and such terrible aching. There were many friends who came to us, helping us through the worst time of our lives, and we felt blessed because we had our two older children. They stayed in the background when we were visiting with our friends who were offering their condolences, but always both of them were right there offering their comfort.

When Matt Tschirgi and his wife Bertha heard of our loss, they came right to Hardin to offer their sympathy. It was still war time, and we had only a pickup to drive. They insisted we use their car for the funeral and to take a trip. They felt that the two of us needed to be together, away from everything, to get our thoughts and feelings sorted out.

We drove to Wyoming, where our good friends Frank and Doris Greenough had bought a ranch. They were comforting people to be around, and we did get our thoughts somewhat straightened out, but I missed Stan and Christine so much and was anxious to get home to try to get our lives back on track.

30
GETTING OUR LIVES BACK ON TRACK

◆

November was a very busy month for Myron, as he still had work to do and was now behind. It helped in easing the pain of losing Casey. At the ranch on Beauvais, there was alfalfa seed to cut and thrash, and he had a sizable crew to manage.

The lambs had to be shipped, and it was time to set the sheep camps for the winter. The herders had to be taken to Billings for their fall break and there was the juggling them back and forth.

For me it was lonely. Stan and Christine were in school and for the first time I was really alone. With so much time to think I kept searching for the answer to my life. Always I came up with, "WHY? WHY ME?" I was a good mother. I wanted my children. Then I thought, "I'm not the only mother who has gone through this, many of them alone. I have my older children, family and friends. Truly the Lord has blessed me..." I thought of the many, many mothers who were losing their sons in the terrible war. I began naming off the bereaved mothers I knew, but I wanted answers for me.

Who could give me the answers? If man can't, surely God can. I searched the Bible. I didn't find the exact answer I was looking for, but in my search I came to know God better, and I found peace for myself. Yet there is something about grief that, even though I found peace with the Lord, there was this well of tears that kept filling up and running over, especially in the evening. I didn't like to upset my family, so I'd take a walk to the outhouse. I'd stop at the yard gate and have my cry and talk to God as I looked up at the stars.

Now I pushed myself to get involved in club work. I was getting better acquainted with the community, and I took a club office. Stan and Christine came down with the mumps and had to stay home from school, so they kept me company for awhile.

Myron and Matt had the opportunity to buy more sheep, so they expanded the Beauvais Sheep Company to 10,000 head of breeding ewes. Since the man who sold the sheep was going out of business, they were able to hire the men who worked for him.

Now we had to find a larger bank for financing and chose the PCA in Helena. I would have liked to have gone with Myron on this trip, but I couldn't because the children had the mumps.

Just before Christmas, while Myron was in Helena, he came down with the mumps. He was very sick and was awfully glad to get home.

He was still feeling rotten on Christmas Day, when we were invited to have dinner with his family. He said, "I don't think I should go. I might give some of the children the mumps."

Smiling at him I said, "Don't worry about those kids; they've all had the mumps. That is how you got them. If you'd like to go, I'll go start the pickup so it will be warm. If you bundle up, I'm sure it won't hurt you to go."

We enjoyed a delicious dinner and had a nice time, but we didn't stay long since Myron didn't feel good.

While Myron was convalescing, he kept worrying about the men and the sheep at the ranch. He knew a crew was coming to wool blind the sheep. (They would be shearing the wool from around the eyes so they could see to eat.) Also, they'd be tagging the ewes (trimming wool away from their teats and hind ends so they would be clean when they lambed).

Being too sick to go to the ranch, he asked George Cooley, his brother-in-law, to tell the camp tenders to go ahead and get the sheep in so the shearers could trim them. "Be sure to count each of the bands carefully (each band should have 2,500 head of ewes), then return them to their special part of the range."

Each band counted out right and the men were elated. They had only one more band to go. The last band was wool blinded, tagged and counted but they came up 500 head short. Feeling there must be a mistake, they put them back in the corral, counted a second time and came up with the same count. There was no doubt about it—they were 500 head short.

George came back to Lodge Grass to tell Myron. Very upset Myron said, "I can't imagine how that could have happened. I've had a herder with those sheep. He's a good man and a good herder."

Myron thought a bit. "What about my two camp tenders? It's their job to see everything is as it should be. They should have seen lost sheep someplace. With all the other bands of sheep out there, one of those herders should have picked up the loose 500 head and been long on their count."

Even though Myron was still sick, he had George call the Yentzer Brothers' Flying Service from Sheridan, Wyoming, and ask one of them to come to Lodge Grass and fly Myron to the Beauvais Ranch.

Dick came after Myron. When they got to the Beauvais Ranch, Myron had his men put the sheep back in the corral, so he could count them. After his count, he was satisfied. The 500 just weren't there. He called Matt, and they decided on an aerial search. Both Jack and Dick Yentzer brought a plane from

Sheridan. Myron flew with Dick; Jack brought a friend to help him search. Matt asked his friend, Wales Wolf, to fly his plane while he searched. These three planes flew back and forth, as the men searched that big country, knowing if the sheep had drifted with the wind and piled up in a deep ravine, there would have been coyote tracks for miles that could have been easily seen in the snow covered terrain.

Their great search availed no sign at all. They had to give up and return home. There was only one conclusion—someone had stolen them. Myron was resting at home still trying to get over the mumps. He reasoned they had been stolen, but it had to be in the early fall before the snow. The only time he wasn't there was during the period of time when we lost Casey. Who in the world could or would have stolen them—especially at that time? The loss was becoming an obsession with Myron.

One day Myron was reading the want ads in the *Billings Gazette*. A man on Pryor Creek was selling 500 head of three-year-old ewes at a price far below market value. This was January, and no one sold breeding ewes at that time of year. Something was wrong and if not, it was much too good a buy to pass up.

Myron hurried to the Pryor Creek ranch to look at the sheep. The owner was not at home, but his young daughters took Myron out to look at them.

As Myron told it, "The minute I saw them, I knew they were my sheep. First glance told me they were sheared by a fast shearing crew like the Portors. I could also see the unusual blue paint brand. No one else was using that kind of blue paint. I had asked the company to mix it special for me. Most of the paint brands had been combed out, but you could still see where the brand mark had been because the wool was cleaner. Here and there were blue spots of paint they had missed."

Myron told the girls he was interested and would come back on Saturday when their father was home.

On Myron's way home, he reported his findings to the Big Horn County Sheriff and the Stock Inspector but was disappointed. They told him, since the sheep had been grazing on Federal land, he would have to make his report to the Federal Bureau of Investigation. To Myron this sounded overwhelming for something as simple as 500 head of stolen sheep.

The next morning, Myron started off for Billings, where he located the FBI office. He was dreading the brush off he thought they might give him, but the agent greeted him in a friendly manner. After carefully listening to Myron, two agents made arrangements to go with him to our Beauvais Ranch. Myron showed them the wooden branding irons which still had blue paint on them and the paint can the blue paint had come in.

On the way back to Billings, they stopped at the Pryor Creek Ranch. The sheep were in the pasture and no one was home. It was a good time to show the two FBI agents the blue paint marks. The two officers sheared off several tufts of wool with bits of blue paint and put them in a plastic envelope. The paint can and the envelope were sent to their laboratory in Washington, D.C. The report substantiated, they called back. The paint was the same.

As Myron told it, "The officer and I went back to the Pryor Creek ranch. When the rancher came out, he figured the officer was the buyer. The officer said, 'We've decided to take the sheep, and we'll be back with trucks tomorrow.'

"The next day we arrived, and the men driving the trucks were sheep ranchers. Svere Berland, Bill Prante and Henry Esp were my friends who came to haul my sheep. They all knew my sheep, could see the paint combed out, and now and then a drop of blue paint and a trace of the brand.

"One of the men who rode along was George Yeoman, my regular herder who had worked for us several years. At one time, he had herded this very bunch of sheep. Also he was a great one to make pets of some of the sheep.

"When George stepped into the corral, several ewes came right up to him. He knew them by name. He looked at me and smiled, then quietly said, `This clinches it as far as I am concerned. These are my pets.'

"When the trucks were loaded, Officer Vince went to the rancher's house. The rancher assumed he was going to write a check to pay for the sheep, but instead he showed his FBI identification and served the papers which indicated the sheep were stolen and would be impounded until the trial."

"The FBI began building their case. They came out to the Beauvais Ranch, and Vince questioned the herder, who was herding this band of sheep at the time the 500 were stolen, and took his statement."

"The people who came to steal the sheep brought whiskey to his camp. Being an alcoholic, he passed out. When he regained consciousness, his faithful dog Chief had been shot and his sheep were scattered. After the herder gave his statement, he was allowed to leave. I had to hire another herder."

Myron continued, "The officer questioned my camp tender and took his statement. He too was allowed to leave, so I had to hire another camp tender."

"He questioned my cook. She was a good witness and he took her statement. Thank heavens she wanted to stay because she would have been difficult to replace; she was a fine person."

STILL TRYING TO GET OUR LIVES ON TRACK

Myron was losing control over alcohol, and it was very hard for me to accept his unexplained absences. Rumors often came my way, but when I questioned him, he was evasive. Why was he in Billings? Or Hardin? He had to wait for something or other...He got to drinking with friends...He had to stay over night because...

We had a special invitation from friends in Sheridan to attend a formal party at the Elks Club, and a few of our Lodge Grass friends were going. I felt a real need to get out and do something different, and to me this was special. We hadn't been any place socially since before Casey was born. When Myron started to leave for the Beauvais Ranch, I reminded him how important this dance was to me. Would he please be sure to get home early so we could go? He promised.

When he didn't get home, I knew why. Two days later when he did get there, I was calm. "I hear you have been in Hardin. Why couldn't you have at least come home and spent that time with us? Why couldn't you have made a real effort to take me to that formal party at the Elks Club? You know how much it meant to me."

He sheepishly glanced out the window. He couldn't look at me. Hesitating he said, "Well, you've no doubt guessed I got to drinking with some guys. Maybe you don't believe it, but I really didn't mean to. I know how much that party meant to you. I'm awfully sorry."

I sighed, "It's pretty much the same story isn't it? Alcohol seems to be controlling you instead of you controlling it. If you'd like to know it, I need someone I can lean on."

Myron turned toward me, but he didn't look right at me. "I know you do. The kids need me too. My main problem is that I miss Casey so much, and I don't know what to do about it. I talked to Father Owens, and he said the best way to get over the loss of a child is to have another one."

I studied Myron a moment. I could see he was baffled about himself. Until now he'd been able to curb his drinking—he could stop when he wanted to.

This situation was new to me and I didn't know what to do about it. I said, "Yes, I know you hurt because we've lost Casey, but I hurt too. Not being able to depend on you has been awful. The children need both of us, and they need you to spend time with them. I don't think another child is the complete answer to anything. God gave us the last two babies that we never got to raise. Maybe he wants ME to do something else. Something that I can't do if I have more children. Had you ever thought of that?"

He was surprised. "You aren't thinking of leaving me are you?"

I took a deep breath. "Well, you've certainly been giving me plenty of reasons and a lot of time to think about it. I can't see why the kids and I shouldn't live in Billings instead of here on the ranch alone. If I lived there, I could get a job and have a life of my own."

Shock registered on his face. He put his head in his hands and said painfully, "Oh, Ellie! I don't know what I'd do without you and the kids. You make everything worthwhile. I see where we have to make a plan for our lives then try to live accordingly."

I sighed. "Yes, this surely gives each of us something to think about."

Later that evening, when the children were in bed, we were listening to the radio. Myron got up and shut it off. "That isn't much of a program. I'd rather talk." I came up with a flip answer.

A bit annoyed he said, "Listen, Ellie. Here is what I've been thinking." Then he paused, trying to verbalize his thoughts. "The sheep are bred to start lambing April 1st. It's terribly important that I be there. Couldn't we leave the children with my folks until school is out? Then you could come out to lambing camp and stay with me. We have the new sheep wagon, and we can use it for our living quarters. I'll park it right beside the cook shack, but you won't have to cook or anything like that. You can just ride around in the pickup with me.

I smiled at his eagerness. "If I go, I could probably help Reggie a little."

Sensing I was about to give my consent, he said, "Oh! You'll like Reggie. She's a fine person, a good cook and very efficient."

I greeted the first of April with mixed emotions. I hated to leave our children, yet I knew Myron needed me, perhaps more than they did right then. I did a lot of praying and thinking about what was best for our family. The children had gone through a lot. I talked to them, and they seemed to think it best for me to go with Myron.

I wanted so much to do what was best for everyone. My thoughts were going something like this: "Myron is basically a kind, generous person, and he has always been good to us. He makes a better than average living, but he has been doing a lot of drinking. We've been hurt because of the things he didn't do that he should have done, but we still love him. The children are a part of him and they will always have a deep feeling for him. He will always love them, regardless of his drinking. We share many happy memories so I guess it is best for us to stay together as a family. Maybe we can help him with our prayers and love to conquer his dependence on alcohol."

The spring weather and all the signs of spring in that beautiful untamed country were a soothing influence. I felt a peace and serenity I hadn't known since we lost Casey.

On our first trip to Billings, I saw my doctor for a checkup. He said, "Having another child is good for easing the hurt you've suffered, but you are the only one who really knows the discomfort you felt during your last pregnancy. You can be sure you'll be going through that again. You will need surgery to correct your problem, and that can't be done until you are sure you've had enough family."

31

OUR NEW DAUGHTER

◆

I wanted so much to do what was best. I prayed continually. Finally, it seemed God wanted me to have another child. Everyone had been through such a time of unrest with the war, and nothing seemed stable, but living out in nature in the Beauvais country, with the sheep lambing, I found peace. It was just what I needed, and my being out there helped Myron. We had a nice spring.

My being out there helped Reggie, too. It gave her someone to talk to. She was able to get her hurts and feelings out and we talked about them. Because I had lost two children I'd been studying the Bible to try to find out why. Reggie began talking of losing her children. She had lost twins when they were babies. A short time ago, she had lost her only son in the war. She couldn't understand the purpose of life here on earth.

We worked together to prepare the meals, but we talked together all day about life and its purpose. Finally it dawned on me. By sharing our grief and suffering, we were no longer trying to push it back. Now, sorrow was like a raw sore exposed to the air, and it could heal. My time with Reggie was a soothing therapy. I had two children and could have another child, but what about Reggie? She had lost all that she had.

One day as we talked, I felt particularly close to God. I said, "Reggie, one thing I'm sure of. God has put each of us here for a special purpose, and someday we'll find out what it is. God never takes away anything without giving back more than he takes. You have been a blessing to my children by just being you, but someday God may give you someone else's child to love. Some child who needs you badly."

She smiled, and it was good to see her smile.

Because I was at camp with Myron, he wasn't drinking. The crew was happy and everything seemed to go better. After lambing and shearing, I checked with my doctor. Sure enough, I was pregnant with our fifth child.

The children were with us through shearing, and now it was time to take the sheep to their range on the mountain. Then came the job of putting up hay on the ranch.

We had just finished that job, and Myron was about to take his hay machinery and crew to Lodge Grass when Matt showed up. He said, "Myron, as long as you have to go by our ranch on Rotten Grass, could I get you and your crew to put up the hay on that place? It seems impossible to find enough men to put up our hay."

Myron and his crew put up that hay, and when they were about finished with the job, Harry Sharp asked Myron if he would stop at his place and put up his hay. They put up Harry's hay; after all, his place wasn't very big.

Finally, they got to Lodge Grass and put up all of our hay. The crew was looking forward to a nice rest, but Matt showed up. He had a broken arm. "I still haven't been able to gather up enough of a crew to put up the hay at my Wyola ranch. Won't you do it?" he asked.

Myron tried to say no, but Matt looked pathetic with his broken arm. He was small in stature and really wasn't well. Myron said he would, but when he told his crew they wanted to quit. Myron really had to give them a pep talk, hinting at their patriotic duty. After the men had a few day's rest, they were in a better mood, but by the time they got that hay put up, even Myron was mighty tired of haying.

That winter we had lots of snow. It was good that Myron had been able to get so much hay put up for the cattle. The deep snow made it difficult for Stan to get all his chores done before school, and I didn't feel good enough to help when Myron had to be away. In the evening, Stan always tried to get enough extra buckets of coal to last me all the next day.

One evening, he was much longer than usual getting the coal. I became concerned, so I stepped out on the porch, planning to call to him. Then I heard him talking. I wondered who he was talking to, so I listened. He was saying the Gettysburg Address, loud and clear, just as Abe Lincoln must have said it, except every now and then there was a <u>plunk</u> when he tossed another chunk of coal in the bucket.

It was difficult to get out because of the snow, so I stayed in much of the time, unless Myron was home and could take me in the car. My main hobby was sewing for Christine. She seemed to love anything I made for her, and that winter was a good time to make a lot.

In late January, I went to Billings to wait for our baby. It was a very drab time. The old snow was on the ground, and there hadn't been any new for a long time, so the snow was worn and dirty and the sky often overcast.

I was especially glad when it was time for me to go to the hospital. I wasn't able to get a hold of Myron, so I called a cab to take me to St. Vincent's Hospital. When we got there, my doctor had left me a note saying that if I planned to have the corrective surgery, I would also have to have the sterile surgery, and that would have to be done at Deaconess Hospital so I should come over there. I didn't feel up to walking on the icy street, so I called another cab. Of course I was late for my appointment, and my doctor was unhappy with me. None of this did anything for my sagging spirit.

The nurse took me to the delivery room where the doctor broke the water to start the birthing process. Then I was taken to the room I was to have. Again I was disappointed. I'd asked for a private room, and I especially wanted one, but with the crowded conditions, I would have to share a room. That meant that I couldn't be alone, which I wanted more than anything. The doctor carefully explained that because the labor room was in use at this time, I would only have to stay in my room until the nurse felt it was time, and then I'd be taken to the delivery room.

None of this was going as I wanted it to, but I'd just have to go along with it. I was glad that our room was semi-dark; the lady in the other bed was having a hard time, and her husband was with her, helping in whatever way he could. It was visiting hours and there were many guests in the hall.

Finally about 8:30, I told the nurse, "You'd better call the doctor. My baby is coming."

She checked and said, "Oh, no. It will take several hours as the bones haven't started to spread." I was too sick to argue with her, but I knew she was wrong.

My baby was born in my room at 9:00, and I heard the one thing I was listening for - a big, healthy cry. It was a beautiful sound that woke everyone up. The head nurse and an assistant came hurrying in. My doctor wasn't there, so a doctor who was on the floor had to come in and take over.

Someone had called my doctor. He came when it was all over and really chewed out the head nurse. "When a woman is giving birth to her fifth child, you'd better listen. She's sure to know what is happening to her." Our room was very close to the desk, so I heard it all.

When Myron arrived, they let him in for a brief visit. Finally, I was able to have a peaceful sleep. I would be having surgery in the morning, but after that, I'd be able to truly enjoy my last baby.

Myron, who had thought he wanted another boy, now was bragging about his beautiful daughter. We just had to decide what to name our beautiful blue-eyed, brown-haired daughter. She was so special that we wanted to give her a special name. First we thought of family names, but they had been used by other members of the family. We both liked the name of Lorretta, using two R's and two T's so the name would be spelled just a little different for our special child. For a second name, we chose Colleen, because it went well with her first name.

We were so happy to take her home to share her with her brother and sister. Ten-year-old Christine was thrilled to have a baby sister and she took over caring for her. Stan liked her, but liked babies better when they were a bit older. Lorretta was a child that seemed to be in a hurry to get on with her life and did everything a little earlier than other babies her age. Some of our friends were concerned when our child crawled, walked and talked before theirs did. Then I'd explain: "It's just our Lorretta."

When spring came, I missed going out to the Beauvais lambing camp, but I was busy and happy with the children. When it was nearly time to shear, Myron asked, "Ellie, won't you and the children come out and stay during the shearing? You won't have to do anything except be there. I need the family, and Stan can help with the wrangling."

I answered, "Well, I suppose; but Lorretta is only four months old."

He quickly answered, "Yes, I thought about that and I know she needs her crib, but instead of using sheep wagons for bedrooms I'll have the men set up one of the large army tents and we can set up a cot for Christine and a bed for us, and we'll take Lorretta's crib with some mosquito netting. Stan can have a cot in the men's bed tent."

I was just a bit amused that Myron had it so planned out for all of us. We truly enjoyed being out at shearing camp amid all the activity. It gave me a chance to get the lambing books straightened up and check the expense account before adding the large expense of shearing. Each thing I could do to help was a load off of Myron's shoulders. As it was, he was doing too much—which was typical of him. He often told me, "Ellie, I appreciate you coming out here among the crew. I need you to sound off to and hear your common sense approach to problems."

I was thankful that, if Myron wanted to run this big sheep outfit, at least he had very good men. Each of his eight herders had 1,200 head of ewes and 2,400 head of lambs, give or take a few. During lambing season, Myron hired extra help to herd the small bunches until the lambs were strong enough to travel with their mothers.

Many of these men were quite young, and some of them were just home from the war where they had seen very bad times. One pilot had flown too many night raids into Germany, and his nerves were shot. When he came out to our camp, he couldn't sleep at night. He'd walk around in the dark, but eventually the quietness of the night had a healing influence on him, and all of us were so thankful.

OUR NEW HOME

My greatest desire, since the war was over, was to have a comfortable home for my growing family. Our little house on Lodge Grass Creek was now much too small. Stan and Christine wanted to have company stay over, but it was difficult in our crowded house. During the war, it had been impossible to build, but in the summer of 1948, most of the soldiers were home and we found we could order a pre-fab house. We decided to build in town, so the children could attend school functions without always having to drive to get there. I was also concerned about raising Lorretta alone in the country, remembering how lonely Casey used to be.

In Lodge Grass, we bought two lots from Bill and Olive Footit. Ray Prine was our carpenter and he built a fine house. My family of brick layers built two beautiful fireplaces, very nice brick steps, a glass brick wall in the bathroom and glass walls in the basement. It was special.

The beautiful house was a thrill of a lifetime. We all loved the luxury of five rooms on the main floor, five in the basement and the wonders of having two bathrooms.

R.E.A. was now in Lodge Grass, so we had the latest appliances; a refrigerator, an electric stove and even a garbage disposal in my beautiful divided kitchen sink, with nice soft running water. I now had a good-sized utility room just off the kitchen, a shiny new automatic washing machine and a dryer. I mustn't forget our beautiful shiny electric iron and the handsome electric sewing machine Myron bought for me.

I don't know if anyone ever moved into so wonderful a new home and was as thrilled with it as I was with mine. I would walk through the house just to touch my many beautiful new things. I truly appreciated the way God had showered so many blessings on insignificant me. Having a door bell and a telephone seemed like paradise to me.

Living in town made it easy for me to go to club meetings, and Myron and I even joined a square dance club. I was most thankful that the children and I could walk to church. No more did we have to wait for a car. The short walk gave me a chance to meditate before entering the church.

Soon Mrs. Florence Westwood, the Sunday School superintendent, asked me to teach fourth and fifth graders. Then I was asked to take the high school class, which I truly enjoyed. They had a great desire to learn about the Bible and how it applied in their lives. My having studied so diligently, when I was seeking answers for my life, was a real help in answering their questions.

The large basement in our home was a fine place for the children to have their parties. I think Myron and I enjoyed having them entertain their friends as much as they did!

Lorretta was a climber and was always finding a way out of her high chair, so I got out the old youth chair and decided to give it a coat of paint. I took it to the basement where it was warm enough to have our twenty-month-old Lorretta with me.

I had just finished painting the chair, when the doorbell rang. I put the lid on the paint can, set it up where Lorretta couldn't reach it, and hurried upstairs to the door. It was the man from the dry cleaners. I accepted the clothes, wrote him a check, and hurried back to the basement.

The freshly painted youth chair had a number of saw marks all along the edge of the seat. The meat saw I'd used to put in a new dowel lay on the floor with paint on it. How could a toddler handle that big saw? But no one else had been in the basement since the chair was painted. I picked her up and she had paint on her. I was too amazed to be really annoyed. I couldn't bring myself to paint the chair again, until the family came home and saw the wonders of our Lorretta. We still have the chair with its saw marks, and I still marvel at that little child's ability.

We loved our home. Everything was so convenient, that I didn't mind cooking for the men whenever it was necessary. It was hard for me to leave all that luxury when it was time to go to the Beauvais to stay in a sheep wagon. Sometimes, when a cook was needed unexpectedly during lambing, I'd have to go and take over. That outhouse didn't even have a roof. The water still had to be hauled in barrels, and the washing still had to be done on a washboard in the wash tub. Baths were taken or given the same way.

But it was important for me to be there. Myron was still having problems with alcohol, so I'd take Lorretta and go to the Beauvais Ranch. Christine often had a friend stay with her in our home. She was such a dependable child, that I didn't worry about her. When school was out, she'd come out to the sheep ranch and stay with us.

In 1949, Stan graduated from high school. We'd never taken the children on a real vacation, so we bought a new car and got ready to go to California. Our friends, the Balls, were going to Seattle with two of their sons, and we traveled together. It was a pleasant trip, and we had a good time at the Seattle Zoo, the first large one we'd ever seen. In Portland, we visited Myron's aunts and went on to California to visit other relatives. All of them were wonderful, showing us many of the wonders in that great state. We had a good time and knew we wanted to take more trips.

That fall, we took Stan to Missoula to attend the University of Montana. He wanted to major in art. We felt he also had a talent for writing, so it was decided that he would major in journalism and minor in art. In journalism, he could always make a living.

When we left Stan and a friend at the college, we started home with mixed feelings. We were thankful that we were financially able to send him, but sad because from now on, he was on his own. The family tie we'd enjoyed so many years now was broken—but that is life. Each of us shed tears as we drove away from the college.

In Stan's second year of college, the Korean War broke out. Many of his college friends were quitting school to do their part in the service. Stan joined the Navy. Myron and I cried again, but he was happy as he went through basic training. Then he was a scribe aboard a ship, before being stationed at Guam. There he got a chance to work on the military newspaper called the *Marianas' Mariner*, which he enjoyed. When the cartoonist on the paper returned to the states, Stan got that job and began his cartooning career with his strip "Ty Foon," which was about two sailors.

In 1954, Christine graduated and went to college in Bozeman, as she planned to be a nurse. When we left her there, Myron and I shed more tears, but felt thankful that we still had Lorretta.

Myron, Lorretta, age 10, and Ellie.

32

WINTER TRIP TO CASHEN RANCH ON BEAUVAIS

◆

In the fall of 1949, Myron's parents decided to sell their ranch which joined our leases. We decided to buy it, and then gradually sell off the sheep until we had all of our interests on Lodge Grass Creek. As we sold off the sheep, we'd have money to pay off the ranch. But for now, we had enough money to make the down payment, and the sheep on Beauvais would help to pay for the repairs that were so badly needed.

Myron was enjoying the work repairing the ranch and making plans to build a sheep shed, although he too appreciated the comforts of our new home and found it hard to drop everything to go to Beauvais country.

In December, we had a heavy snow fall, and as Myron watched the snow pile up outside our picture window, he became increasingly worried. Finally he said, "If this storm gets any worse, I'll have to get to the sheep somehow."

I always felt concern when Myron had to travel that road of 45 miles through uninhabited country. If he had trouble, there was no help available. I answered, "I don't see why you have to go, when you've hired Bud and Marvin to tend camps for you. Won't they see that the herders are okay and the sheep taken care of?"

Impatiently he said, "Well, it's George Yeoman's sheep that I'm most concerned about. They're still in the farming corporation. When the wind blows across that flat, there's not a darn thing to stop it. George is one of the best herders we've got, but last fall he had trouble with both Bud and Marvin and was going to quit. The only way I could get him to stay, was to promise I would personally tend his camp. Besides, at times like this, there are decisions that only I can make, and the men can't know what I want unless I tell them.

"Most of all, I'm concerned about how violently that wind can blow. Remember last year? We lost 300 head of damn good three-year-old ewes when they drifted with the storm until they piled up in that deep ravine. I don't ever want anything like that to happen again."

Hesitant, I answered, "I'm sure you're right, but both of your four wheel drives are at the ranch. In this storm Yentzer can't fly you. How will you get there?"

He pulled on his overshoes and warm jacket. "Right now, I'm going over to the garage to see if there is someone with a four wheel drive who can take me."

Soon he was back to the house, tromping off snow, "This storm is a bad one. Everyone with a four wheel drive is hauling feed to someone's cattle who are worse off than the sheep. The corporation road is closed, so I'll have to go by the Snyder Ranch. As long as I have to go that way, I'll go into Billings and get that long wheel base Jeep I have up there for sale. I'll catch the evening bus to Billings and leave from there early tomorrow morning."

I was glad he'd come up with a solution to his immediate problem, yet I felt deep concern knowing how deep snow could pile up in the coulees he'd have to cross. "Maybe you ought to hire a man to go with you," I said.

"I've already thought of that," he answered, "so I asked Ralph. He's home from college, and I figure he can do a lot of shoveling. How about packing me a couple changes of clothes and helping me find my warm packs and wool socks? I'll need my warm sourdough pants, my scarf and scotch cap. I'm glad I bought that new down-filled-jacket because I'll be needing it."

Getting on the bus, he said, "I don't know when I'll be back, but I'll get back as soon as I get everything is taken care of with the sheep."

In Billings, Myron and Ralph checked into the Grand Hotel and called a cab to go after the Jeep. They got it serviced, ate a late supper and went to bed. Early the next morning, they ate a good breakfast and started out. It was still snowing and blowing, and the temperature was 40 degrees-below-zero with 40 miles to go.

A LONG COLD NIGHT
(Myron's Story)

The highway had been cleared, so we sailed right along until we reached the Snyder Ranch turn-off, when we started bucking snow. Visibility was very bad, but I had been over this road so many times, I knew the terrain well. We had little trouble, although every now and then we'd get stalled and have to get out and do some shoveling.

I was looking forward to seeing the first sheep camp, but that was 15 miles away. Suddenly the Jeep gave a great clatter and came to a halt; the rods had burned out.

I was real disgusted with myself, because I remembered that the Jeep had been sitting out in the cold weather for a couple of months. Condensation had caused water to form in the oil line and it froze. "Lucky we got this far, I thought.

Now there was nothing we could do but start walking. I said, "Ralph, we can make it to the ranch by dark if we just take off. Do you think you can make it?"

Both of us realized we had no choice, and he answered, "Oh, sure. When I'm hunting I walk great distances."

We started out walking at a pretty good pace, and every now and then, we would pause and rest a bit before going on. I noticed Ralph eating snow and warned him, "Ralph, you shouldn't be eating snow. It's bad for you."

I guess he figured that wasn't much of a reason. I had wondered about it myself. All that I could go on was that old timers had told me eating snow would make you colder. Ralph kept on eating it.

When we got to Big Woody Creek, he seemed unusually tired. I was tired too, so we set about gathering wood for a fire. Because of the snow, there wasn't any dry wood so I peeled some bark off an old cottonwood tree and broke off some dry twigs. It was vitally important to start our fire on the first try. My mittened hands were numb with cold and Ralph's were too. Both of us went through our pockets to see what bits of paper we could find. I found the hotel receipt and a few other bits of paper. This gave us enough to start a fire right up against a fallen tree. The big old cottonwood got to burning and we were reasonably comfortable. We'd get very warm on one side, then turn and warm the other side.

However, the ranch, food and comfort were still a long ten miles away, and I was mighty worried about George's sheep. The wind was blowing bad enough where we were, so I knew it must have been blowing a gale out on that windswept plain. I knew George would do his best, but sheep will drift with a strong wind in spite of all the herder's and his faithful dog's efforts. There was no doubt George needed help.

It was about three-o-clock P.M., when we decided we would walk to the ranch. We still had two hours of daylight. When night came, it would be even colder.

We hadn't walked far, when I again noticed Ralph eating snow. I was sharp with him and told him not to eat it. He no longer talked to me and was lagging behind. I could see he was having trouble walking. I put his arm around me, so I could help him walk. I kept wondering why a kid like him would play out. I was twice his age and wasn't having that kind of trouble. He was wearing a long, heavy army coat. I was wearing my down filled short coat and I decided it might help if we traded coats. It didn't help. He just sat down, and I was scared. I knew that giving up was a sign he was freezing to death.

I was desperate. I had to get him to Little Woody Creek somehow. With trees there, I could build a fire. But right now he was as big and heavy as I was, and Little Woody was nearly five miles away. Soon it would be dark.

Being scared, I thought of all the trials he was putting me through. I could easily lose my life trying to save his. I thought of all the people depending on me and became angry. Old timers, especially old time cowboys, had told about making a victim mad enough to fight, to bring him out of his lethargy. So I let go of all my fears and frustrations. I swore at him, calling him everything I could think of. I told him he was yellow, and he was going to freeze both of us to death. He didn't respond. He was in a world of his own.

I had to drag him, and every so often I stopped to rest. It became drag, rest, drag, rest, drag him some more. I was so weary. Finally, we were no longer climbing up a hill. We'd reached the top and my spirits rose when I discovered we now had a down hill go, so I just dragged him down like a toboggan. Fortunately we came to a shallow, cave-like shelter.

I left Ralph at the shelter and looked around in the snow to try to find a little fire wood. Finally I had a small pile made—enough to get the fire started. I was cold, especially my hands. They were stiff and I dreaded taking them out of my mittens. I needed something dry like paper. I thought of my pockets but I'd used up all the bits of paper for our first fire. Then I decided my pants pockets were dry—why not tear them out and use them? So I did. Then I thought they just might lay there and smolder. I needed something that would ignite immediately. To tell the truth, I was plenty scared we'd both freeze to death right there on Little Woody. Again I went through my hip pockets. All there was in my billfold was my driver's license and a little folding money. Realizing I wouldn't be needing either if we froze to death, I put them on the pile.

I lit a match and breathed a prayer as the flame ignited my little fire. I pulled on my mittens to gather more wood, as this was where we'd be spending the night. I tried to talk to Ralph, but he just didn't seem to be with me. The wood was all snow covered and hard to find. However, it was a starlit night, so surely I could find something. A number of times I had to climb a tree to break off a dry branch. All night long, I wished I could find a whole tree like the one we found at Big Woody, but I didn't. Each trip I had to range out a little farther.

One time when I came back, I could smell rubber burning. I dropped my wood and ran back. In his delirium, Ralph had rolled into the fire, and his overshoes were burning. My new down filled jacket was also on fire. I drug him out and rolled him in the snow until the fire went out. I was even more worried, wondering how long I could hold out. As I looked into the beautiful clear, cold star-filled night, I talked to God and told him how much I needed His help. I told Him the only way we could possibly make it would be with His help.

The night was long. I looked at the sky often. Sometimes I'd see an airplane with its lights blinking, and I wished there was some way for me to talk with the pilot or passengers. I wondered if they could see our pitiful little campfire in this 50 degree below zero temperature.

When dawn came, I was thankful that we'd made it through the night. Even though it was very cold, the sun was shining, which raised my spirits considerably. But Ralph was no better, so we started off again in the same dragging, resting fashion.

Without food or water and sleep, I was weakening. I managed to keep going until we were about a mile from my first sheep camp. I was exhausted, but I just had to get to Shocky's wagon for help. The thought hit me, "Why not set Ralph against a large clump of sage brush and get to Shocky as fast as I can walk?" I did. When Shocky looked out and saw me he couldn't believe I'd walked. I climbed into the warmth of Shocky's wagon leaned back and told him about what happened, and where I'd left Ralph.

Shocky pulled on his warm clothes and started off to get Ralph. I climbed up on Shocky's bed and went to sleep, knowing he could take better care of Ralph than I could. Shocky was an ex-oil driller and a very large, powerful man. He found Ralph, put him over his shoulder and carried him back to the wagon.

The warmth of the wagon, the rest, and the breakfast Shocky cooked were wonderful. Our bodies and spirits were restored, but I was so dehydrated, I didn't think I'd ever get enough water.

While Ralph and I rested, Shocky walked to the ranch to get help. Both camp tenders with the four wheel drives had gone out to the camps. Shocky saddled two of the horses and brought them back to the wagon for us. My energy was renewed and Ralph was well enough to ride to the ranch. There, we examined Ralph's frozen feet and began doctoring them.

When the two camp tenders came in, I hoped to find out how all of the sheep and herders had gotten through the bad storm. They said all of them were okay, but they didn't know about George. The wind was still blowing a gale out where he was.

LOTS OF SNOW AND PLENTY OF WIND

I had the men service the cab-over army truck because it was high off the ground and had lots of power. We loaded it with extra gas and groceries for George. Most important, I had them load it with plenty of pressed cotton seed pellets, which was good feed for sheep. Each ewe needed a fourth of a pound a day. They also needed grass or hay for roughage, which they had been without since this snow began.

While we were loading the hay, I wished I could haul more; but I planned that as soon as I got there, we'd start the sheep to the ranch. What I could take would have to do until we got them moved.

As soon as everything was ready, I went to bed and was lost to the world until early next morning. The cook had a good breakfast ready, and I ate a large stack of hot cakes, ham and eggs, then got in the army truck and started out.

The wind was blowing violently and causing extreme blizzard conditions, but the dependable old truck faithfully took me the thirteen miles to George's camp. He was glad to see me, as the sheep hadn't been able to get any grass. The cotton seed pellets I'd stored there were nearly gone. We fed the sheep hay and pellets and spent the rest of the day visiting and getting everything ready to move first thing in the morning. We even hooked George's wagon to the truck.

Early next morning, George cooked us a big breakfast, hot cakes, ham, eggs and fried potatoes. We were going to have a rough day and didn't know what might delay our next meal.

While I did the dishes, George put on his heavy clothes and his homemade knapsack filled with cotton seed cake and started out, his five pet ewes following him. The rest of his band, 2,500 head of ewes, followed them.

I came behind with the truck pulling the wagon. With me was George's faithful dog, Skunk. He was black with a white stripe down his back. We traveled this way until three o'clock, when we stopped and fed the sheep their pellets. They ate and bedded down where they would stay until morning. Knowing the sheep were okay, we got in the wagon and cooked something to eat.

This is the way we spent each night, knowing the next day would be the same. We considered ourselves lucky if we made two or three miles a day.

When we got to Hay Coulee, the wind was blowing so violently the sheep refused to follow George, so we had to camp. We were concerned, as the sheep needed more than cake. They needed hay for roughage. We were only about two and a half miles from Campbell Farming Corporation's Camp Four, and they had hay there but no livestock. I decided to see if they had some hay I could buy.

The only person there was the caretaker. I asked him if he would sell me some and explained how desperately the sheep needed it, but he said, "No."

Almost begging I said, "Couldn't I even borrow some and return it as soon as we get to my ranch?" Still he refused. Reluctantly I understood. He had not been given the authority to sell hay.

I hated to go back and tell George the discouraging news, as he always put the welfare of his sheep ahead of his own. When I did tell him, his temper flared. He picked up his handgun—he always kept it handy—and began checking it, "By God, I'm going down there to see that son-of-a-bitch, and I'll damn sure get it."

I knew that was exactly what he would do, because he felt such a keen responsibility for his sheep. I was scared of what he might do and said, "George, we've been having a hell of a lot of trouble. We sure don't need any more. I know its hard on these sheep and we may lose some, but most of them will make it to the ranch somehow."

All that day we sat in the wagon listening to the wind howling and blowing snow around the wagon. It was real blizzarding conditions. Having to be cooped up made me thankful George always bought a large bundle of paperback books when he made his yearly trip to Billings. With nothing else to do, we sat there and read.

Next day, the sheep willingly plunged through the deep snow following George to the Beacon. When the sheep looked off into Muddy Valley, where the wind had whipped off much of the snow, exposing great patches of bare range grass, they started running. When they got to the grassy spots, they settled down and began grazing. To them it must have seemed like paradise. George and I just stood there and watched the sheep. It truly was a beautiful sight, and we hadn't lost any sheep.

I set George's wagon above the bridge on Muddy Creek. Then, on the way back to the ranch to get George more groceries, I thanked the Lord it had turned out so well. It wouldn't take long to get George settled, and then I could visit the other herders, although I knew things hadn't been as bad for them. But first I had to find a way to get Ralph to a doctor to see about his feet.

Early the next morning, the Lord again answered my prayers. My friend Dick Yentzer flew into the ranch with skis on his plane to see how my sheep made it through the storm. When I went out to greet him, I said, "Dick, you old son-of-a-gun, I've never been so glad to see you in my life." I explained what had happened and asked Dick to take Ralph to the doctor in Sheridan. "Then call my wife to let her know that I'm okay. And come after me tomorrow morning."

I spent the rest of the day talking to the herders, getting everything shaped up so I'd be ready to go home the first thing in the morning.

33
PLAN TO GO SOUTH

◆

Myron and Ralph had come so close to death. Myron and George brought the sheep through a bad storm. If George had been alone, he might have killed to get feed for his sheep. To Myron these had been such moving experiences, that he kept wondering, "Why? Why? Was this all there was to life?"

I knew Myron was going through a bad time. I suggested, "Why don't you and I get away, a trip where we can have complete privacy. We need to get off alone where we can get our thoughts and feelings out and talk about them. Maybe we can come to understand each other better, and if you are away from your problems, perhaps you can see them in a different light. It seems that in everything we do, we are involved with other people. Your work, your drinking, and even here at home, there are always other people who come by for many different reasons. It seems we can never really say what we feel."

Because it was January, we decided to go south. I suggested Mexico.

But Myron said, "No, we'll just go as far as Texas. Then maybe swing over to California, but that is far enough."

A bit disappointed, I said, "Couldn't we even cross the Texas border into Mexico?"

Now that our plans were set, we both got enthused. We had a number of things to take care of before we could leave. Myron had to go back over to the Cashen Ranch on Beauvais to talk things over with his men, who would be taking care of the sheep. I had to get things lined out for our two daughters.

We asked our neighbor and friend, Mrs. Shipley, who usually baby-sat for us, if she could stay with the children while we were gone. She said she'd be happy to. Then the only thing I had to do was to pack our suitcases. Myron had Yentzer fly him over to the sheep outfit. He had the car serviced and all there was for him to do was to help his parents figure out their Federal Income Tax, go to the bank for our travelers' checks, and we'd be ready to leave.

It was a cold icy morning. Myron decided it would save time if Lorretta and I went with him up to the ranch, so he could get an early start on the tax forms.

While he was doing that, I could take the car and Lorretta and drive to the bank in Wyola to get the travelers' checks. When we got back, we were to drive on to the ranch and wait for him until he was finished.

As Myron was driving up the creek road, I said, "I don't know about me driving over these icy roads to Wyola."

Frowning he said, "I know its icy, but the car is all serviced. I had new knobby tires put on so you and Lorretta won't have any problems. When you get back, just drive up to the ranch. I think I'll be through by then."

Driving out of the ranch, down the creek road, I thought the icy ruts were even worse than they were when Myron was driving. I was relieved that the highway to Wyola had been plowed. Even though it was icy there were no ruts.

When we got to the bank our three-year-old Lorretta and I went in the bank and got our checks. It was so cozy inside, I hated to go back out in that below zero weather and start our icy trip home, but I consoled myself. I had made it okay to the bank, and surely I would be able to make it back home. When we drove by our town house, it looked so cozy I wished we could stop, but Myron was expecting us so I drove on.

About two miles out of town, we met a truck load of cattle and after that the ruts seemed worse. We were about a mile and a half from the ranch, when I hit some really bad ruts, so I crept along. Suddenly I realized I'd lost control of the car. It swerved and then slowly it rolled over in a barrow pit with the driver's side down. Lorretta fell on top of me, then scooted down on the floor by the clutch and huddled there. She seemed to be all right.

I chatted to her. "I hope someone will come along soon." No one did. With the motor shut off, there was no heat. It kept getting colder, and I knew that I had to get out somehow. It might be a long time before anyone came up the creek road. I climbed up on the steering column and tried to force the door open, but I couldn't open it wide enough to make it stay open. If only I could find a tool in the car that would prop the door open until I could pull myself up. I remembered Myron kept a small bag of tools under the front seat, but with the car on its side, it was awkward to get the bag, and then get a tool out of it. Finally, I got a hammer and stepped back up on the steering column. I got the door open a little and wedged the hammer so it wouldn't slam shut. I had a hand hold so I could put more pressure on it, opening the door enough to crawl out.

All this time, Lorretta was huddled comfortably in her little corner and wouldn't talk to me. When finally I was on top of the car I said, "Now Lorretta, you step up on the steering column like I did. Then hold up your hands so I can reach you and pull you out."

She just stayed huddled in her corner, not talking to me. Annoyed I said, "Lorretta, we are going to freeze if we don't get out of this car." Still she ignored me. I was desperate. I was also annoyed because she refused to cooperate in this below zero weather, and I had about all I could stand.

Scolding, I said, "Lorretta, we've just got to get out of this car and walk up to Grandma's or we'll freeze. If you won't climb out where I can reach you, I'm coming back down there and give you a good spanking."

She knew I meant business, but didn't know I'd have done a lot of begging rather than to crawl back in that car. She climbed up on the steering column and I pulled her out. I had her sit on the side of the upturned car while I slid down in the snow. Then she slid in my arms. I was relieved and thankful neither of us were hurt. I hugged her close and started our mile and a half walk.

After I had carried her about a mile, she got awfully heavy. I tried to set her down, but she clung to me so tightly I couldn't release her. Knowing how frightened she must be, I asked the Lord to give me the strength to get there. We were almost to the ranch when Myron looked out and saw us walking. He jumped in his father's car, came after us and took us back to the ranch house.

I related our story to his parents and went into shock. I started to shake. I couldn't stop even though I was cuddled up to the warm furnace vent with my fur coat wrapped tightly around me. Lorretta was fine because she was with her Dad in the familiar house.

Myron took us home and went for the wrecker. There didn't seem to be much damage to the car, but he was afraid to take it on a long trip without a good overhaul. He decided to buy a new car and had to get it ready.

It was dark when Myron got back from Hardin. We ate our supper and were just beginning to relax when the door bell rang. It was friends who lived down the street and had come to visit. We welcomed them and got out the card table and cards to play Rummy. That was a common way to entertain guests.

After we played a while, Myron yawned. "I'm just going to have to quit playing cards. I've had a mighty busy day, and we plan to get up early tomorrow as we are leaving for the south. We feel the need for a vacation."

Kathryn said, "Why, we are planning a trip south, too. Do you care if we go with you?"

I was caught by surprise. "Sure you can come, but we'll need to take two cars because on our way back we plan to visit relatives in California."

Myron sighed and stretched. "We are all packed and ready to leave early in the morning."

Buster said, "We can't leave until the bank opens."

We stopped playing cards, and they hurried home to pack. We went to bed.

Next morning, as we drove toward Wyola, we met all the school bus traffic and people going to work. I couldn't help saying, "Our plans really got changed, didn't they? If we'd known about having to stop at the bank this morning, I wouldn't have had to go yesterday and might not have wrecked the car."

Myron looked at me and smiled a bit. "Oh, Ellie. Quit thinking negative thoughts. Remember this is going to be a fun trip. As for the car, it may have had a fault and something could have happened on our trip to spoil it. I didn't tell you, but Buster said he thought it was the knobby tires that caused the wreck. The same thing happened to him. He wasn't able to control the front end, and the back just kept pushing until he turned over."

I felt better. Now I was ready for a good time.

34

LEAVING FOR THE MEXICAN BORDER

◆

We waited for our friends in Wyola and then continued on toward Denver. The roads were icy and snowy all the way, but from Denver on, we had good roads. Neither of us had been south of Denver, so we enjoyed seeing the country. In New Mexico, we were happy to see historical sites we'd been reading about.

Texas was a state we'd heard much about. We knew many cowboys who had been raised in Texas, came to Montana when cow herds were brought north, and stayed because they found jobs. These men talked of the places where they were raised. Now we got to see their country.

While we were sightseeing in Texas, the four of us talked it over, and all were in favor of crossing the border at Laredo, Texas. We were interested in the Pan American Highway. Myron and Buster talked with a border guard, telling him that we were only interested in crossing the border to see something of Mexico.

"You'll be making a real mistake," the man said. "The border towns aren't at all like the real Mexico. Why not go as far as Monterrey? It's only 240 miles. It is a nice city and is true Mexico."

We went to Monterrey as he suggested, and felt rewarded. We saw ox teams and carts, beautiful automobiles, and fine buildings. There were also adobe huts with thatched roofs and children begging. We were told of families who had many children and were not able to feed them. It made our hearts ache.

California Courts Motel had been recommended to us. After we got rooms there, we asked the attendant to call a guide for us, as we wanted to see the sights.

That evening, our guide drove us through the wealthy part of the city and then up to a mountain top overlooking Monterrey. The view was breathtaking. There was even a mountain top resort with horses for those who wanted to ride.

We had a choice of eating our dinner indoors or on the patio. It was a nice evening, so we chose the patio where we enjoyed a wonderful dinner while we looked up at the stars that were just beginning to be seen. From the patio, the lights of Monterrey were so beautiful. Musicians came to our table and played to us for a tip. The evening was very romantic for two sheep herders from Montana.

We had a good night's sleep, and woke up when we heard birds singing. We chuckled when we thought of the 28 degrees-below-zero weather at home. Myron said, "You'll have to pack my long johns. I'm not wearing them in this balmy weather." Then we noticed the sounds of busy activity outside. It sounded so exciting that we couldn't stay in bed.

Myron and I walked over to the swimming pool. From there we could see farmers hauling their produce to market in ox carts, donkey carts or whatever they had for transportation. It was all so fascinating that we bought souvenirs from peddlers and the children who were selling wares. When we got back to the motel, Kathryn, Buster and the guide were ready to start out.

The guide took us to a very nice cafe where we enjoyed our breakfast. Myron picked up the ticket which was $21.00 in Mexican money—$2.50 in our money. We couldn't believe how cheap it was for us. The Mexican dollar was only worth twelve cents of our money. It made us sad that there was that much difference.

At a leather factory, we bought purses and a little suitcase, and I bought some sandals. We went to a factory where they were weaving rugs so we bought some of them and some beautiful handmade linens.

Next, our guide took us to a huge cathedral which took three generations to build. He started to take us inside then stopped. "Oh! First you've got to put on hats." We didn't have hats. "Just put the men's handkerchiefs over your heads." Catheryn and I laughed, realizing we probably didn't look our best, but at least we could go in. The cathedral was so gigantic, they could have four different services going on at the same time.

We stopped at a small sugar mill. A man and his horse were going around and around, grinding sugarcane. His daughter was selling preserved oranges in squash and cane syrup. They gave us a taste, and we bought some. They also gave us a taste of pecan candy. We sampled that and bought some. The guide told us the young girl dressed in black was in mourning. Her mother had died and she would be in mourning for a full year.

Our guide took us to the Grand Monterrey Hotel, which Poncho Villa had taken over as his headquarters. It had been beautiful, but he and his men had no respect for the grandiose old hotel. They rode their freshly shod horses over the beautiful tile leaving ugly scars, and they stabled their horses there. The bar room was all paneled in beautiful dark wood, but the soldiers had shot around in there, leaving bullet holes in that polished wood. I felt sad seeing this evidence of the worst in mankind.

We then went to the oldest hotel in Monterrey, built in 1798. The patio in the center really had charm. That evening, our guide took us to a promenade, which 4,000 young people took part in. This was held for the middle class, in the park, with chaperons keeping a watchful eye. Young girls, dressed in their best, walk together in twos. They promenaded the sidewalks of the park. Coming down the sidewalks, meeting the girls, are the young men also dressed up, and walking in twos. Boys and girls who find each other attractive, smile and eye each other each time they meet while walking around the park.

When the promenade was over, a girl went back to her chaperon, hoping her special young man would show up. But first, he had to find someone who could introduce him to her and her chaperon. Then maybe she could talk to him briefly. If the chaperone and girl were satisfied with his actions, he might have been asked to the girl's home. If not, there will be other promenades. This is how middle class girls met their future husbands. The rich have a hotel where they get together, not so closely chaperoned.

It was fun watching the young people and their chaperons, so much like the young people we knew, and the parents who had the same feeling for their young that we had for ours.

The whole visit to Monterrey, and the help of our guide, made our trip worthwhile. In fact, Myron had gotten so enthused, that he decided we should go to Mexico City. We had been studying the map. There was a ferry which went from the west coast of Mexico across the gulf of California to Baja. If we took that we could cross the border at Tiajuana. That would save us many miles and time, and we'd be seeing something different.

I was really happy about the opportunity to see more of Mexico, even though I had bought all the things I'd wanted. Myron had even bought me a gorgeous Jade necklace and bracelet that I had admired.

As the Pan American Highway is very mountainous, we'd stop frequently to admire some magnificent view—and some Mexican children were sure to pop up to sell us some trinkets. We couldn't help admiring the enterprise of these children; surely they would become good businessmen.

Of course Myron and Buster were very interested in Mexico's cultivation of their soil. We saw different methods, but the most interesting was the way they tilled steep hillsides with oxen; sometimes they used mules. At times it was one oxen and one mule hitched together, because that was the only way it could be tilled. A tractor could never be used on steep hills like that. Often we saw a single tree in the middle of a field. When we asked about it, we were told that the tree was there for the farmer to tie a rope to, in order to support him and keep him from falling out the field while he tilled the field by hand. We were also told they didn't have to be concerned about watering these trees because of the nice mountain mists; the ocean being near and the warm climate produced plenty of humidity.

As we were driving along, I kept smelling coffee. I couldn't imagine why I could smell fresh roasted coffee way up here on a mountain. Then Myron noticed a small sign and turned off. Buster, who was following us, turned off, too. There were workers bringing in coffee beans and roasting them—thus the aroma. These people were not interested in Touristas, but they were kind and let us look around. One young man, just home from the Mexican Army, was still in uniform and very proud of it; He talked to us and I took his picture. We appreciated talking to him because he spoke some English and answered our questions.

Upon arriving in Mexico City, we had to stop for a traffic light. A couple of boys were waiting at the intersection. One came to our car and asked, "What hotel do you want to stay at?"

Myron said, "The Geneva."

"I'll show you how to get there," the boy said. He climbed in with us, and told Myron where to go. This was truly appreciated and was another example of enterprise. He had been a help to us, so we were pleased to give him a tip.

We checked into the Hotel Geneva and were thankful that the staff catered to English-speaking people by hiring help who could understand us. After supper, we hired a guide to take us to some night clubs. The one I got a big kick out of was called the Catacombs. The guide parked the car, then said, "We'll have to go through this dark alley so watch your step." We sure wondered where he was taking us.

Finally we got to a dark doorway. He opened the door and we went in. The host, in a dark robe, greeted us rather mysteriously. We sat in a booth lit by a candle. After we were served, we became used to the dark interior and began to relax.

Then a very large spider came down on his web and would swing towards Kathryn, then towards me. He sure was an ugly looking spider. We were fascinated and finally figured he was a fake. The guide laughed and said, "You ladies are supposed to jump up and scream."

This guide was good about taking us to all the places we wanted to see, but he wasn't as much fun as the one in Monterrey. Mexico City, in many ways, was more cosmopolitan, so we did a few things on our own. Before we left Lodge Grass, a friend emphasized that while in this city, one really missed a lot if they didn't go to Sandborn's Cafe, an interesting spot which caters to Americans. As this was about our last evening in Mexico City I didn't want to go home and tell her we hadn't been there, so Myron and I decided to take in Sandborn's.

Our friends said they'd rather eat in the hotel dining room. We asked directions from the desk clerk, and he said it wasn't far. We eagerly walked in the direction we thought he told us to go but could see no sign of the cafe.

Reluctantly we started back to the hotel. Nearly there, I complained, "I'm so disappointed. I really hoped we could eat there. It would be something different to do."

Myron noticed a taxi cab stand, "Let's take a cab. They'll get us there." Two men were in the cab. Myron asked the driver, "Do you know where Sandborn's Cafe is?"

"Sí, sí, Señor. I know where it is." He opened the cab door for us. We got in and started off.

It wasn't supposed to be far from the hotel, so we were surprised that he didn't get there quickly. Soon Myron nudged me. I could tell from his expression that he was suspicious and quietly said, "This is the way we came into town." He then said to the driver, "You aren't taking us in the right direction to get to Sandborn's Cafe."

A bit uneasy, the driver said, "Oh! I thought you wanted to go to Carla's Little Cafe. That's out this way about three miles and is very nice."

Then he seemed to be going in a different direction, and I hoped we were going back to Sandborn's or to our hotel. Then the other man asked Myron where he worked. Myron didn't think it was any of his business, but said, "I'm a rancher and work for myself."

Twice, in different ways, the man asked if he worked for the United States Government. This caused both of us to be very uneasy. Finally Myron said, "Why do you ask?" Both men were quiet, but they still weren't taking us back to the city. We were in heavy traffic and a policeman was directing. Our cab had to stop for the many people who were crossing the street to get to a carnival. Myron nudged me. "We're getting out of this cab." I opened the door, and we got out, joining the large crowd of carnival goers.

I was badly shaken, but thankful Myron had the presence of mind to act quickly. We walked around, watching the children and parents buying tickets and helping the little ones get up on the merry-go-round. It made me lonely for our own children. Tears started to come, and Myron said, "Come on, let's get out of here."

As we walked toward the street where the policeman was directing traffic, we saw another officer was standing by the curb. Myron asked him about a cab. He didn't understand English, but with Myron's sign language and limited Spanish, the policeman hailed a cab for us. The driver wanted to know, "Where?"

Myron told him "Geneva Hotel." The driver had no idea of where that was. He kept talking to us in Mexican, and finally it dawned on that we weren't giving him the Mexican name. But how could we tell him?

I remembered I hadn't left our room key at the desk when we left the hotel. Quickly I got the key. As soon as the driver saw the name on the key he said, "Oh, sí! Gracias, gracias."

Away we went, straight to the hotel. We were so glad to get there, Myron gave him a generous tip. We walked into the dining room for our evening meal, but somehow we were no longer hungry. As we were being seated, Myron said, "Wasn't there a lot of difference in those two cab drivers?"

I smiled, tired but relieved. "Yes. I hope we never see any more like those two in the first cab."

35

WISE ADVICE, SEE VOLCANO

◆

It was almost time for us to leave Mexico City, and we still hadn't gotten in touch with our lifetime friend Margaret Ping. I'd been a little hesitant because she was Administrator of the YWCA and no doubt a busy lady. Finally, in late afternoon, I called her.

When I told her where we were staying, she said, "I'll be right over!" Bless her heart. As busy as she was she came to see us.

We had a nice visit, and Margaret said she'd come after us at two-o-clock the next day to take us to the floating gardens.

In the morning, the guide took us to the Government Buildings and then took us to the Palace that had been built for Emperor Maximillian and his wife Carlotta. Maximillian's reign was brief, but I wanted to see the palace because I'd never been in one. It was huge and therefore seemed cold to me. I thought, "I'm glad I don't have to live in a palace; it would be hard to feel intimate in those huge rooms." I decided fairy tales are false. They always said the young lady married the prince and lived happily ever after. We'd lived in all kinds of places and had lot of problems, but I knew my life had been a lot happier than the Emperor's and his wife's.

At two-o-clock, Margaret and a friend came after the four of us and took us to the floating gardens. We took a boat ride on the canals and learned the history of the gardens. We enjoyed a lovely dinner with Mexican musicians playing for a tip. It was fun to be with Margaret, because she spoke Mexican so well and really knew her way around. On our way back, she took us to a lovely Spanish home owned by a lady she knew. She also took us to a family owned factory where they spun and dyed their own wool and wove shawls, blankets, rugs and ponchos.

We were impressed with their operations, and I wished I hadn't bought all the things I'd wanted in Monterrey.

Margaret told us she had been to see the volcano south of Mexico City near the town of Uruapan. It was so awesome, she felt we'd be making a mistake if we didn't go to see it. "After all, how many volcanoes does one see in a lifetime?"

Next morning, we left Mexico City and drove along in a leisurely fashion having decided we'd like to see the volcano at night, as Margaret had told us, "If you have to make a choice, be sure and see it at night."

On our way down the highway, we saw a long mule train loaded with fire wood on its way to Mexico City. It was a beautiful sight. Since Myron's father had been a horse trader and Myron had learned to appreciate a good horse at an early age, he exclaimed, "Man! Those mules are the best I've ever seen, and those men are certainly well dressed. Their saddles and bridles are the best."

We wished we could talk to them, but they wanted nothing to do with Touristas from the States. They wouldn't even allow anyone to take pictures of them; in fact, they saw to it that we all stayed in our cars. If anyone started to get out, one of the men would be sure to ride over with his big bull whip cracking. Everyone got the message.

At Carapan, we stopped at a gas station, and a pleasant appearing man who spoke English well asked if he could ride with us to Uruapan, as he had to leave his car at the garage. Myron said, "Sure you can go with us. We're on our way to see the volcano." He climbed in and we visited. He told us that he often guided people to the volcano and suggested we take a taxi as the road was hard on cars.

As we neared the town, Myron asked about a good hotel, as we would be staying the night. He smiled and said, "I'll take you to the best hotel in town." It was an old Spanish style hotel including an inner court with a fountain, and charm which I found very appealing. Our suite of rooms was on the ground floor. When the clerk handed Myron the key, we both had to smile. It was huge—about eight inches long and as big around as a man's finger. Attached to it was the hotel name on a board a foot long by two inches wide. No one could run off with that key.

The keyhole was large enough to look through so we left the key in the lock for a little assurance. The hotel seemed very old. The windows were long and went down to the floor. They had ornate bars on them so no one could get in. I stood back of the drapes and looked out on the street, watching the people who couldn't see me walk by our windows. I felt I'd gone back in time and wished I could spend more time there. It was relaxing and made me feel welcome. The large dining room was pleasant, the hotel was warm and accommodating. I'd never felt so pampered.

We decided to nap, as we wanted to see the volcano at night, and it would be late by the time we got to bed. It was nearly dark, when we hired a taxi to take us there. Guides were sitting around a campfire with their serapes wrapped snugly around them, making an impressive sight, as they waited for tourists who would come to see the volcano.

A guide took us out, stopping at a safe distance. What a sight! Red hot lava was spouting out and running down the cone. Gigantic boulders shot out from the earth with a terrific force. It was awesome. God's works make man's feeble ones look so puny.

Standing in the dark and feeling awed, I thought it easy to understand why primitive man felt he had to offer sacrifices to appease a volcano. It was a terrifying God. We were so fascinated, we stayed late watching the red lot lava move and move. Finally, we decided to return to the hotel and come back in the morning to see how far the lava had moved during the night.

When we got to the hotel, the door was locked, so we had to awaken the night watchman who slept just inside the door. It was an eerie feeling to be standing in the dim light, waiting for him to unbolt the door, and seeing him waiting there with a gun until we identified ourselves.

At breakfast next morning the same gracious hostess took our orders; sliced oranges, hotcakes and bacon. A young waitress brought a bowl of fruit we hadn't ordered, and a large bowl of baked beans. We smiled at the mistake realizing that Mexicans loved beans.

The four of us were excited about seeing more of the volcano, and were chatting away, when the hostess came to our table and asked, "What's matter with beans?"

Myron said, "We just don't want any for breakfast."

The dear lady had been trying to be kind to us. She shook her head at these strange foreigners. "No beans for breakfast? No beans?"

We checked out, and Myron decided to take our car. "The road out there isn't any worse than our ranch roads." It was a pleasant day as we drove to the volcano. Guides waited around the campfire, and one asked what we wanted. Myron and I decided to ride horses out to the volcano in order to go farther and see more. The place where we'd been standing the night before was now was covered with lava and the stream had flowed a considerable distance beyond that. Again, we felt insignificant as we witnessed God's great powers.

A guide took us to see where two towns had been covered with lava except for the very top of the houses. We could see where the streets had been. A church had been partially spared, but a wall of lava had crowded around it. As we stood on top of it, and looked down at the church, a very reverent feeling came over us.

36
HOME, BUT NOT FOR LONG

◆

Now it was time for us to hurry back to the States and our world, but we had much to think about. No longer would our problems seem quite so large or consume us quite so much as they had in the past.

After a brief visit with family and friends in California, we hurried back to the snow and cold in Montana. The nicest part of our trip was returning to the children in our home.

Myron called Dick Yentzer to fly him to the Cashen Ranch on Beauvais to see how the men and sheep were doing. The folks at the ranch said there had been no problems. Then Myron visited each of the herders. They were glad that we had a good trip and that we were home again.

We'd been home about a week, when Myron asked me to look at the bump on the back of his shoulder. "It bothered me some in all the driving I did, but riding in the airplane seat really caused it to hurt," he said.

I looked at it. "It has grown. I don't see why you won't go to a doctor rather than worrying about it. In fact, I don't see why you didn't have Matt's doctor friend from Mayo look at it when they spent the day at lambing time. We should have gone to Rochester instead of going to Mexico."

He looked at me and grinned. "Well, there is no reason why we can't go to Rochester right now is there?"

This surprised me, but as long as he was in the notion, I quickly answered. "That sounds like a good idea, if Mrs. Shipley can stay with the girls again."

She could, so I packed our suitcase and we started out. The roads were snow covered, and in South Dakota, the highway was even worse, and people were having problems. Fortunately Myron had his overshoes and warm clothes. He had a shovel so helped those who were not prepared and happened to get stuck in front of us. We weren't making as good a time as we had hoped, but we got there soon enough to keep his appointment at the clinic.

After an examination, the doctor decided to remove the tumor, but its tentacles had wrapped around the shoulder muscle, so it was more of an operation than he'd thought it would be.

We were thankful it wasn't malignant, and Myron wouldn't have to stay in the hospital. He had to stay in the hotel and take it easy for a day and a night, though. When we checked with the doctor, he said, "You can go home now but have your wife do the driving."

The streets were covered with about ten inches of heavy snow, making driving difficult. When we were checking out of the hotel, we noticed an elderly lady with whom we'd gotten acquainted. She was quite upset, so we asked her, "What did you find out about your checkup yesterday?"

"They tell me that I have terminal cancer, and I have an appointment at the hospital this morning," she said. "The hardest part is not having any family to be with me at this time. But right now I an upset because of the snow. The cabs are running late, and I'll be late for my appointment at the hospital."

We both felt so much compassion for her, that Myron said, "Don't worry about getting a cab. We'll take you. We are just ready to leave." Myron carried her suitcase with his good arm. I was about to slide into the driver's seat, when he said, "I can drive with my right hand." I wanted to argue, but because the lady was upset, I let it go, realizing it was his shoulder and he'd have to decide.

Myron carried the lady's suitcase into the hospital and we started home. The Minnesota highway had been cleared, and we went right along until we reached South Dakota. There the wind had really been blowing, but we were able to travel as far as Chamberlain. There the patrol was stopping traffic; two snow plows were stuck because they'd stopped to help a motorist in trouble. We got a hotel room, but Myron was restless, because he felt we could have made it in our car.

Later, Myron was talking with a rancher from Murdo who said, "The roads around Murdo and on west are bare. I made it fine in my pickup. I'm sure you can make it, as you say you are used to snow, and you have a stick shift. It is the people who have automatic shifts that get into trouble because when their cars hit those big drifts, their automatic shifts and they are stuck."

We drove on to Murdo, and by then, Myron was tired enough to want to go to bed.

THE END OF AN ERA

When we bought Myron's parent's ranch, we felt it was the ideal thing to do, but it was an added strain for Myron when he should have started taking it easy. Now he had many miles of fence to build; the house, the bunkhouse and the barn needed a good deal of repair; and because we were planning to have sheep there as soon as we could, he had a large sheep shed to have built.

Again he was expecting too much of himself, and his control over alcohol was getting worse. He decided to go to a Seattle Sanatorium to take the cure. I went with him, and for a while it helped, but he still had all the frustrations of building up the ranch and trying to handle the sheep and the ranch at Beauvais.

Then he went into partnership with his parents and bought purebred cattle, which caused nothing but aggravations. Soon he was drinking again.

When school was out, the girls and I went with him back to Seattle. There he talked with a doctor who made him see that he had to get rid of the problems that were causing him so much frustration. Selling the purebred cattle was a great relief, but we took an awful loss. While some of our problems diminished, others sprung up to take their place.

For example, one fall day, Myron gathered up his crew in Lodge Grass and drove the 75 miles over the dirt road to the Beauvais Ranch where the alfalfa seed had already been cut and bunched in fork-sized piles, then left in the field to dry and cure. Ten days later, the thrashing machine had gone out to the ranch and was ready to start as quickly as the crew of eight men got there.

There needed to be four men in the field pitching bunches on the sleds pulled by tractors. Often, when they picked up a bunch of hay with their pitch forks, there would be a rattlesnake in the hay. They crawled under there because it was warm and comfortable. Most of the regular men kept an eye out for the snakes and accepted them as part of the job. However, Charlie and Cal weren't too fond of working so far out of town, and they were afraid of snakes.

Everything was running full blast when Charlie came over to one of our top hired men and said, "Hank, I hate these damn rattlesnakes. I'm going to the bunkhouse and put on my white shirt. You tell Myron I quit and he can just take me into town."

Cal was with him, and he spoke up. "I'm going with you. I'm quitting too."

Soon Myron noticed he was short two men in the field, so he went to Hank, "Say, where's Charlie and Cal?"

Hank began to chuckle, "Oh! They decided to quit because they are afraid of the snakes. I don't know why they came out here; they knew there were snakes in these fields. Anyway, they went to the bunkhouse go get cleaned up so you could take them to town."

Fuming, Myron hurried to the bunkhouse, hoping he could talk them into staying, because he was now short two hands. There they were, all dressed up, just lolling around as if there wasn't a thing in the world to do.

Myron exploded. "Just what is the idea of taking this job and coming all the way out here and then quitting when you are so badly needed and leaving me shorthanded?"

Charlie hung his head. "I don't like those damned snakes. Every time I move a bunch of seed there's a rattler under it, so I'm quittin."

Then Cal spoke up. "I don't like them either so I'm quittin too, and you can just take the two of us into town."

Still fuming, Myron said, "Well you two can just keep sitting in this bunkhouse, but I'll be damned if I'll take you into town just because you don't want to work. In the meantime you can eat in the cook house with the rest of us." Quickly he wrote each of them a check for the brief time they worked, saying as he hurried out the door, "If someone comes along, I'll tell them that you want a ride."

He hurried out to the thrashing machine, grabbed a pitch fork and began pitching bunches off the sled into the machine, relieving Ed so he could go out to the field.

Soon Ed came to Myron and said, "Well Cal and Charlie pulled out."

Myron was very surprised. He looked at Ed and said, "How? No cars have left here."

But Ed was really chuckling, "Oh, they left on foot. See, there they go."

They were beyond the meadows when Hank came up chuckling. "They'll be back as soon as they see a snake."

At noon, the thrashing machine shut down and the crew went to the bunkhouse to wash up. They all went to the house for dinner except Ed. He seemed to be delayed. As they gathered around the table they all laughed and joked about Charlie and Cal having to walk to the highway—twenty five miles across the prairie and two creeks in the hot sun. They figured they'd be plenty hungry and thirsty with very sore feet.

Just then Ed came to the table grumbling, "Them dumb boneheads. I know they are scared of snakes, but that doesn't give them the right to walk off with Hank's and my rubber irrigation boots. Everyone laughed and remarked how "hot" those rubber boots would be on this extremely warm fall day. The merriment made the dinner more pleasant.

We were short handed and the fact that the others didn't even complain but cheerfully accepted the extra work made Myron appreciate their loyalty so much that he vowed to himself he'd reward them with extra pay when the job was done.

When Myron got back to Hardin, he met Bob, his patrolman friend, who greeted him. "Well, where have you been lately? I haven't seen you around."

"Oh, I've just been out to the Cashen Ranch on Beauvais thrashing alfalfa seed. Why do you ask?"

Bob looked down and smiled. "Well, a while back, at night, two men ran out on the highway and waved me down. When I stopped, they said their names were Charlie and Cal, and they sure needed a ride to Hardin because their feet really hurt. Of course I was curious, so I questioned them. They said that they were working for you at your Beauvais Ranch, but that was all they said about that before they began talking about other things. Well, I figured something wasn't quite right or you'd have taken them to town yourself."

Myron broke out laughing and explained about what had happened. Then, both he and Bob had a good laugh.

During the winter it was easy for Myron to slip back into his old pattern of drinking. This was perhaps the most depressing time of my life, and I guess it was for Myron too, because he didn't seem to know what to do. He'd tried the two trips to the Sanitorium and still hadn't been able to stop drinking as he wanted to. Then he learned of the Alcoholic Anonymous group in Sheridan, Wyoming, so he began attending their meetings. There he met many fine people, but the important thing was that he learned "your own therapy comes from helping others." Soon, Myron asked the Sheridan Group to come to Lodge Grass to start a group, as the Indian people were having a real bad time with alcohol.

They held meetings in our house until they got organized. It was good for these young men to see that there was a way to overcome alcohol. That winter was especially pleasant for all of us.

When spring came, there was the lambing, shearing and then haying. There was trouble with the haying equipment, so we decided we'd better buy a new baler. Myron looked around and found just what he wanted. We both felt good about it, because now we wouldn't have to make the many trips after parts, thus saving much expense and time.

In striving for an alfalfa seed crop, it is important to get the first cutting of hay off as early as possible in the spring, so the second cutting of hay can get an early start. It produces the seed which needs to be cut before the frost.

The crew of men were in good spirits as they started haying, feeling all would go well, and they wouldn't be out to the Beauvais ranch long.

However, they had a breakdown on the new baler, so Myron made the 75 mile trip back to the dealer in Lodge Grass to get the part and hurried back to the crew. They put it on and started baling again, but right away a different part broke, so back to Lodge Grass Myron went. It was dark when he returned, but as soon as it was daylight, he and his mechanic put the new part on the baler so as not to lose any more time. Right after breakfast, the crew was in the field ready to go to work, but before the baler had really got to bailing a third part broke.

Myron was furious as he drove back to the dealer in Lodge Grass. He told the dealer just what he thought of that new baler and of the company that would make a piece of machinery that was always breaking. Myron insisted that the dealer go out to the ranch to see if he could figure out what the problem was.

The dealer came out, but couldn't see what was causing the breakdowns. He went back and called the factory. They said they would send out their trouble shooter, but he was tied up and couldn't come right away.

While we were waiting, Myron had business in Billings to take care of, and we needed more groceries. With the baler problem constantly on his mind, he decided to talk with the Billings dealer. As they talked, Myron told the dealer that if he could come out and look at the problem, we'd pay his expenses. He did come and looked the situation, over but he had no solution.

When the trouble shooter from the factory did arrive in Billings, there was so much interest that quite a number of people came out to the ranch. The trouble shooter couldn't see the problem either.

Finally the parts man from Billings, who had just come along for the ride, spoke up. "The part that is giving you all the trouble does not belong on this machine. It belongs to an older baler and it is causing all the other parts to break. Whoever sold it to you sure didn't look at the number."

After all the delay, trouble and expense it was now too late for a seed crop. Then, because the hay wasn't needed on the Beauvais Ranch, Myron decided to haul it to Hardin and sell it there. It was sold, but we didn't end up getting paid for it. We didn't even get our trucking expense out of it.

We were having our share of financial hardships when we had to make a trip to Billings. While we were still out in the country where there was no shelter, a violent storm hit us with golfball-sized hail. We were helpless as we sat there with every window in the car being smashed, covering us with shattered glass. Even the top of our car was dented.

Both Myron and I received minor cuts, but Lorretta huddled down on the floor boards in the back seat and didn't get hurt. We were surprised and thankful that she was smart enough to think of that.

When the storm was over, we drove right to the insurance agent. He looked it over and said, "Are you sure you didn't get on top of your car with a ball peen hammer?" We sure didn't appreciate his humor. The insurance covered the glass but not the dents. We had to spend the next day getting glass put in before we could go back to the ranch.

As we thought of our many problems, we felt like Job in the Bible. Then we decided that God was trying to tell us to give up the Beauvais ranch. Surely there was a way to make a living without so much anxiety. Both the older children were married; Stan was in New York cartooning and Christine, now a nurse, and her husband lived in Butte.

Myron had planned to talk it over with Matt, but before he got to see him, herder Alex quit, so Myron had to go to Billings to get another herder. He got the new man settled and came home to Lodge Grass and called Matt's ranch. When he learned that they had guests, he decided to wait a while, knowing a little later was the best time to sell sheep.

Again, he became involved in the Lodge Grass ranch. Soon, Myron went back to check on the herders and see how the sheep were doing. As he drove toward the new herder's camp, he could see the sheep, but couldn't see the man with them, so went right to his wagon. There he saw Bud stretched out on his stomach, a hasty note scribbled on his writing tablet: "Lightening struck me, the sheep are east of the wagon."

Myron roused him, but he was somewhat delirious. His back had really gotten badly burned and so had his feet. Myron helped Bud into the pickup and drove by the ranch to tell the camp tender to herd the sheep until he got back with another herder. The trip to Hardin was difficult; he wanted so much to get Bud to the doctor but he didn't dare drive fast over those rough country roads which might cause Bud more misery.

In the Hardin Hospital, Bud recovered slowly, and he was so despondent that he often made his way to town where he would drink and not get back for his treatments. Myron tried to talk to him, hoping to make him realize that he wasn't helping himself, the hospital or us, and that we had to pay for the treatments whether he took them or not. Myron felt he got his point across and went about taking groceries to the ranch, stopping to see how the new herder was getting along. On his way home from the ranch, he stopped to see Bud. The hospital staff was quite upset, because Bud had left and not returned nor taken his suitcase.

Myron hurried to the cafe and bar where Bud hung out. They too had been wondering about Bud, for he hadn't been in for quite some time, so Myron notified the sheriff that the man was missing. Nothing was heard of him. Often Myron wondered if Bud had become so despondent that he'd made his way to the Big Horn River and jumped in. From then on, whenever a body was found, we'd feel anxiety until it was identified.

We didn't hear what happened to Bud until years later. Our son Stan happened to be in a Billings barbershop, when a man in the barber's chair recognized him as Myron's son, and began to tell about working for us when he was struck by lightening. He had caught a ride to the Veteran's Hospital in Sheridan, Wyoming. There they amputated his feet and healed up his back. He then went into Wyoming and started a sheep outfit of his own, married and had a family. That was a happy discovery for us.

Finally, Myron got around to talk to Matt about selling the sheep company. It was agreeable with Matt because his health was bad. The sheep were sold to several different buyers.

It was a melancholy time when we said good-bye to the herders, who were now friends, and the dogs and horses, for they had been so loyal to us. It was even sad to see the wagons leave. Of course we both shed tears, but as Myron said, "This is the end of an era. We won't be seeing any more big sheep outfits in this part of Montana. There is no longer room enough."

As soon as we moved off the Beauvais Ranch it became a cow ranch. The big sheep shed, corrals and wool house were torn down. The cookhouse was dragged to the ranch, and horses were pastured in the beautiful alfalfa meadows, so they were ruined. Now there is no evidence that it had ever been a sheep ranch, except where the corrals used to be. The sheep had fertilized them so well in the spring of the year that, what is now a part of the prairie, has areas of very green grass, and the plots are the exact size of the old corrals.

Stan, Ellie and Christine at the Cashen place, remembering.

AFTERWARDS

◆

Several years ago, Myron and I led a small expedition of our children and grandchildren to see the old ranch. Nostalgia surrounded all of us, and the men married to our daughters caught a glimpse into the past that captured their imagination.

The terrain was the same except for the fences and a paved road, not the old dirt road, that led to the ranch. It was no longer in use, erasing the memories of events that happened along it.

When we finally reached the old log house, we felt sad, because it hadn't had care. The once beautiful lawn was now overgrown with tall weeds, making it difficult to get in the door. The creek had overflowed, flooding the house, leaving dried silt on the floor that I'd spent so much time cleaning.

We paused to look at the old root cellar that had stored huge supplies of groceries for the sheep company, but now was caved in.

We walked up the hill to the old log barn. It stood there like a sentinel, waiting for the many horses and tack it had held over the years. The Beauvais wind rattled the tin roof as we stood there, remembering.

Before leaving, we felt we should pay tribute to the ranch graveyard, but it was covered with weeds, making it hard to find the markers. I sighed as I thought of the Cashen family who had built up this once beautiful ranch, giving it so much loving care, and I was thankful they didn't have to see the ruins.

Standing there in the wind, gazing at the panorama, I smiled thinking, "All of this is the past, and I'm glad that I was part of it. Now we are in the present, enjoying life on our beautiful ranch on Lodge Grass Creek just four miles from town, living in our comfortable modern home with all the conveniences I could ever have dreamed of."

I don't know the future, but I've become well acquainted with Who holds the future, so I'm looking forward to many happy times and more great memories.

978-0-595-43142-7
0-595-43142-9

Made in the USA
Las Vegas, NV
27 June 2023